LEADERSHIP AND MANA(
FOR EDUCATION STUDIE

C000131778

This book introduces theories of educational leadership and management and provides examples of their translation into practice. Many students studying education no longer go directly into teaching, but instead follow a diverse range of careers associated with the education sector more widely: local authorities, think tanks, charities, school trusts, administrative, and managerial roles. This book highlights and explores these diverse pathways. For staff in schools who are currently on a National Professional Qualification (NPQ), this book gives an overview of differing leadership pathways, including senior leadership (NPQSL) and headship (NPQH), whilst also discussing the impact of system reforms (NPQEL).

Topics covered include:

- strategies for leadership across primary, secondary, and higher education settings;
- school leadership and management through the challenges of the pandemic and beyond;
- equality and diversity and inclusive practice;
- non-teaching leadership roles.

By offering an introduction to leadership and management discourse not usually encountered until postgraduate study, this lively and accessible book is an essential read for all students of Education Studies as well as those embarking on CPD or National Professional Qualifications.

Deborah Outhwaite is the Director of DTSA and an EdD Supervisor in the Centre for Higher Education Studies at the University of Liverpool, UK.

Catherine A. Simon is a Visiting Fellow and PhD supervisor at Bath Spa University, UK.

The Routledge Education Studies Series

Series Editor: Stephen Ward, Bath Spa University, UK

The Routledge Education Studies Series aims to support advanced level study on Education Studies and related degrees by offering in-depth introductions from which students can begin to extend their research and writing in years 2 and 3 of their course. Titles in the series cover a range of classic and up-and-coming topics, developing understanding of key issues through detailed discussion and consideration of conflicting ideas and supporting evidence. With an emphasis on developing critical thinking, allowing students to think for themselves and beyond their own experiences, the titles in the series offer historical, global, and comparative perspectives on core issues in education.

Philosophy and the Study of Education
New Perspectives on a Complex Relationship
Edited by Tom Feldges

Sociology for Education Studies
Connecting Theory, Settings and Everyday Experiences
Edited by Catherine A. Simon and Graham Downes

Understanding Education and Economics
Key Debates and Critical Perspectives
Edited by Jessie A. Bustillos Morales and Sandra Abegglen

Understanding Contemporary Issues in Higher Education
Contradictions, Complexities and Challenges
Edited by Brendan Bartram

Education in Europe
Looking out for what the neighbours do
Edited by Tom Feldges

Pedagogies for the Future
A critical reimagining of education
Gary Beauchamp, Dylan Adams and Kevin Smith

Understanding Education Studies
Critical Issues and New Directions
Edited by Mark Pulsford, Rebecca Morris and Ross Purves

Leadership and Management for Education Studies
Introducing Key Concepts of Theory and Practice
Edited by Deborah Outhwaite and Catherine A. Simon

For more information about this series, please visit: www.routledge.com/The-Routledge-Education-Studies-Series/book-series/RESS

LEADERSHIP AND MANAGEMENT FOR EDUCATION STUDIES

INTRODUCING KEY CONCEPTS OF THEORY AND PRACTICE

Edited by
Deborah Outhwaite
and
Catherine A. Simon

Routledge
Taylor & Francis Group

LONDON AND NEW YORK

Designed cover image: © Getty Images

First edition published 2023
by Routledge
4 Park Square, Milton Park, Abingdon, Oxon, OX14 4RN

and by Routledge
605 Third Avenue, New York, NY 10158

Routledge is an imprint of the Taylor & Francis Group, an informa business

© 2023 selection and editorial matter, Deborah Outhwaite and Catherine A. Simon; individual chapters, the contributors

British Library Cataloguing-in-Publication Data
A catalogue record for this book is available from the British Library

Library of Congress Cataloging-in-Publication Data
Names: Outhwaite, Deborah, 1973- editor. | Simon, Catherine A., editor.
Title: Leadership and management for education studies : introducing key concepts of theory and practice / edited by Catherine A. Simon & Deborah Outhwaite.
Description: First edition. | New York : Routledge, 2023. | Includes bibliographical references and index.
Identifiers: LCCN 2022059731 (print) | LCCN 2022059732 (ebook) |
ISBN 9781032343013 (pbk) | ISBN 9781032343020 (hbk) | ISBN 9781003321439 (ebk)
Subjects: LCSH: School management and organization. | Educational leadership. | Teacher educators–Training of.
Classification: LCC LB2801.A1 L42 2023 (print) | LCC LB2801.A1 (ebook) | DDC 371.2–dc23/eng/20230322
LC record available at https://lccn.loc.gov/2022059731
LC ebook record available at https://lccn.loc.gov/2022059732

ISBN: 978-1-032-34302-0 (hbk)
ISBN: 978-1-032-34301-3 (pbk)
ISBN: 978-1-003-32143-9 (ebk)

DOI: 10.4324/9781003321439

Typeset in News Gothic
by KnowledgeWorks Global Ltd.

MIX
Paper | Supporting
responsible forestry
FSC
www.fsc.org   FSC™ C013985
Printed in the United Kingdom
by Henry Ling Limited

Contents

List of Abbreviations   *vii*
Series Editor's Preface   *ix*
List of Contributors   *xi*

1 Introducing Educational Leadership and Management   1
  CATHERINE A. SIMON

2 The Intersection of System and Distributed Leadership   9
  IAN POTTER

3 Equality and Diversity and Inclusive Practice: Significance for Organisations
  and Individuals   23
  SHEINE PEART

4 Resilience and Vitality as Necessary Leadership Traits   33
  MARK T. GIBSON

5 Effective School Management: Leadership Capacity of the School Principal   46
  PINAR AYYILDIZ AND ADEM YILMAZ

6 Observations of Classroom Management and School Leadership in the COVID-19   59
  PURVI (VI) GANDHI

7 Pedagogical Leadership in Early Childhood Education and Care: What Is It,
  Why Do We Need It, and How Do You Do It   71
  MONA SAKR

8 The Role of Primary Headteachers within School Trusts: English Landscape
  Divergence in a Post-Pandemic World   81
  MEGAN CRAWFORD AND DEBORAH OUTHWAITE

9 Crisis Leadership in English Secondary Schools: Its Effects on School
  Leaders' Long-Term Visions of Education   89
  JACQUELINE BAXTER AND ALAN FLOYD

10 Leading a Large and Disparate School in Higher Education   102
   PETER WOLSTENCROFT AND TRACK DINNING

11 Leadership of International Schools   114
   MARK T. GIBSON AND LUCY BAILEY

12 Leadership for Flourishing Schools: From Research to Practice   127
   ANDY WOLFE AND LYNN E. SWANER

13 A Practical Exploration of Non-teaching Leadership Roles within
   the Further Education and Skills Sector (FES)   140
   BRENDAN COULSON, JOHN EVERSON, AND SHERIDAN BROWN

14 Charitable Education Organisations in England: The Case of Teacher
   Educators   153
   BETHANY KELLY AND DEBORAH OUTHWAITE

   Index   *164*

Abbreviations

AB	Appropriate Bodies
AL	Ambition Leadership
APPG	All-Party Parliamentary Group
BLM	Black Lives Matter
CEO	chief executive officer
CLASS	classroom assessment scoring system
CPD	continuing professional development
CQI	continuous quality improvement
CRT	Critical race theory
DAN	Disabled People's Direct-Action Network
DBS	Disclosure and Barring Service
DfE	Department for Education
DfES	Department for Education and Science
DL	distributed leadership
DWP	Department for Work and Pensions
ECEC	early childhood education and care
ECF	Early Career Framework
ECT	Early Career Teacher
EF	Education Endowment Fund
EFL	English as a foreign language
EHCP	Education, Health and Care Plan
EI	emotional intelligence
FES	further education and skills
FSM	free school meals
GEO	Government Equalities Office
GTP	Graduate Training Programme
HE	higher education
HEI	higher education institutions
HMG	Her/His Majesty's Government
HR	human resources
IB	International Baccalaureate
ICT	information and communications technology
ILEA	Inner London Education Authority

IQ	intelligence quotient
IT	information technology
ITT	initial teacher training
ITTE	initial teacher training and education
KPI	Key Performance Indicator
KSB	knowledge, skills and behaviours
LA	local authority
LGBTQ+	lesbian, gay, bisexual, transgender, queer, and others
LEA	local education authority
MAT	multi-academy trust
MS	Microsoft
NASBTT	National Association of School-Based Teacher Training
NCSL	National College for School Leadership
NIoT	National Institute of Teaching
NOR	pupil number on roll
NPQ	National Professional Qualifications
NQT	newly qualified teacher
OECD	Organisation for Economic Co-operation and Development
OfS	Office for Students
Ofsted	Office for Standards in Education
PGCE	Postgraduate Certificate of Education
RD	Regional Director
RSC	Regional Schools Commissioner
SIP	School Improvement Partner
SMART	specific, measurable, attainable, relevant, and time-based
SSAT	Specialist Schools and Academies Trust
STA	strategic thinking in action
TDT	Teacher Development Trust
TF	Teach First
TSA	Teaching School Alliance
TSH	Teaching School Hubs
TTA	Teacher Training Agency
UCET	Universities Council for the Education of Teachers
UKRI	UK Research and Innovation
UN	United Nations

Series Editor's Preface

Education Studies has become a popular and exciting undergraduate subject in many universities in the UK. It began in the early 2000s, mainly in the post-1992 universities which had been centres of teacher training. Gaining academic credibility, the subject is now being taken up by pre-1992 and Russell Group institutions. In 2004, Routledge published one of the first texts for undergraduates, *Education Studies: A Student's Guide* (Ward, 2004), now in its fourth edition (Simon and Ward, 2020). It comprises a series of chapters introducing key topics in Education Studies and has contributed to the development of the subject. Targeted at students and academic staff at levels 5, 6, and 7, the Routledge Education Studies Series offers a sequence of volumes which explore such topics in depth.

It is important to understand that Education Studies is not teacher training or teacher education, although graduates in the subject may well go on to become teachers after a Postgraduate Certificate of Education (PGCE) or school-based training. Education Studies should be regarded as a subject with a variety of career outcomes, or indeed, none: it can be taken as the academic and critical study of education in itself. At the same time, while the theoretical elements of teacher training are continually reduced in PGCE courses and school-based training, undergraduate Education Studies provides a critical analysis for future teachers who, in a rapidly changing world, need so much more than simply the training to deliver a government-defined school curriculum.

Education Studies is concerned with understanding how people develop and learn throughout their lives, the nature of knowledge and critical engagement with ways of knowing. It demands an intellectually rigorous analysis of educational processes and their cultural, social, political, and historical contexts. In a time of rapid change across the planet, education is about how we both make and manage such change. Education Studies, therefore, includes perspectives on international education, economic relationships, globalisation, ecological issues, and human rights. It deals with beliefs, values, and principles in education and the way that they change over time.

Since its early developments at the beginning of the century, the subject has grown in academic strength, drawing explicitly on the disciplines of Psychology, Sociology, Philosophy, History, and Economics. But it has also broadened in scope to address the many social and political questions of globalisation, international education, and perceptions of childhood. A glance through the list of book titles in the series on page 2 reveals the ever-growing range of topics which Education Studies embraces.

Much of the early thinking about education studies has focused on its development as a 'pure' university academic subject. But more recently course leaders have been paying attention to the way the subject can prepare students for their working lives as graduates. For example, Jim Hordern and Catherine Simon's (2017) book on placements and work-based learning looks at the possibilities for careers other than teaching. This book on management in education takes that process further in helping students to visualise a role for themselves in the world of work in education. There are contributions from a wide range of education managers from different contexts who share their experiences and advice. The book is invaluable for professionals looking to enhance their career prospects. If you are still an undergraduate and wondering whether you will ever need to know about management, be assured that leadership roles come along surprisingly quickly, and an awareness of the issues will strengthen your potential. And, of course, how leadership and management work in education settings is an important part of our understanding of the education landscape.

Stephen Ward
Bath Spa University

British Education Studies Association

Many of the editors and contributors to Education Studies book series are members of the British Education Studies Association (BESA). Formed in 2005, the BESA is an academic association providing a network for tutors and students in Education Studies. It holds an annual conference with research papers from staff and students; there are bursaries for students on Education Studies programmes. The Association funds small-scale research projects; the support for the writing of this book was one of those.

The website offers information and news about Education Studies and two journals: *Educationfutures* and *Transformations*, journals for student publications. Both are available without charge on the website: https://educationstudies.org.uk/

References

Hordern, J. and Simon, C.A. (Eds.) (2017) *Placements and Work-Based Learning in Education Studies*. Abingdon: Routledge.
Simon, C.A. and Ward, S. (Eds.) (2004) *A Student's Guide to Education Studies*. Abingdon: Routledge.
Ward, S. (Ed.) (2004) *Education Studies: A Student's Guide*. Abingdon: Routledge.

Contributors

Dr Pinar Ayyildiz is an interpreter, sociologist, and teacher trainer and owns MA and Doctor of Philosophy degrees in Educational Management alongside a Cambridge Diploma in Teaching English to Speakers of Other Languages (DELTA). She acted as a DELTA trainer as well. She works on areas like Epistemology of Educational Sciences, Equity in Education and Educational Leadership. She has various academic memberships and is the editor of a number of international journals. She is an assistant professor of Management Information Systems Department today and also the coordinator of education in Ankara Medipol University, Türkiye.

Dr Lucy Bailey has degrees from the Universities of Oxford, Bristol and London. A highly experienced educational leader, who has developed professional development programmes to upskill teachers across Asia, Dr Bailey has also published extensively on the internationalisation of schooling and higher education. Her current position is as Head of Education Studies at the Bahrain Teachers College (University of Bahrain).

Dr Jacqueline Baxter is a Professor of Public Policy and Management in the Department of Public Leadership and Social Enterprise at the Open University Business School. She is a Fellow of the Academy of Social Sciences, Principal Fellow of the Higher Education Academy and Director of the Centre for Research and Innovation in Online education. Her current research focuses on strategic planning for digital learning in schools, and introverted leadership. She tweets as @drjaquebaxter and you can find her profile here: https://www.linkedin.com/in/professor-jacqueline-baxter-53206a12/

Sheridan Brown is an assistant course leader for the PGCE in Post-Compulsory Education and Training, and module leader on the MA in Education at Nottingham Trent University. She has worked in further and higher education, for more than 20 years, undertaking a range of teaching, course leadership, and research roles.

Brendan Coulson is the Head of Technical Education at Nottingham Trent University; his role includes leading the development of higher technical skills-based courses, advising on technical educational policy, and skills pedagogy. His experience encompasses teaching, leadership, educational governance, and research in the Further and Higher Education sectors.

Professor Dr Megan Crawford is a Professor of Education in the Centre for Global Learning at Coventry University. She is a Fellow of the Academy of Social Sciences, Visiting Professor at several universities internationally, and author of several books. Her current research focuses on flourishing leadership, and the relationship between identity and emotion in leadership. Megan is Deputy Editor of Educational, Management, and Leadership (@EMALjournal) and tweets as @drmegancrawford. Her profile is here: https://pureportal.coventry.ac.uk/en/persons/megan-crawford

Dr Track Dinning is a Deputy Director at Liverpool Business School, part of Liverpool John Moores University. Her research focuses on Entrepreneurial Education and explores how it can be used to foster employable and enterprising students through various approaches to both pedagogy and assessment.

John Everson is a principal lecturer and member of the Post-Compulsory Education and Training Team at Nottingham Trent University. His experience encompasses teaching, leadership, and research in the Secondary, Further Education and Higher Education sectors.

Professor Alan Floyd is a Professor of Education at the University of Reading where he is also Research Division Lead and a member of the Senior Management Group for the Institute of Education. His research interests focus on key issues related to educational leadership and management including how people perceive and experience being in a leadership role, leadership development, distributed and collaborative leadership, and academic careers. His web profile is here: https://www.reading.ac.uk/education/about/staff/alan-floyd.aspx.

Purvi (Vi) Gandhi, MA; MBA, switched from being a practising psychologist to teaching psychology in 2003. As an African of Indian origin, she has experienced the Kenyan, American, and British educational systems. Over the past 20 years, Vi has been a passionate middle leader in a variety of schools from 'inadequate' to 'outstanding' across the UK, where she undertook action research to bring about improvements for my colleagues and students. Currently, Vi's research interests include flourishing in schools, CPD for middle and late-career teachers and diversity, equity, and inclusion in education.

Dr Mark T. Gibson is a Senior Lecturer at The School of Education, Oxford Brookes University, UK and was previously an Assistant Professor at the University of Nottingham Malaysia. His primary research and teaching are in the field of Educational Leadership and Management; he is the Strand Leader for the MA (Educational Leadership and Management) at Oxford Brookes. His research is primarily within two areas of educational leadership and management, those of International Schools and structural reform in England such as Academy Schools. He has published widely in these areas.

Dr Bethany Kelly is the Director of Programmes at the Faculty of Education at the University of Buckingham. Bethany taught in schools for over twenty years culminating in senior leadership positions in different UK schools. She is a member of the BELMAS council. Her current area of research focus is leadership identity, with a particular interest in the identity of Teacher

Educators in England. She tweets as @imisschalk and you can find her profile here: https://www.linkedin.com/in/bethany-kelly-imisschalk/

Dr Deborah Outhwaite is Director of DTSA and an EdD Supervisor in the Centre for Higher Education Studies at the University of Liverpool. She is incoming Chair of BELMAS 2023-2026, a Fellow of the RSA, a Fellow of CollectiveEd, a Fellow of the IESE, a Fellow of the Chartered College of Teaching, and a Senior Fellow of the Higher Education Academy. Her current research focuses on the changes in English systems leadership. She tweets as @deb_outhwaite and you can find her profile here: https://www.linkedin.com/in/dr-deborah-outhwaite-fcct-7a329843

Dr Sheine Peart began working at BGU in 2019 and is a Reader in Access, Equality, and Inclusion at BGU, the Programme Leader for the Education Doctorate and leads the Social Justice RKEU. Her research covers multiple aspects of equality with a particular focus on race. She led the 2020 internal Telling It Like It Is project on the experience of Black and Brown students at the University and co-ordinated the production of racially inclusive teaching resources in collaboration with Black History Month Magazine and Museumand. She supports students on the Professional Studies and Masters in Education courses. Before teaching in higher education, she worked in the further education sector for 15 years, teaching numeracy to learners on a wide variety of vocational programmes, and managing the College's teacher education programmes. Prior to being based in HE, she worked as a local authority adviser, a secondary school teacher and a youth worker.

Ian Potter is currently working as CEO of a Multi-Academy-Trust in the South of England, following several decades in school leadership. He is the present Chair of BELMAS, a member of the Association of Education Advisors (AoEA) Board with whom he is also accredited as a Senior Associate. Co-opted onto the Conference and Events Committee of BERA, is a Trustee of two further charities and was voted by peer Vistage group members as Inspirational Leader 2022. His research interests are in system and distributed leadership, coaching and mentoring, and social justice leadership. He has been involved in the coordination of the International School Leadership Development Network (ISLDN) for nearly ten years.

Dr Mona Sakr is an Associate Professor of Early Childhood and Education at Middlesex University. Her research focuses on leadership development in the early years' policy context in the UK and internationally.

Dr Catherine A. Simon is an experienced teacher, Teaching Fellow, Visiting Research Fellow at Bath Spa University (BSU), PhD supervisor and Education Studies consultant in Higher Education. She is co-editor of *A Student's Guide to Education Studies* (Routledge, 2019) with Prof Stephen Ward. Catherine was a longstanding Council member for the British Educational Leadership, Management and Administration Society (BELMAS) (Director of Publications) and sits on the editorial boards of *Educational Management, Administration and Leadership* and *Management in Education* (Sage Publications). She co-convenes the BELMAS Research Interest Group (RIG) on Structural Reform. She is a Fellow of Advance HE and Senior Fellow of the Higher Education Academy.

Dr Lynn E. Swaner is the chief strategy and innovation officer at the Association of Christian Schools International, where she leads initiatives and develops strategies to address compelling questions and challenges facing Christian education. Swaner serves as a Cardus senior fellow and as a non-resident scholar at Baylor University's Center for School Leadership. She is the co-author or editor of numerous books on Christian education, including *Flourishing Together: A Christian Vision for Students, Educators, and Schools* (Eerdmans, 2021). Prior to joining ACSI, she served as a professor of education at the university level and a Christian school administrator in New York. She holds an EdD in organisation and leadership from Teachers College, Columbia University.

Andy Wolfe is the executive director of education at The Church of England. He has national oversight of the Church of England Foundation for Educational Leadership, which runs programs, networks, and research focused on leadership development. Previously, he worked as a senior leader in a large high school, where he oversaw the development of teaching and learning and the school's Christian ethos. He is the co-author of the book *Flourishing Together: A Christian Vision for Students, Educators, and Schools* (Eerdmans, 2021).

Dr Peter Wolstencroft is a Deputy Director at Liverpool Business School, part of Liverpool John Moores University. He has written extensively about leadership and a range of other educational issues and is the co-author of the bestselling teacher training textbook 'The Trainee Teacher's Handbook'.

Dr Adem Yilmaz is an academic, analyst, educational researcher, and a measurement and evaluation specialist. He holds a PhD in Measurement and Evaluation. His fields of expertise are as follows: teaching and learning of science, science education, scale development, measurement and evaluation, SPSS, LISREL, AMOS, EFA/DFA analyses. In addition, he concentrates upon topics like teacher training, quality in higher education, and accreditation. He is currently a faculty member and is working as an associate professor of education in Kastamonu University, Türkiye. He is also a member of several committees in the same university.

1 Introducing Educational Leadership and Management

Catherine A. Simon

Introduction

Leadership is one of the most widely used terms in many areas of human activity (Silva, 2016). Think, for example, of sectors such as the armed forces, business, politics, religion, or sport. All interpret leadership differently and how it translates into practice. The concept of leadership, therefore, has proved notoriously difficult to define. To date, there is no one accepted definition of leadership, although researchers and practitioners have tried to capture the nuances of leadership over time. Early definitions of leadership were influenced by traditional hierarchical organisational structures which attributed leadership to a single individual, namely Thomas Carlyle's eponymous 'Great Man' (Carlyle, 1840/2011), where leadership was as much about *the character of the individual* as it was about their success in setting and achieving a specific goal. Think of historical characters, often put in this category such as George Washington, the Duke of Wellington or Winston Churchill. By the second half of the twentieth century, however, research indicated that leadership was more to do with the *act of influencing* others rather than any specific personal character traits of the 'leader'. In other words, leadership was now understood as a 'process': that of 'influencing the activities of an organised group in its efforts towards goal setting and goal achievement' (Stogdill, 1950: 4). The focus on influence and process has remained over time, to which has been added an emphasis, at the end of the twentieth century, on 'followership' as a necessary determinant of 'leadership'. One cannot be a leader without anyone following. Who was following and how they expressed their followership was of specific interest to researchers. More recent conceptualisations during the first quarter of the twenty-first century emphasise the role of context, the primary purpose, and organisational structures as key components of leadership. Research continues to make sense of the nature, purpose, and contexts of leadership in all its diverse guises.

The study of leadership, by necessity, involves the study of management and administration. Although connected, management, administration, and leadership all mean different things that cannot be ignored. Indeed, Dimmock (1999, cited in OECD, 2008), with reference to educational leadership, sets out the distinction as follows:

> Irrespective of how these terms are defined, school leaders experience difficulty in deciding the balance between higher order tasks designed to improve staff, student and school performance (leadership), routine maintenance of present operations (management) and lower order duties (administration).

DOI: 10.4324/9781003321439-1

Whilst not necessarily involved in the day-to-day activities engendered here, leaders will, inevitably, have interest in and be ultimately accountable for all three practices of leadership, management, *and* administration. A more nuanced distinction between educational leadership and management is provided by Connolly *et al.* (2019: 3)

> Educational management [...] entails delegation, which involves being assigned, accepting and carrying the responsibility for the proper functioning of a system in which others participate in an educational institution, and implies an organisational hierarchy.

According to this definition, 'responsibility' is a metaphor for 'a state of mind and does not necessarily entail actions, though it implies them and frequently prompts them' (*ibid.*: 3).

Leadership, on the other hand, 'is the act of influencing others in educational settings to 'achieve goals, and thus necessitates actions' (*ibid.*: 3). The authority for exerting influence comes from hierarchical relationships as well as other sources. Significantly, unlike educational management, educational leadership 'does not entail carrying the responsibility for the functioning of an educational system in which the influence is exercised' (*ibid.*: 3). The concepts of educational management and educational leadership are therefore different.

There is now wide agreement that leadership does not necessarily sit with a single individual. Modern organisational structures are such that leadership can operate at all levels of an institution, and for a variety of reasons, including sustainability, distributed across the workforce. In terms of educational leadership, for example, OECD (2008: 3) suggests that:

> Leadership is a broader concept where authority to lead does not reside only in one person, but can be distributed among different people within and beyond the school. School leadership can encompass people occupying various roles and functions such as principals, deputy and assistant principals, leadership teams, school governing boards and school-level staff involved in leadership tasks.

Leadership has thus acquired significant importance for policymakers and researchers alike, and this interest has gained prominence in education.

Why educational leadership?

Whilst the account of leadership so far is largely generic, educational leadership is different from all other forms of leadership in that its primary focus is on the aims and purposes of education: in other words, on pupil and student success, the development of staff, parent satisfaction, and community outcomes. To this end, the study of educational leadership is deeply embedded in the socio-political context of the nation. Educational institutions operate within a legislative framework set out by national governments. These centralised systems determine many of the policies that govern school business, often embedded in law. The most recent Education Act in England (2011), for example, covered issues such as early years' provision, discipline, the school workforce, academies, post-16 education, and student finance.

School leadership

Ever since the introduction of the 1988 Education Reform Act in Britain, the significance of school leadership has grown as schools became autonomous institutions in their decision-making processes regarding such matters as finance, staffing, and educational outputs. At the same time, standards and accountability measures were centralised. A national curriculum was introduced, shortly followed by standard assessment tests at ages 7, 11, and 14. The Office for Standards in Education (Ofsted) was set up in 1992 to provide a centralised system of school inspection and accountability. These processes ensured that school leadership and management became a core component of the school improvement and effectiveness movement, which was gaining particular prominence in England, for example, with the establishment of the National College for School Leadership (NCSL) in 2000.

Bush (2022), in writing the 50th Anniversary editorial of the *Journal of Educational Management, Administration and Leadership* (EMAL), charted the name changes of the journal since 1972, providing an interesting snapshot of the changing interests and developments in the field of educational leadership, including school leadership, both in the UK and internationally, First published as *Educational Administration,* the journal attracted authors interested in exploring understandings of educational theory and practice. By 1982 the journal had changed its name to *Educational, Administration and Management*, signalling the growing interest in New Public Management and the growth of managerialism at the time (*cf.* Clarke and Newman, 1997), which foreshadowed the 1988 Education Reform Act. It was this act that brought in seismic changes in the UK educational landscape, promoting the local management of schools and curtailing some of the responsibilities of local education authorities (LEAs). By 2004, the year in which LEAs became effectively obsolete, the journal adopted its current title of *Educational, Administration, Management* and *Leadership*, reflecting the growth in interest in educational leadership as school headteachers (principals) steered their way through seemingly uncharted territories.

Many of these changes, as already indicated, were also evidenced internationally. By 2008, the Organisation for Economic Co-operation and Development (OECD) had published extensively on school leadership and management, providing a clear rationale for policymakers globally, to invest in school leadership policy as a means of responding to rapidly changing expectations of national education systems in the developed world. The OECD (2008) argued that effective school leadership stands as an intermediary between the classroom, the individual school and society and is essential to improving the 'efficiency and equity of schooling' (*ibid.*: 16). Not only do school leaders provide the conditions and climate in which improved teaching and learning can occur, they also have influence beyond the school gate, connecting and adapting to changes in society and acting as the bridge between internal school improvement processes and externally initiated reform. It is school leaders, therefore, who take on a prominent role in initiating change in schools (Fullan, 2001). The overall argument is that a school leadership system, designed for the hierarchical industrial age, is no longer fit for purpose, and it is incumbent on policymakers to create new conditions for school leadership better suited to respond to current and future environments' (OECD, 2008: 16).

Recognising that policies to enhance school autonomy do not necessarily translate into autonomy in practice, international research by Neeleman (2019) explored the activities of school leaders as self-determined entities. Asking which school interventions did school leaders consider and initiate in the context of increased school autonomy and intensified accountability, Neeleman was able to create a classification of enacted autonomous activities practice. The resulting typology was divided into three areas of activity:

1. **Educational:** this included pedagogical approaches, educational programmes; systematic pathways through the education system such as accelerated pathways to a diploma: learning environments and methods for teaching, learning, and assessment.
2. **Organisational**: the organisation of school culture, structures, teaching and learning; quality assurance; student care and support; stakeholder relationships: financial resources and facilities and accommodation.
3. **Staff:** professional autonomy and culture; teaching and school-related assignments; staffing policy, assessment and payment, recruitment, and employment.

This framework demonstrates that school leaders have a range of responsibilities and activities that can be called 'autonomous' within the confines of their institution and which, at times, extend beyond those boundaries into the local community. The emphasis here is on school outputs rather than curriculum design which had once been at the heart of the headteacher's role. School leadership thus gained greater bureaucratic and strategic importance in the brave new world of new public management and centralised control.

The significance of school leadership for national government was laid out in an NCSL report (Leithwood *et al.*, 2006: 3) that emerged from a review of the research literature at the time:

1. School leadership is second only to classroom teaching as an influence on pupil learning.
2. Almost all successful leaders draw on the same repertoire of basic leadership practices.
3. The ways in which leaders apply these basic leadership practices – not the practices themselves – demonstrate responsiveness to, rather than dictation by, the contexts in which they work.
4. School leaders improve teaching and learning indirectly and, most powerfully, through their influence on staff motivation, commitment and working conditions.
5. School leadership has a greater influence on schools and students when it is widely distributed.
6. Some patterns of distribution are more effective than others.
7. A small handful of personal traits explains a high proportion of the variation in leadership effectiveness.

Whilst the authors admit that these claims 'are not all strong in the same way' (*ibid.*: 3), significant amongst them is the emphasis on influence – influence on student learning and staff development. Although originally posited as a controversial claim, the authors, in reviewing their 2006 report (Leithwood *et al.*, 2019), acknowledged the wide acceptance and endorsement of the impact of strong leadership on pupil attainment. Subsequent evidence similarly endorses the modest yet consistently significant indirect impact of leadership on pupils, staff, and the wider school community.

Indeed, Bush and Glover (2014) identify influence as one of three dimensions of school leadership:

• Leadership as influence independent of positional authority or intentional influence. Leadership thus understood can be exerted by both individuals and groups.
• Leadership and values where leaders ground their actions in clear personal and professional values; there may, of course, be a tension between personal and professional values and those 'imposed' through government policy.

- Leadership and vision also present tension in that a leader's vision will need to conform to centralised expectations and external bodies such as Ofsted.
- Influence, values and vision are thus key characteristics of educational leadership and are closely linked to the many models and styles of leadership reported on in the literature.

Models and styles of leadership

The evolution of definitions of leadership indicated earlier has moved from ideas and characteristics associated with the 'great man', or trait theories to more recent definitions that consider the role of followers and contexts. In the chapters that follow, several models of leadership are explored. 'Transactional' and 'distributed' are just some of the adjectives applied to leadership theories.

Connolly *et al.* (2019) created a typology of leadership theories, including:

- leadership theories and the purpose of the influence;
- leadership theories that describe the resources for leadership;
- leadership theories and the process of leading.

Furthermore, the OECD (2008: 19) identified four major domains of school leadership:

- supporting, evaluating, and developing teacher quality;
- goal-setting, assessment, and accountability;
- strategic financial and human resource management;
- collaborating with other schools.

Such summaries have gained popularity recently and have led to leadership frameworks such as those for the National Professional Qualifications and the Early Career Framework in England, which act as a training and assessment tools for middle and senior leaders.

In summary, the work of school leadership can be defined in terms of:

- context: the local and national contexts in which educational leadership takes place;
- core purpose: the personal and professional vision and goals of educational leaders together with centralised aims and purposes of education;
- character: none of the above can be divorced from the individual character traits that leaders bring to their roles.

In the chapters that follow in the book, context, core purpose and character are all evident in the accounts depicting leadership in a diverse range of educational settings.

Summary of chapters

In producing this first book on educational leadership and management directed towards undergraduates, masters students, and practitioners working towards national professional qualifications, we have taken a fresh look at leadership and management issues across a range of educational contexts.

In the opening chapter, Ian Potter, considers a new perspective on leadership and management as the driver for sustainable school improvement in the current schooling landscape. In this way, 'systributed' leadership brings together models of distributed and system leadership, where the notions of system leadership are conceptualised through the lens of distributed leadership. The new model challenges traditional understandings of the solo leader and presents the case that (eco)systems perceived as organisms for distributed and shared leadership is how the schooling landscape in England, transformed by the rise of multi-academy trusts, can be improved sustainably.

Similarly, Megan Crawford and Deb Outhwaite explore some of the challenges that recent changes in the English education system have made to the role of primary headship. In this way, Chapter 8 discusses the tensions between a principal's personal and professional core purpose when set against centralised aims and objectives for school leadership, where the UK government proposed that all schools in England, both primary and secondary, should be nested within a multi-academy trust.

The notion of primary purpose is also explored in Chapter 12, where Andy Wolfe and Lynn Swaner consider the notion of the Flourishing Schools Culture model. The chapter describes the research findings in the five domains of Purpose, Relationships, Learning, resources, and Wellbeing, with a particular focus on the interdependence of educators and students. The call is for schools to prioritise the learning, growth, and wellbeing of staff alongside children and young people. The Church of England is a key provider of National Professional Qualifications (NPQs).

Wellbeing presents a strong theme in several of the chapters. In Chapter 6, Puriv Gandhi, for example, presents a fascinating insight into the classroom during the Covid-19 pandemic. Profiling teacher leadership, she takes us through the day-to-day realities of working online and through the transition of a safe return to classroom teaching. Empowered by new circumstances, the chapter illustrates how teachers can take a leadership role in sharing knowledge and expertise with colleagues for the good of the school community. Jacqueline Baxter and Alan Floyd, also reflect on lessons learned during Covid-19 in Chapter 9, with a particular focus on how Covid changed school leaders' vision for digital education in schools and the impact this had on senior leaders' strategic planning.

It has been well reported in the press and elsewhere that the recent pandemic highlighted the inequalities in access to quality education encountered by many children and families. Shein Pert in Chapter 3 explores the evolution of debates on equality, diversity, and inclusive practice, arguing that such knowledge is essential for all senior leaders, providing a framework for better understanding of current situations.

Equality of access remains an issue for all sectors and levels of the education system. In Chapter 10, Peter Wolstencroft and Track Dinning consider the challenges of leading a large and disparate school (or department) in higher education with a small leadership team. In attempting to bring in a culture of empowerment, the chapter focuses on how both communication and community can be used to ensure that everyone is working collaboratively with a consistency of approach, whilst at the same time ensuring those working within the system are empowered to work towards objectives in the best way possible.

The context of educational leadership is considered in Chapter 11 on International Schools by Mark Gibson and Lucy Bailey, offering a unique understanding of the nature of international schools. The authors highlight the specific leadership challenges, the typical leadership and governance structures, and the implications for leadership preparation. Whilst working in such schools brings issues of leadership and management common to all schools, there are specific challenges which come from working in another country, not least the notion of leading a for-profit organisation, and contributing to the mainly white talent bled from Western countries.

It becomes clear throughout the book that leadership demands not only a keen understanding of the system and contexts in which education takes place but also the ability to use personal character traits for the betterment of the education community. Mark Gibson's Chapter 4 discusses the little reported concept of resilience and vitality as required overarching traits in all leaders, irrespective of other traits or 'leadership styles'.

If character traits and experience are helpful determinants of successful leadership and management, so too is the ability to focus on clear purposes and objectives. In Chapter 7, Mona Sakr introduces students to the idea of pedagogical leadership in early childhood education and Care (ECEC) and enhances our understanding of why it matters and how it can be developed. In emphasising three essential aspects of pedagogical leadership: a holistic approach to leadership work, distributing leadership roles and responsibilities, and building a community of leadership, she considers how pedagogical leadership in ECE can be fostered through the five key practices of coaching, reflective practice, pedagogical conversations, action research and storytelling.

Chapter 13 by Bendan Coulson, John Everson and Sheridan Brown shines an important light on professional leadership roles within the education sector other than teaching. Focusing on the further education and skills (FES) sector, their chapter considers roles within four areas of work: leadership in supporting learners and learning; leadership in encouraging and supporting employer engagement; leadership of activities that support staff, and leadership of corporate systems. These areas of work indicate the breadth of the FES sector and of the non-teaching leadership roles within it. It underlines the opportunities the sector presents for establishing and developing a varied and stimulating career that encompasses multiple areas of work.

The final Chapter 14 also looks beyond the standard institutional contexts of educational leadership including schools and universities and considers the role of not-for-profit organisations. As governments continue to outsource essential services following the demise of LEAs, Bethany Kelly and Deborah Outhwaite focus on government policy as leadership and pay particular attention to the changing face of teacher training following the Education White paper (DfE 2022).

In presenting this first book on leadership and management for all students of Education Studies at both undergraduate and Master's level we believe the chapters outlined above will offer a valuable resource, not only in adding new perspectives and knowledge to the field but also in widening student expectations about the graduate leadership roles available across the wider education sector. We also see this volume as offering practical and accessible reading for busy professionals engaged on any of the national professional qualifications for education.

References

Bush, T. (2022) EMAL Is 50: Celebrating Half a Century Disseminating High-Quality Research and Scholarship. *Educational Management Administration & Leadership* **50**(1), pp. 3–5.

Bush, T. and Glover, D. (2014) School Leadership Models: What Do We Know? *School Leadership & Management*, **34**(5), pp. 553–571.

Carlyle, T. (1840) *On Heroes, Hero Worship and the Heroic in History.* Online. Available at http://public-library. uk/ebooks/44/74.pdf (Accessed 13 October 2022).

Clarke, J. and Newman, J. (1997) *The Managerial State: Power, politics and ideology in the remaking of social welfare.* London: Sage.

Connolly, M., James, C. and Fertig, M. (2019) The Difference between Educational Management and Educational Leadership and the Importance of Educational Responsibility. *Educational Management Administration and Leadership* **47**(4), pp. 504–519.

DfE (2022) *Opportunity for All: Strong schools with great teachers for your child.* London: HMSO.

Fullan, M. (2001) *The New Meaning of Educational Change* (3rd ed.). New York, NY: Teachers College Press.

Leithwood, K., Day, C., Sammons, P., Harris, A. and Hopkins, D. (2006) *Seven Strong Claims About Successful School Leadership.* Nottingham: National College of School Leadership. Available at: https://dera.ioe.ac.uk/6967/1/download%3Fid=17387&filename=seven-claims-about-successful-school-leadership.pdf

Leithwood, K., Harris, A., and Hopkins, D. (2020) Seven Strong Claims about School Leadership Revisited. *School Leadership and Management* **40**(1), pp. 5–22.

Neeleman, A. (2019) The Scope of School Autonomy in Practice: An Empirically Based Classification of School Interventions. *Journal of Educational Change* **20**, pp. 31–55.

OECD (2008) *Improving School Leadership Vol. 1: Policy and practice.* Online. Available at: https://www.oecd.org/education/school/Improving-school-leadership.pdf (Accessed 26 August 2022).

Silva, A. (2016) What Is Leadership. *Journal of Business Studies Quarterly* **8**(1), pp. 1–4.

Stogdill, R.M. (1950) Leadership, Membership, and Organization. *Psychological Bulletin* **47**(1), pp. 1–14.

2 The Intersection of System and Distributed Leadership

Ian Potter

Introduction

This chapter draws on my experience of school leadership in England over several decades and from reviewing the literature. My argument is that typical notions of what is a 'system leader' are less relevant when the idea of non-solo leadership is gaining traction. The notion that every school is a 'great school' because it has a 'great leader' is challenged as a dominant model for school improvement. I contend that the perception of Transformational leadership as charismatic leaders is not how the whole system is best transformed. The case argued is that (eco)systems perceived as organisms for distributed and shared leadership is how the schooling landscape can be improved sustainably. It is recognised that the transformation of self is a crucial ingredient in transformation of the system. The chapter begins by discussing a context for appreciating the leadership and management landscape across the schooling landscape in England.

Theoretical perspectives

The numerous attempts to theorise what senior leadership in schools looks like, or should look like, vary around the historically contested issue of the importance, or not, of the dominant solo senior leader. It is a case of contention whether that individual leader is working, or should be working, within a collective, shared approach to leadership or within a status-orientated, hierarchical, and bureaucratic scenario. It is probably simplistic to characterise the discourses as being 'from solo to distributive leadership' because it may be conceptualised better as 'solo *and* distributed' (Crawford, 2012). Indeed, Gronn (2010), having established the historical significance of leadership in various societal arrangements, provides a genealogy of leadership and describes the phenomenon of 'reverse dominance hierarchy'. He reveals anthropological evidence about hunter-gatherers that suggest a culture of leadership by groups. This 'order of things' existed in order to prevent leadership by a top individual because such a thing would destroy the balance required in hunting and gathering. It was only when settlements emerged that institutionalised authority came into being, and the monopolising impact of dominant hierarchy was realised.

Gronn (2010) builds on the reverse dominance concept to argue for an understanding of leadership that he calls 'leadership configuration'. His idea of the egalitarian relationship enjoyed by hunter-gatherer leaders resonates with the idea that strong management cultures protect the collective from the dominance of the individual.

DOI: 10.4324/9781003321439-2

Zalenzik (1977), however, identified the stultifying impact that this can have, particularly when change is required. A culture of managerialism in an organisation ensures succession to power through the development of managers, as opposed to the growth of individual leaders. Managerialism is a power ethic that favours the collective over individual leadership; the cult of the group over that of personality (Zalenzik, 1977). The bureaucratic ethos of such organisations protects the business from the impact of the dangerous individual, the maverick. However, it was against this 'conservatism' that Zalenzik championed a concept of leadership which promoted the idea that it takes 'great' people to become leaders. They are the people who can act out a psycho-drama of the brilliant, lonely person who gains control of themselves as a precondition for control-ling others and enabling change.

This emphasis on the personality of the individual led to constructions of leader-managers that are prevalent today and which celebrate individuals who are risk-takers, divergent thinkers, and visionaries. These leaders, according to Zalenzik, achieve followership through presenting an image of idealism, and gain emotional buy-in because they are perceived as less manipulative and con-trolling as the dispassionate 'manager'. In other words, the discourse of 'leader as controller', or transactional leadership, gives way to a discourse that is 'leader as messiah' or transformational leadership (Western, 2012: 12).

Question for discussion

Can you think of examples from your own experience where you have been led by someone who fits the manager description above and perhaps another who has been more like the leader, as described?

Bush (2011) outlines six models of management that he identifies as existing in education, and associated with these is a set of educational leadership models. Together they provide a helpful number of 'lenses' through which to try to understand leadership and management in schools (Mongon and Chapman, 2012). Bush points out that no single model should be applied and, in order to understand what is happening in schools, it is best not to even try to. Nevertheless, according to Bush (2011: 15), educational leadership and management has progressed from being 'a new field dependent upon ideas developed in other settings' and becoming an estab-lished discipline with its own theories and significant empirical data testing their validity in education.

It is a contested point whether or not education is simply another field for the application of gen-eral principles of leadership and management, typically drawn from and dependent upon industrial and organisational models, or is a special case justifying a distinct approach with its own body of knowledge.

Question for discussion

To what extent do you think leadership and management thinking is generic to all contexts or is better understood within the context of its application?

The theory/practice divide can cause school leadership to be dismissive of theories because of their seeming remoteness from the 'real' school situation (Bush, 2011: 23). Yet, it is not sensible to dismiss them as irrelevant because they provide mental maps and cognitive frameworks for interpretation of practice and experience, as well as potentially to inform future activity. Furthermore, a dependence on personal experience is narrow because it denies the knowledge of others. Therefore, the 'relevance of theory should be judged by the extent to which it informs leadership action and contributes to the resolution of practical problems in schools' (Bush, 2011: 26). Hence, my appreciation of my practice has been enhanced by the literature and theorising, and indeed the theoretical model I present in this chapter is generated from both types of knowledge.

System leadership

In my time in school leadership in England, the concept of a 'system leader' gained currency alongside the orthodoxy that every school could be a great school if only it had a great leader (Hopkins, 2007). Such a perspective encourages the notion of the individual leader who is charismatic in making a difference to the system, because it is thought that policy needs to enable these individuals to increase their sphere of influence beyond the single school they lead. Thus, system leadership is perceived through the lens of the solo-leader who is given parts of the system to lead. This is what makes them 'a system leader'. This chapter gives a profile to another way of thinking about system leadership.

Senge (2000) presents a notion of 'system thinking' that has the implication that leaders need to look beyond their own discrete activity to consider wider interconnections through which they can collectively lead change. Higham *et al.* (2009:8) argue for 'the central state...to play a more enabling role'. Their argument is for government to facilitate the conditions for a new professionalism of headship in which headteachers provide an alternative to reform driven in a top-down way. Their ambition is that '...such professionalism should be capable of harnessing local ownership and ideas...' (*ibid*). In other words, system thinking can be interpreted as a lateral approach to leadership that generates a leadership ethos which is more about distributing the power that comes with knowledge creation and decision-making.

A system leadership perspective encourages a disposition that the system needs to self-consciously build professional capacity within itself and that this 'implies a rebalancing towards greater internal evaluation' (Higham *et al.*, 2009:10). Dimmock's (2012) definition of leadership illuminates how leadership is about capacity building. He writes:

> Leadership is a social influence process guided by a moral purpose with the aim of building capacity by optimising available resources towards the achievement of shared goals (2012: 7).

He presents a construct of leadership that is not necessarily about 'a' leader. He draws on Leithwood and Reihl (2003) and their finding that leadership is primarily a set of group-orientated processes. This resonates with Gronn's (2010) idea that distributed leadership (DL) needs to be perceived not as one leader distributing leadership, but rather as a concept of leadership being collective and properly distributed. DL is discussed further later in the chapter, but the important point here is a perspective on school leadership that is about capacity building in order to bring about school improvement.

System leadership theory demands that school leaders engage in a much deeper and wider development of learning communities, widespread horizontal and lateral ways of working and, above all, the leadership of learning by schools. And yet, as Higham *et al.* identify: 'The difficulty is that, in imagining this new professionalism, the thinking of many stakeholders is constrained by their experiences within the existing power structure' (2009: 10). It is intended that this chapter is a contribution to that mindset shift and new imagining.

Questions for discussion

If you are, or are planning to become, a teacher, how keen are you to understand how the system of your classroom is impacted by the wider system into which it was nested? Why might an understanding of the system be significant?

Jackson (2003) challenges leaders to learn to be holistic in their thinking. His idea of 'holism' to the education sector requires schools to see themselves as constituting the system and for 'a multitude of new lateral interactions between schools to rebalance or rival central power structures?' (Higham *et al.*, 2009: 15).

Goodson (2003) and Bottery (2006) favour the term 'collaborative working' to describe the inter-professional paradigm of leadership today, and what Gibbon *et al.* (1994) refer to as 'cross-professional' working. Cox (2010) describes it as 'shared leadership', whereas Dunford (2010) uses the term 'partnership working'. There is also Lumby's (2009) term 'collective leadership'. In this seeming myriad of definitions for collaborative leadership; each author is attempting an exposition of the changing paradigm of school leadership towards non-solo leadership. Each is trying to describe what the new professionalism looks like and how it differs from what was the condition of being a headteacher in the past. The signifiers chosen to highlight the shift in emphasis – or fresh lens through which to perceive school leadership – although different, may in fact be related to the same phenomenon that is being signified: a new professional identity of headship which is a leader who has the ability to work collaboratively with others. They are system leaders because they contribute collaboratively, collectively, in a shared way, to system improvement.

Question for discussion

Have you found yourself frustrated by the slipperiness of language, or do you enjoy a debate about defining what is meant when a term is used?

Distributive leadership

DL has emerged as the dominant discourse in school leadership in England and many jurisdictions around the world. The OECD has 'highlighted the prime importance of DL in transforming schools' (Hall *et al.*, 2011: 32).

The National College of School Leadership in England (NCSL) presented DL as a model of good practice as reflected in their training materials (2007). The Specialist Schools and

Academies Trust (SSAT) endorsed DL (Harris, 2005, 2008), as did Leithwood *et al.* (2006) in their literature search for a New Labour government project. The DL project asserted 'that school leadership has a greater influence on schools and students when it is widely distributed' (Hall *et al.*, 2011: 32).

The literature that challenged the 'distributed leadership' movement argued that it is used within schools to mask the harsh realities of central government prescription (Hartley, 2007) and that, too often, it is used by school leaders as a tactic for delegation rather than as a strategy (Hartley, 2010). This resonated with Hatcher's (2005) view of the contradiction inherent in leadership distribution to lower levels of management in schools against a backdrop of government-driven managerialism of headteachers. Indeed, more recently, O'Sullivan and Mac Ruairc (2022) provide evidence that the Irish government's preference for delegation in leadership is masquerading as DL. Hence, the concept of DL employed within schools remains somewhat slippery and elastic (Hartley, 2007).

Notwithstanding these contentions, Hall *et al.* (2011) find that the concept has emerged strongly into the discourse of English schools. How that discourse is translated into practice will vary from school to school and school leader to school leader, hence the slipperiness identified in what it means. A significant interpretation of why it has proved useful in schools is the shift it represents away from a dependency on the 'talents and energy of one influential and dominant individual' (Spillane, 2006 in Hall *et al.*, 2011: 33). The 'all-knowing' school leader no longer reigns. Instead, as Gunter (2005) argues, there is an alternative to the model of the heroic transformational 'super head' that was becoming somewhat discredited as a sustainable solution to longer term school improvement. This democratisation of decision-making in schools and the lateralisation of leadership resonates with the discourse above about system leadership.

The key resonance, however, is with the traits required for effective collaborative leadership. To be truly collaborative requires the ability to be distributive rather than protective. A leader who has struggled to share authority within their own school may find it difficult to do so with another headteacher. Someone who has learnt that a professional identity for headship is about being the charismatic leader of the school, one who is the ultimate authority on what the organisation is supposed to think and stand for, may find working laterally with a leader of another school too great a challenge. Thus, in order for them to work effectively together, it cannot be a partnership of equal respect: the collaboration relies on one partner acquiescing to the 'superiority' of the other. In this scenario, system leadership becomes the extension of an empire for the 'super-head' rather than a mutual understanding about how collaboratively headteachers work well together for the good of all their pupils and the wider community. Thus, my argument is that a self-improving system in which school leaders can truly work collaboratively together probably needs a new lexicon to describe the professional identity of such headship. It will need to be able to describe the traits, attributes, and behaviours of headteachers who can work effectively together in collaboration within an actually DL context.

Question for discussion

Have you experienced a boss who invites you to be 'part-of-the-process' in order to control you rather than to really include you in what they are doing?

It is often a challenge for school leaders to be collaborative. As Bush (2011) explains,

> Since the 1980s education has been framed by masculinist discourses and I have observed during my teaching career how the language of business and the corporate world has been adopted in education. School leaders have learned to be fierce guardians of the reputation of their schools, and often the school is an extension of their own ego. Thus, the ability to perceive leadership in the way Rubin articulates it will be a challenge to these leaders.

Rubin (2009: 2) states:

> You are a collaborative leader once you have accepted responsibility for building – or helping to ensure the success of – a heterogeneous team to accomplish a shared purpose…collaborative leadership is the skilful and mission-orientated facilitation of relevant relationships.

Those 'masculinist discourses' (Bush, 2011: 38) have informed the professional identity and self-construction of the highly ambitious traditional headteacher looking to lead systems that are, in effect, extensions of their empires. Their mindsets are a barrier to making the transition to real collaborative system leadership and a truly self-improving school system. They are too steeped in the historic 'king-like' construct of headship to be able to understand the concept of the collaborative leader. They will not comprehend what is so beautifully expressed here with:

> Let's be very clear: 'collaborative' leader does not prescribe the context in which leadership happens, rather it modifies 'leader' to describe the type, style, and purpose of the leader. In other words: *Collaborative leaders do not necessarily (or only) lead collaboration, they lead collaboratively'* (Rubin, 2009:3).

Furthermore, Glanz's (2007) notion of collective leadership initiating things is helpful. It is a leadership that is sustainable because everyone is involved in being 'sustainers'. Initiatives are sustainable because of a culture of engagement in the processes of managing the organisation and system. As Glanz (2007: 9) states:

> 'Engaging and encouraging collaborative decision making is the heart of collaborative leadership'

The following section explores interpretations of how evolving perspectives have impacted on policy evolution in England.

Implications of policy evolution in England on perspectives of school leadership

I have tabulated interpretations of the evolution of policy in England over a 10-year period at the start of the twenty-first century as researched by different scholars (see Figure 2.1 over page).

The parallels across the commentaries outlined in the above table illuminate a direction of travel towards schools as more autonomous +entities, adopting an identity of being self-managing units. This is common in all of the narratives. The drift towards (or back towards) the school leader being

Chronology	Simpkins (2012, p. 622–627)	Ball (2008, p. 57)	Taylor (2013)	Higham et al (2009, p. 128/9)	Hargreaves & Shirley (2009, p. 3–15)	Glatter (2012, p. 526–564)
1870 Education Act		**Modern State (1870–1944)** Liberal resistance to state intervention is overcome				
1944 Education Act	**The Era of Administration** 1944 - mid 80s (p. 623)				**The First Way of Innovation and Inconsistency** (End of WW2 till mid-1970s) Innovation without Cohesion	
1976 The Ruskin Speech		**Welfare State (1944–1976)** National system of education provision, administered locally	Pre Ruskin: **Solidaristic (1970s)** Belief in egalitarianism	Pre LMS: *Laissez-faire and paternalistic culture of leadership [Secret classroom]*		*1960s liberal, optimistic mood* *1970s 'battle for ideas': Publication of 'Black Papers' from 1969*
1988 (LMS) The Education Reform Act (after Thatcher's 3rd election victory)	**The Era of Management** Mid 80s – 97 (p. 625) ERA is defining legislative moment in management era (p. 624)	**Neoliberal state (1976–97)** End of professional autonomy for teachers and schools as the emerging comprehensive national system breaks down	Post Ruskin: **Hierarchical (1980s)** Belief in policy, command, audit, government control	Post ERA: *Locally Managed Schools within devolved autonomy tempered by national accountability framework*	**The Interregnum of Complexity and Contradiction** (Mid-70s to late 80s) **The Second Way of Markets and Standardisation** (Late 80s to late 1990s)	*1972: BEAS formed* *1976: Ruskin* *1985: No Turning Back Group ILEA abolished* *1988: The Self – Managing School published*
1997 'New Labour' Govt. elected	**The Era of Leadership** 1997 – date (p. 625)	**Managerial or Competition State (1997–2007)** End of national system administered locally	**Individualistic (1990s)** New Public management encourages belief in markets and individualism	Mid 1990s: *Pressure from league tables and inspection regime leads to high degrees of competitiveness between schools* Late 1990s, 2000s: *Commitment to collaboration to ameliorate competitive environments with initiatives such as*	*Top-Down Government, Bottom-up Support* **The Third Way of Performance and Partnerships** (from 1990s) *Government demands and performance targets met through lateral energy achieved from partnership working*	*1992: First Publication of School performance tables* *1993: Creation of Ofsted New Labour continue market and privatisation route, as well as increasing central steerage of system including National Strategies.*
2000 National College established	Leadership development framework established (p. 626)		**A post modern, uncertain frame of a non-classicist perspective in which the three beliefs chaotically conflict with each other**	*'Excellence in Cities, LIG, New Relationships with Schools (SIPs)*		*2000: introduction of Academies to replace schools in difficulties* *2010: academisation of higher performing schools, including 'free schools'.*

Figure 2.1 Evolution of Policy in England

a leader of a business is evident in the chronology. There are variations in interpretation about the role of the state and the system in how things evolved.

Ball (2008: 76) argues that policymakers felt that what was needed was 'more market, less state', that is to say deregulation, liberalisation, and privatisation. He suggests that it was 'an antagonism towards the welfare state that signalled this "neo-liberal outlook"' (Ball, 2008: 77). Consequently, any special status that public services may once have had no longer applied. This was to the extent that some such as water, gas, electricity, and telecommunications were sold off. Others, including education, were expected to adopt the cultures and corporate sector ways of working.

An impact of this neo-liberalising of the public sector brought with it changes to the development of school leaders. A paradigm shift in the professional identity of school leaders led to them operating more like chief executives (Bolam, 1997; Simkins, 2012). The implication of introducing a competitive environment to the schooling sector produced school leaders who were fierce defenders of the reputations of their own schools, even if that meant denigrating the reputation of other schools and, at times, their leaders.

The challenge in such 'solo-orientated' competitiveness is ensuring justice for those who are not catered for by the vested interests of individual leaders. Which schools and school leaders will serve those learners who no one else wants to teach (Potter, 2017a)? Therefore, a schooling landscape that encourages non-solo perspectives of school and system leadership provides an antidote to the neo-liberalising impact.

Question for discussion

What is your view of school systems where the market ideology of competition between schools is seen as fundamental to improving schools?

Figure 2.2 illustrates a continuum upon which a conceptualisation of school leadership can be placed. It is a typology of perspectives on school leadership: a 'slippery' continuum from a solo conceptualisation of leadership towards a non-solo construct. Hence, it divides the theoretical perspectives propounded by academics into three categories: the first is those that perceive the leader as an individual. The third category includes scholars who theorise leadership as something that is non-solo. The second group of researchers located in the middle of the continuum interpret school leadership as a phenomenon that is *moving towards* a non-solo construct. Their research finds leadership to be about how school leaders are reinventing themselves.

The inexorable logic of a direction of travel towards non-solo leadership is that educational leadership is no longer about the position one holds but rather the way the organisation and/or system behaves to improve opportunities for learning for all. The word 'leadership' signals the energy, impetus, and collective action needed for change and improvement to occur (Robertson, 2008). It is how, collectively, schooling provision is more socially just and how the whole ecosystem of education works interdependently (Western, 2012).

Leadership becomes about the multitude and diversity of voices within and across schools. This potential for a morass of cultural mores within the system is recognised by ambiguity theories and 'the ambiguities of purpose, power, and experience make it difficult for leaders to distinguish between success and failure' (Bush, 2011: 162).

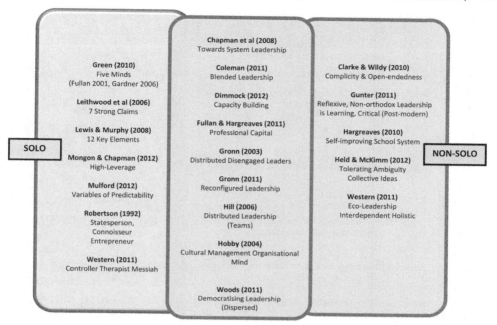

Figure 2.2 Conceptualisations of School Leadership

I interpret the appetite for theories and models of school leadership towards the non-solo end of the continuum is due to the increasing complexity of school leadership that I have experienced. It needs to be recognised, however, that the perspectives in category three of the typology in Figure 2.2 are based more on conjecture or scholarly theorising rather than on data collected from the field. It has been an emerging theory. Indeed, my autoethnographic research (forthcoming) is a contribution to the new knowledge required. I contend a necessity for non-solo perspectives on school leadership is, in part, because of the open-endedness and unpredictability of the context school leaders find themselves operating within; it is a situation best managed, and made sense of, through human relationships (Potter, 2013). Furthermore, I argue that there needs to be a dimension in leadership that is more than corporate targets and results. It should look more like this:

> ...transcendental, distributive, servant and quantum leadership are seen as representing more appropriate approaches to the contemporary school environment because of their emphasis on open-endedness, unpredictability and interpersonal relationships. It is these kinds of leadership...that are best suited to harnessing organisational learning through the development of organisational intelligence and an ability to learn from internal and external environments.' (Clarke and Wildy, 2010: 7)

Question for discussion

Do you agree that people are seeking the paradigm shift in leadership where leaders provide certainty, or do you think that people generally still expect leadership to have all the answers?

2003	Systems thinking within the closed system of a school	A Hargreaves, 2003 [Senge, 1990]
2004	Looking beyond one's own school Standards of System Leadership	Fullan, 2004 Collarbone & West Burnham, 2008
2005– 2007	"Successful, highly effective leaders" leading other schools within the system	Hopkins, 2007 O'Leary & Craig, 2007 Collarbone & West-Burnham, 2008 Higham et al., 2009
2008	System redesign: all within the system reconfigured	D Hargreaves, 2008 Williamson, 2008 (Gronn, 2010)
2009– 2011	Sustainable collaborations require mutuality rather than the leadership of an individual	(Smith, 2009 & Leana, 2011) Halinger & Heck, 2010
2012	Dispersed leadership for 'holistic democracy', enabling increases in 'professional capital'	Woods, 2012 A Hargreaves & Fullan, 2012
2012	Self-improving, self-correcting school system of collective social capital	D Hargreaves, 2012
2013	Whole system educational leadership (All Systems Go: whole system reform)	Campbell, 2013 (Fullan, 2010)

Figure 2.3 Chronology of a Decade of Research Discourse on System Leadership 2003–2013

The impact on the policy direction of systems thinking in the education landscape in England is now examined.

Figure 2.3 illuminates how, within a decade, the literature on system leadership took us from Senge's (1990) introduction of systems thinking and how that might be applied to the classroom and the closed system of the school to a perception of the whole system being a combination of all systems within it. A way of thinking was reached that was about a self-improving, self-reforming school system.

As can be seen, within a decade, the literature on system leadership moved from system leader as a solo leader applying systems thinking to their leadership to a conception of system leadership that is about the non-solo. The system as a whole leads itself, and it does so through a construct of leadership that is distributed throughout the system.

The discourse tends towards an interpretation that leadership is inherently a collective enterprise, and so what is the role of the individual leader in making leadership collaborative and shared? And what are their motivations for doing so? Is it part of a neo-liberalising hegemony to ensnare all into a corporatising ideology? Or is it an emancipatory movement of reducing hierarchies and empowering every learner? Is it that the building of a culture of continuous improvement is a distributed activity (Bennett *et al.*, 2003)? Or is it the case that leadership is already distributed (Woods and Roberts, 2013; Youngs, 2009), and the purpose of a debate is whether or not power, as well as influence, have been distributed?

Woods and Roberts (2013) argue that leadership *is* a distributed phenomenon; it is not a matter of whether or not leadership *should be* distributed, it *is* distributed. 'The consequence is that everyone concerned with school education needs to understand and work with this fact – and consider how in practice leadership is distributed and whether it is distributed fairly and for the benefit of students' learning' (*ibid*: 1).

Question for discussion

How does the idea that everyone is a leader, whether we like it or not, resonate with you?

My model for systributed leadership

Linking thinking about leadership within and across schools with theories of distributing leadership of learning within and across classrooms will develop a holistic conceptual framework that is powerful in how we understand what collaborative, interdependent, empowering learning communities can look like in school systems (Macdonald *et al.*, 2020; Ritchie *et al.* 2021). There is still a place for DL in the discourse on school leadership. It has gained unprecedented purchases. It is, therefore, pragmatic to make use of a term that has such a constituency and to push for an interpretation of it that is of greater value to the school system and its learners. Leadership has never really been the domain of one individual; it is structures, traditions, hegemonies, and vested interests that have sustained a 'preferred' dominant view of individualism and hierarchies.

The signifier of DL supports a leadership discourse in schools that is about creating and sustaining collaborative learning communities. DL 'works' because it signifies the process by which we shift from the individual leader to collective leadership. DL is the solo to non-solo signifier. It is the construct that exemplifies the journey school leaders need to take within their own schools, and the route schools need to take within the system. What is called for is a concept that transforms that 'siloised' school leader into a way of thinking that I refer to as 'Systributed' Leadership (Potter, 2015).

The model is a theory generated from both the literature and an auto-ethnographic method of research; it is a synthesis of the perspectives in the literature and empirical evidence of my lived professional experience, found from a reflexive enquiry (Potter, 2017b) using the data from my own career and informed by the literature.

Systributed leadership is when school leaders know how to distribute leadership in their own schools and how to share leadership of their schools and other schools with colleagues.

It requires an understanding and application that demands considerable reflection and deep thought. It is not about delegation, or strategies to cope with an ever-increasing workload. It is more fundamental than that. It is philosophical.

The transformation from the headship of a single school to 'collaborative' system leadership has to be at the core of a 'self-improving system'. School leaders have to engage in recording the narratives of their journeys from 'traditional' headship to a new professional identity of 'systributed' leadership. An autoethnographic reflexivity will engender a culture of social justice in schools because it will develop a construct of leadership that is synonymous with collaborative learning. The transformation from headship of a single school to 'collaborative' system leadership will be at the core of a 'self-improving system' that is socially just.

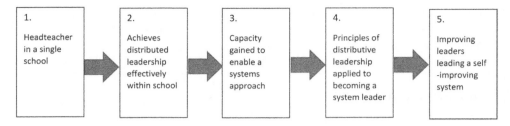

Figure 2.4 The Process of Transformation

The theory is that to 'really' be a system leader, of the collaborative type, requires one to be effective in 'distributed leadership'. I use the term 'distributed' to represent, as explained above, the range of various signifiers for shared, collaborative leadership, and recognise that within the literature, it is a contested concept. It is a five-stage model for the transformation to an 'authentic' system leader. This is a transformation from 'solo-leadership' and is predicated on the leader having been effective in 'really' distributing leadership within the single school context. Figure 2.4 outlines the process of transformation.

Implicit in my theoretical proposition is that within a self-improving system there needs to be self-improving school leaders. I summarise my proposition in Figure 2.5, which is a conceptual map of what would be the outcome of the five-stage process in Figure 2.4. It illuminates how the transformation from the headteacher of a single school to 'collaborative' system leader is at the core of a 'self-improving system', and for it to occur, there needs to be headteachers who are effective at distributing leadership, taking an 'authentic' collaborative and partnership approach to their leadership.

The conceptual leap is from a 'closed system' (Senge, 2000) approach of distributing leadership within one's own school or schools towards an 'open' system approach in which the distribution of leadership happens across the ecosystem. It happens because a new way of thinking and working, and a 'new' professional identity, has developed.

Figure 2.5 A Conceptual Map of What Would Be the Outcome of the Five-Stage Process

Summary points

The chapter outlines

- The contribution systems thinking has made to leadership discourse;
- the unprecedented use of the term DL in the literature and in policy;
- the impact of both in developing a non-solo perspective on school leadership;
- the challenge for many school leaders' professional identity to be non-silo;
- a model for enabling transition from headship to systributed leadership.

Recommended reading

Crawford, M. (2012) Solo and Distributed Leadership: Definitions and Dilemmas. *Educational Management Administration and Leadership*, **40**(5), pp. 610–620.

Gronn, P. (2003) *The New Work of Educational Leaders: Changing leadership practice in an era of school reform*. London: Sage.

Macdonald, I., Dixon, C. and Tiplady, T. (2020) *Improving Schools Using Systems Leadership: Turning intention into reality*. Abingdon: Routledge.

Senge, P. (1990) *The Fifth Discipline*. NewYork: Doubleday

References

Ball, S. (2008) *Education PLC*. Abingdon: Routledge.

Bennett, N., Wise, C., Woods, P. and Harvey, J. (2003) *Distributed Leadership*. Oxford: NSCL.

Bolam, R. (1997) Management Development for Headteachers: Retrospect and Prospect. *Educational Management Administration and Leadership* **32**(2), pp. 265–284.

Bottery, M. (2006) Education and Globalisation: Redefining the Role of the Education Professional. *Educational Review* **58**(1), pp. 95–113.

Bush, T. (2011) *Theories of Educational Leadership and Management* (4th ed.). London: SAGEe.

Bush, T. and Crawford, M. (2012) Mapping the Field Over 40 Years: A Historical Review. *Educational Management Administration and Leadership* **40**(5), pp. 357–543.

Clarke, S. and Wildy, H. (2010) Preparing for Principalship from the Crucible of Experience: Reflecting on Theory, Practice and Research. *Journal of Educational Administration and History* **42**(1), pp. 1–16.

Cox, K. (Ed.) (2010) *Distributing and Sustaining Leadership*. Leicester: ASCL.

Dimmock, C. (2012) *Leadership, Capacity Building and School Improvement*. Abingdon: Routledge.

Dunford, J. (2010) Vital Cooperation' Leader. *The Education Leader Magazine* **48**, pp. 16–17.

Gibbon, M., Limoges, C., Nowtny, H., Schwartzman, S., Scott, P. and Trow, M. (1994) *The New Production of Knowledge*. London: Sage.

Glanz, J. (2007) On Vulnerability and Transformative Leadership: An Imperative for Leaders of Supervision. *International Journal of Leadership in Education* **10**(2), pp. 115–135.

Glatter, R. (2012) Persistent Preoccupations: The Rise and Rise of School Autonomy and Accountability in England. *Educational Management Administration and Leadership* **40**(5), pp. 559–575.

Goodson, I. (2003) *Professional Knowledge, Professional Lives*. Oxford: Oxford University Press.

Gronn, P. (2010) Leadership: Its Genealogy, Configuration and Trajectory. *Journal of Educational Administration and History* **42**(4), pp. 405–435.

Gunter, H.M. (2005) *Leading Teachers*. London: Continuum.

Hall, D., Gunter, H.M. and Bragg, J. (2011) The Discursive Performance of Leadership in Schools. *Management in Education* **25**(1), pp. 32–36.

Harris, A. (2005) *Crossing Boundaries and Breaking Barriers: Distributing leadership in schools*. London: Specialist Schools Trust.

Harris, A. (2008) *Distributed School Leadership*. Abingdon: Routledge.

Hartley, D. (2007) The Emergence of Distributed Leadership in Education: Why Now? *British Journal of Educational Studies* **55**(2), pp. 202–214.

Hartley, D. (2010) Paradigms: How Far Does Research in Distributed Leadership Stretch? *Education Management Administration and Leadership* **38**(3), pp. 271–285.

Hatcher, R. (2005) The Distribution of Leadership and Power in Schools. *British Journal of Sociology of Education* **26**(2), pp. 253–267.

Higham, R., Hopkins, D. and Mathews, P. (2009) *System Leadership in Practice.* Maidenhead: OUP.

Hopkins, D. (2007) *Every School a Great School: Realising the potential of system leadership.* Maidenhead: OUP.

Jackson, M. (2003) *Systems Thinking: Creative holism for managers.* Chichester: Wiley and Sons.

Leithwood, K., Day, C., Sammons, P., Harris, A. and Hopkins, D. (2006) *Seven Strong Claims about Successful School Leadership.* Nottingham: NCSL.

Leithwood, K. and Reihl, C. (2003) *What We Know About Successful School Leadership.* Nottingham: NSCL.

Lumby, J. (2009) Collective Leadership of Local School Systems Power Autonomy and Ethics. *Educational Management Administration and Leadership* **37**(3), pp. 310–328.

Macdonald, I., Dixon, C. and Tiplady, T. (2020) *Improving Schools Using Systems Leadership: Turning intention into reality.* Abingdon: Routledge.

Mongon, D. and Chapman, C. (2012) *High-Leverage Leadership: Improving outcomes in educational settings.* Abingdon: Routledge.

O'Sullivan, J. and Mac Ruairc, G. (2022) *System level implications regarding distributed leadership in the contemporary era: Discursive change to maintain the old order?* Paper presented to BERA Conference 6/9/2022.

Potter, I. (2013) *Self-improving School Leaders Within a Self-improving School System.* Paper presented at European Educational Research Association ECER on 10/9/13.

Potter, I. (2015) System Leadership in Education. *Bay House Journal of Education* (in house publication), **1**(5), pp. 16–19.

Potter, I. (2017a) Change in Context and Identity: The Case of an English School Leader. In P.S. Angelle (Ed.), *A Global Perspective of Social Justice Leadership for School Principals.* Charlotte, NC: Information Age Publishing.

Potter, I. (2017b) Developing Social Justice Leadership through Reflexivity. In P.S. Angelle (Ed.), *A Global Perspective of Social Justice Leadership for School Principals.* Charlotte, NC: Information Age Publishing.

Ritchie, M., Angelle, P. and Potter, I. (2021) School Leaders in England Transition Through Change: Insider and Outsider Perspectives. *Open Access,* **36**(1), pp. 40–58. https://sciendo.com/article/10.2478/jelpp-2021-0003

Robertson, J. (2008) *Coaching Educational Leadership: Building leadership capacity through partnership.* London: BELMAS; Sage.

Rubin, H. (2009) *Collaborative Leadership: Developing effective partnerships for communities and schools.* Thousand Oaks, CA: Corwin Press.

Senge, P. (1990) *The Fifth Discipline.* New York, NY: Doubleday.

Senge, P. M. (2000) Systems Change in Education. *Reflections* **1**(3), p. 58.

Simkins, T. (2012) Understanding School Leadership and Management Development in England. *Educational Management Administration and Leadership* **40**(5), pp. 621–640.

Spillane, J.P. (2006) *Distributed Leadership.* San Francisco, CA: John Wiley and Sons.

Western, S. (2012) An Overview of the Leadership Discourses. In M. Preedy, N. Bennett and C. Wise (Eds.), *Educational Leadership: Context, strategy and collaboration.* Milton Keynes: Open University/London: SAGE.

Woods, P. and Roberts, A. (2013) Leadership is…Distributed. *European Policy Network on School Leadership.* Online. Available at www.schoolleadership.eu/epnosi_vip/discussion/leadership-distributed (Accessed 14 October 2013).

Youngs, H. (2009) (Un)Critical Times? Situating Distributed Leadership in the Field. *Journal of Educational Administration and History* **41**(4), pp. 377–389.

Zalenzik, A. (1977) Managers and Leaders: Are they different? *Harvard Business Review.* Online. Available at https://hbr.org/2004/01/managers-and-leaders-are-they-different (Accessed 8 November 2022).

3 Equality and Diversity and Inclusive Practice: Significance for Organisations and Individuals

Sheine Peart

Introduction

Debates on equality, diversity, and inclusive practice have been discussed at all levels of society and nation-states for many years, with the Universal Declaration of Human Rights (which established an international benchmark for equality) recognised and endorsed by the United Nations (UN) in 1948. Currently, all 193 member states of the UN (including global superpowers such as the United States of America, the United Kingdom, France, Russia, and China) have all formally ratified this declaration, pledging their commitment to promote equality. However, translating theoretical rights into tangible outcomes and protections for all peoples requires careful planned action, appropriate financial, physical, and human resourcing, political will, and public endeavour. It is through conscious, determined actions that inclusion changes from optimistic wishful thinking to become the everyday reality of people's lives. Because of entrenched, persistent inequalities and challenges created through insular thinking and vested interest, inclusion cannot be left to chance in the vague belief that, given time, it will happen organically. In both contemporary and historical contexts governments have demonstrated a reluctance to engage across communities, share resources; or to redistribute power, as dramatically demonstrated in the persecution of Muslims in Myanmar in 2013. Accepting that equality, diversity, and inclusion remain a proclaimed ambition of the global community; it is concerning that so little progress has been made in some countries and that some UN member states have been charged with overt abuses against human rights.

While the Universal Declaration of Human Rights has established a template for inclusive practice for the world to follow and is a powerful influence on the development of international legislation, it is not a treaty. As such there is no legal obligation for countries to comply with the UN declaration or to enact its goals. In this context, the declaration can be viewed more as a statement of intent rather than an absolute obligation. It remains the responsibility of individual nations to create ethical legislative frameworks, underwritten by corresponding laws and supported by relevant enforcement agencies to create an environment which can realise the ambitions of the declaration. Although legislature may be presented as objective, neutral, and dispassionate, laws are entirely constructed by populations, and can change: they can be brought into existence or removed from statute. All laws are a product of context and are profoundly influenced by history and culture. These three factors (context, history, and culture) act collectively to determine which laws are written, which groups may (or may not) receive protection and how robustly laws are upheld. In addition to offering protection to individuals and groups, legislation through its ability to normalise actions within and across communities, is one of the factors which determines what acceptable and expected behaviour is

DOI: 10.4324/9781003321439-3

and can therefore work to support inclusion or can legitimate discriminatory practice. In education settings, leaders must manage working collaboratively with all users to develop policies and procedures which ensure the rights of all groups are protected and at the same time acknowledge any historic injustice.

Through examining selected pivotal events and using the lens of UK legislation, this chapter considers how historical events have highlighted specific inequalities, and how often grass-roots campaigns have pushed forward debates, forcing action. Taking three specific foci, disability, gender, and race, the chapter explores how individuals and organisations can take ownership and challenge persistent inequalities to produce structural and material changes, governed by an ideology of universal fairness. In organisations, administrative leadership requires the understanding of legal structures to ensure legislative obligations are met; moral leadership demands that frameworks are established to protect dignity and promote agreement across and between groups. Leaders must remain alert to the organisational climate and the needs of groups, and work with communities to generate relevant, collaborative responses to both existing and emerging needs where all voices are actively heard and engaged with in developing co-operative approaches.

Terminology

Debates regarding equality, diversity, and inclusion are in constant flux, as is the terminology used in these discussions. While terms such as 'handicapped' or 'coloured people' have been generally rejected as outdated and failing to accommodate the views of the groups the terms are intended to describe, there is less clarity on currently acceptable terms, partly as a consequence of the evolution of debate and partly as a result of the multiple diverse voices which need to be captured and included in the development of an agreed terminology.

Drawing on legislation, the term 'disabled people' will be used to describe those who have 'a physical or mental impairment, and the impairment has a substantial and long-term adverse effect' (HM Government, 2010). Acknowledging the fluidity of debate, 'women' is used to describe females aged 18 and over, and 'girls' to describe females under 18. Similarly, 'men' is used for males over 18 and 'boys' for males under 18. 'Black or global majority' is used to describe people who are 'Black, Asian, Brown, dual-heritage, indigenous to the global south, and or have been racialised as 'ethnic minorities' (Campbell-Stephens, 2020). This term is used as it reconfigures discussions and obviates the stigma of being depicted as marginal populations.

Disability rights

Before concepts of gender and race equality were protected in UK law, there was an early recognition of disability as an equality issue. As early as 1927, the Mental Deficiency Act acknowledged societal and personal challenges to individuals as a consequence of mental incapacity necessitating some form of intervention including state guardianship. In 1944, following the growing number of people returning wounded from the war, the Disabled Persons Employment Act sought to assist disabled people in finding employment as well as providing rehabilitation and vocational training courses. In the same year, the 1944 Education Act required that all children, regardless of their physical or academic capabilities needed to be in a setting receiving an education, and local authorities should also make suitable provisions for older students with disabilities.

While these were among the first UK equality laws and gave some protection to disabled people, it is important to remember the prevailing attitude towards disability at the time. When these acts were passed, disability was constructed as the problem of the individual; a problem which needed to be fixed so that the individual would then be able to take part in mainstream society. This was a medical model of disability which configured disabled people as a problem to be fixed and was responsible for further 'exacerbating disadvantage and exclusion' (Witcher, 2015: 106), pushing disabled people to the fringes of society. Because the medical model positioned disabled people as incapable of sound, rationale thought and 'not only as a burden but also a threat to the wellbeing of society' (Boronski and Hassan, 2015: 147), they were routinely prohibited from making decisions about their own lives; their voices were unheard and instead decision-making rested with professionals, including doctors, psychologists, and other clinicians.

Medical language which described disabled people, predicated on a deficit approach, permeated everyday language and normalised thinking, which simultaneously configured disabled people as both 'heroic and freakish' (Millett-Gallant, 2017: 428). The medical model was both persuasive and pervasive and dominated thinking about the capability of disabled people until the 1950s where disabled people were seen as helpless dependents reliant on the assistance of others.

In contrast, the social model of disability reconfigured disability as a societal construct, where mainstream culture has created barriers which prevents disabled people from fully engaging with the structures and systems of society. Responsibility is therefore not an individual concern, but one which is borne by the whole of society. The social model represented a significant change in thinking as, rather than holding individuals as being personally responsible for the impact of their disability, 'the model decoupled the causal link between impairment and disability, instead attributing the cause of disability to the impact of socio-cultural context' (Witcher, 2015: 118).

The social model helped to inform the actions of the Disabled People's Direct-Action Network (DAN), a UK organisation established in 1993 by Barbara Lisicki, Alan Holdsworth, and Sue Elsegood. DAN rejected the notion that disabled people were reliant on charity and through a series of high-profile direct-action campaigns including 'handcuffing themselves to public transport' (Webster, 2022). Using the rallying call of 'Piss on Pity', activists drew attention to the different ways society worked to ignore and disadvantage disabled people through exclusion and marginalisation. DAN's tactics were so effective that they 'successfully convinced the Conservative government to pass the Disability Discrimination Act (DDA) in 1995' (*ibid*). Even though this Act helped to strengthen rights for disabled people, for many it did not go far enough, leading a DAN member to comment that 'the real concerns of what disabled people need' (BBC News, 2003) had not been addressed.

Within education, the strengthening of disability rights has been achieved through new legal obligations identified in the Equality Act 2010 (HM Government, 2010), the Children's and Families Act 2014, and the Special Educational Needs and Disability Code of Practice 2014 (revised 2015). Under the Disability Code of Practice, children and young people who had previously received statements to meet their educational needs were to be issued an Education, Health and Care Plan (EHCP). This plan would incorporate all the child's or young person's needs and employed a multi-agency approach, bringing together health services, therapeutic interventions and other identified needs. A particularly important feature of this last piece of legislation is that it foregrounded rather than silenced the voice of the disabled person, and section A of the plan must contain 'the views, interests and aspirations of the child and his or her parents or the young person' (DfE, 2015: 164).

Rieser (2012: 159) states,

> At least 15 percent of the world's people have a significant long-term, physical or mental impairment that can and usually does disable them from taking part in the usual educational, social and economic activity in their community. This is due to barriers in attitudes, in the built environment and the way society is organised.

Change has happened over time and successive amendments to legislation are testimony to the possibility of progress. What remains striking, though, is the pace of change and apparent unwillingness of authorities to listen to groups or to act on their views. This resistance has resulted in individuals feeling compelled to take direct action to bring their issues to the attention of authorities. There is a risk for any leader or leadership group which does not listen to the populations they work with. Further, although legislation may compel action, attitudes can be slow to change and, while the population of disabled people in employment had risen to 4.4 million by June 2021, disabled workers were more likely to be in part-time, lower-skilled positions (DWP, 2021) suggesting entrenched views regarding the capability of disabled people.

Questions for discussion

Carry out an examination of your setting's physical environment. What provisions are in place to support disabled people? For example, is an induction loop available to support staff or students who may have a hearing impairment?

What current processes or procedures exist which may cause challenges to disabled people? For example, is there a 'hot-desking' policy which may cause unnecessary stress to those with social anxiety disorders?

How does your organisation capture the voices of disabled people, and how does it act on this information?

In your organisation how, historically, have leaders managed the demands of marginalised groups? What plans does the leadership team have for working in a proactive way with disabled people to manage possible future demands?

How should leaders address financial issues with regards to making reasonable adjustments for disabled organisation users? How should possible tensions between funding and provision be approached?

MeToo and sex equality

Sex equality in education has not yet been achieved and most leaders would, without a second thought, reject archaic ideas which only allowed women and girls to study solely a non-technical, domestic curriculum based on 'their perceived biological, psychological and social differences' (Inner London Education Authority, 1986: 22). While such ideas are rightly consigned to history, gender debates including the lack of representation of women in leadership positions, and the ongoing challenge of gender-based harassment persists. The 1975 Sex Discrimination Act made sex discrimination illegal in the UK. While focussing primarily on employment and work-based training, education was also included, and the Act set a template to both identify and challenge discriminatory practices.

Like disability, sex equality has been subsumed into the 2010 Equality Act, identified as one of the nine protected characteristics and remains an important local, national, and international priority. In its 2030 sustainable development goals, the UN specifically identified the 'need to achieve gender equality and empower all women and girls' as well as calling for an 'end to all forms of discrimination against women and girls everywhere' (United Nations, 2015: 21). Further, when meeting in London in 2021, the G7 nations reaffirmed their commitment to these goals and agreed to 'sign up to new global targets' (Gov.UK, 2021) to improve the education opportunities of women and girls. In this context, for leaders sex equality is not an option but an imperative.

While national and international frameworks have identified the need for women and girls to be protected in education and the workplace, because of the normalisation of 'sexual harassment, from name calling to physical abuse' (Renold, 2006: 443), women and girls have not always accurately identified abuse when it has occurred, or have not had the confidence to challenge it. Consequently, for many young people education settings have become 'abusive and dangerous spaces' (*ibid*) which have provided them little protection and where abuse, sometimes excused as banter, has proliferated unchallenged.

The prevalence of sexual harassment and violence was bought into sharp focus through the MeToo movement. Started in 2006 by Tarana Burke in America, MeToo was a vehicle for survivors of sexual abuse and harassment to recognise the trauma they had lived through, and provided a space which enabled survivors to share their stories and through supportive, caring empathy begin the process of healing. At the same time, MeToo sought to draw attention to the extent of the problem of sexual harassment and how so many women and girls had been subjected to this kind of abuse. Although MeToo started as a localised grass-roots endeavour, a series of successful criminal convictions against such luminaries as film producer Harvey Weinstein, comedian Bill Cosby, and USA Gymnastics national team doctor Larry Nassar, helped to demonstrate the frequency of sexual abuse and how many influential people had misused their authority so that their actions remained uncontested and hidden, denying justice to survivors.

Sexual harassment, like other forms of discrimination, has evolved to reflect contemporary times and changes in technology. In the UK in 2018, 'almost 100 cases of upskirting were reported to police ... including one in Leicestershire where female pupils said a teacher had taken pictures up their skirts in the classroom' (Times Educational Supplement, 2019). Upskirting is 'taking a sexually intrusive photograph up someone's skirt without their permission' (O'Mallay, 2019), and until recently, this invasive demeaning behaviour was not a criminal offence. However, following a successful campaign by Gina Martin where she used social media to highlight this issue and to gather support, the Voyeurism (Offences) Act became law in April 2019; offences were punishable by up to two years in prison.

In the context of what constituted unacceptable behaviour, the UK government commissioned Ofsted to investigate sexual abuse in schools and colleges. Ofsted's (2021) report found that 'for some children incidents [were] so commonplace that they [saw] no point in reporting them' and found 'the frequency of these harmful sexual behaviours [meant] that some children and young people considered them normal' (*ibid*: np). From 2019, the government have made 'Relationships Education compulsory in all primary schools in England and Relationships and Sex Education compulsory in all secondary schools' (DfE, 2019: 4). However, when asked about the effectiveness of this addition to the curriculum, 'Children and young people were rarely positive about the RSHE they had received. They felt that it was too little, too late and that the curriculum was not equipping them with the information and advice they needed to navigate the reality of their lives' (Ofsted 2021: np).

Thus, while legislation and curriculum changes have provided a framework for action, little appears to have changed for women and girls. Further, leaders have 'consistently underestimated the prevalence' (*ibid*: np) of sexual abuse and, through their inaction, leaders have made it the victims' 'responsibility to educate boys' (*ibid*: np).

Questions for discussion

In some environments, sex discrimination has become normalised and is no longer considered a problem, and those that seek to challenge discriminatory practices are identified as being over-sensitive. What are the responsibilities of leaders to surface and reframe discourse to recognise the damaging impact of discrimination?

Where are the safe spaces in your organisation for women and girls to discuss their experiences of being a member of the organisation?

What support is in place to help women and girls identify and articulate their concerns?

How are men and boys encouraged to review their behaviour and to recognise how their actions might be abusive or biased?

Black Lives Matter and race equality in the UK

In the UK, legislation which offers some security and protection to Black people has evolved gradually over a long period, suggesting a lack of political urgency or lower government prioritisation. The introduction or amendment of race equality laws has often been triggered by defining national events which have exposed some of the deep-rooted tensions between communities, reshaped discussions and public perceptions and led to a demand for change. In 1958, over an 18-month period there was 'a series of attacks on individual black people in Nottingham' (Fryer, 1984: 377) which culminated in a pitched battle lasting '90 minutes between blacks and whites in the St Ann's Well Road area' (*ibid*). Although 'these disturbances were called riots [they] were in reality attacks launched against black people and their homes by white mobs' (Olusoga, 2016: 509). In the same year, in London, there were 'anti-black riots' (Fryer, 1984: 378) which had been 'stimulated by fascist propaganda, urging that black people be driven out of Britain' (*ibid*). The following year in 1959, also in London, Kelso Cochrane was fatally stabbed by a gang of white youths. While over 140 people (72 of whom were white) were charged following the London Notting Hill riots and, after trial, the perpetrators received lengthy punitive prison sentences intended to act as a deterrent against lawless behaviour, no one was ever charged following Cochrane's attack which remains an unsolved murder case. In 1963, a group of global majority activists organised and led a bus boycott against the Bristol Omnibus Corporation who refused to employ black workers and operated a *de facto* colour bar. After four months of action and protracted negotiations, the bus boycott ended when the company finally agreed to employ staff from black communities.

In the wake of continued attacks against black people, widespread social unrest, discrimination in employment, housing, recreation and other areas of life, a small gain was finally achieved by the introduction of the 1965 Race Relations Act. This was the UK's first race law and afforded global majority people some formal legal protection. While it was significant that the government approved this legislation, it is important to note that eight previous attempts to introduce a bill safeguarding black people from 1956 to 1964, were rejected because the bill failed to secure adequate political support. It should also be noted that the 1965 Act was a weak piece of legislation and only prohibited 'discrimination on racial grounds in places of public resort' (HM Government, 1965: 1615), thus allowing shops, private sector rented accommodation, and other environments to continue with discriminatory practice should they so choose. In addition, the Act did little to recognise the impact on victims and, rather than being identified as criminal offences, some actions were classified as less serious civil offences which cannot be punished by imprisonment. The 1965 Act was repealed and replaced by the 1968 Race Relations Act, which strengthened the original legislation by expressly focussing on employment, housing and attempted to address the routine casual racism experienced by many black people, including second-generation citizens who had been born in the UK.

During the 1980s, the UK witnessed nationwide disturbances in larger metropolitan areas including Brixton London, Toxteth Liverpool, Handsworth Birmingham, Chapeltown Leeds, and Moss Side Manchester in addition to problems on the streets in smaller towns and communities. However, rather than the attacks on black people instigated and carried out by white communities as witnessed in the 1950s, these events 'were fought by young black people in response to years of systematic persecution and prejudice' (Olusoga, 2016: 517) who felt 'the need to fight for a place and future in the country; (*ibid*: 518) and were prepared to challenge the state's apparent acceptance of racism. The potential catalyst for these later conflicts was possibly the increased use of 'stop and search', which resulted in large numbers of young black males being detained by police, often to be released later without charge. Following these riots, Lord Scarman reporting on the events in 1983 and, while denying the existence of institutional racism, concluded there had been a breakdown of trust between black communities and authorities requiring positive intervention to rebuild relationships between communities and the police. In 1999, reporting on the murder of Stephen Lawrence in 1993, Macpherson concluded that many of the recommendations of the Scarman report had been ignored and little had been done to try and rebuild trust between state authority and black communities. The Race Relations Amendment Act 2000 addressed some of the concerns raised by both Scarman and Macpherson, and the Act made the police directly accountable for discrimination, with further specific duties placed on the education sector. Partly in response to these harmful, destabilising events. In the latest revision to the law, the 2010 Equality Act recognises race, religion, and belief as protected characteristics under the law.

Most recently, informed by critical race theory (CRT) which identifies race as paramount in determining the life chances, experiences, and opportunities available to both individuals and groups, Black Lives Matter (BLM) (which was started in 2013 in the United States by three black American activists, Alicia Garza, Patrisse Cullors, and Opal Tometi) has drawn attention to the routine killings of black people by police and others. BLM drew attention to the fact that in many areas (for example, healthcare, justice, and education) 'Black lives haven't mattered' (Yates, 2021: 31), and that in the UK and other countries, black people routinely experienced poorer treatment and had worse outcomes than their white counterparts. BLM gained global status following the murder of George Floyd in May 2020 by American police officers and triggered a series of worldwide protests.

In the UK, numerous demonstrations took place to highlight enduring injustices experienced by black communities from worse outcomes for expectant black mothers to harsher treatment in school and care systems. Notably, in Bristol in November 2020, the statue of Edward Colston, a slave trader venerated as a philanthropist, who gave his name to local schools and streets, was pulled down and dumped in the River Avon, sparking a national debate on which figures warranted occupying public spaces and what history should be taught in schools. Significantly, following a debate facilitated by staff and involving the whole school community, several schools in the Bristol area (including a private school founded in 1710 by Colston) decided to drop Colston's name and rebadge themselves to reflect a more positive, inclusive approach.

Questions for discussion

Within your current workplace or residential base, what is your understanding of relationships between different communities and either their employers or neighbours? Do positive relations exist between different racial groups?

In the workplace, what is the policy on fair and equitable recruitment policies? Are provisions made for different communities in terms of fundamental needs such as diet or cultural needs including the provision of worship facilities?

What provisions are made in the workplace to promote positive relationships between communities and advance community cohesion?

Discussions regarding race remain difficult in some organisations with a preference to avoid and not name issues. How should leaders address the challenge bringing difficult issues to the surface so that they may be openly and frankly debated?

Conclusion

Building on the UN's Universal Declaration of Human Rights, 'The Equality Act 2010 consolidated most equality law into one Act' (UK Parliament, 2022) and strengthened existing legislation regarding disability, sex, and race. In doing so, the Equality Act provided an overarching legal framework to direct and govern actions and life in the UK. This chapter has considered the historic and contemporary experiences of those who have experienced discrimination as a consequence of having a disability, being part of the global majority or their sex. While legal frameworks can define social boundaries, this chapter has also demonstrated the power of activism and how grass-roots campaigns have both raised awareness and changed the law. The chapter has raised important issues regarding accountability and leadership and has questioned the role of leaders in recognising and challenging discrimination. Although the chapter has focussed on three principal areas, it is important to recognise that the Equality Act also covers age, gender reassignment, marriage and civil partnership, pregnancy and maternity, religion or belief, and sexual orientation. It is further important for leaders at all levels to understand the dynamic nature of equality and the need for constant vigilance in challenging injustice.

Leadership is a difficult and challenging role. It involves listening to many people, making choices and decisions, and ensuring policies and procedures are implemented as well as challenging inequality and promoting inclusion. It is through positive leadership that the ethos of an organisation is established, and it is through the vigilance of leaders that the safety and security of all groups are assured making equality, diversity, and inclusion a reality for all setting users.

Summary points

- Making inclusion a reality for the many groups and individuals who have been excluded through repeated, structural discrimination requires commitment, endeavour and will. It is only through positive action that discrimination is dismantled.

- New structures which support and sustain inclusion and participation have to be built. This requires vision, creativity, and flexibility. It is likely that solutions for tomorrow's issues will not be met by the systems of today.

- Discrimination acts unevenly and some groups, because of identifiable features or characteristics, will experience a greater level of injustice than others. Discrimination also acts in an intersectional way and individuals may be a part of many marginalised sectors of society at the same time.

- While legislation may change the way society operates, change is also promoted through individual and community activism, which has challenged extant norms and mores to produce cultural shifts in attitude.

- Leadership for equality, diversity, and inclusion requires that all voices are enabled and supported to join the debate and generate actions and solutions for the future.

Recommended reading

Jana, T. and Baran, M. (2020) *Subtle Acts of Exclusion: How to understand, identify, and stop microaggressions.* Oakland, CA: Berrett-Koehler Publishers.

Perry, R. (2018) *Belonging at Work: Everyday actions you can take to cultivate an inclusive organization.* Portland: Academy Press

Ryde, J. (2019) *White Privilege Unmasked: How to be part of the solution.* London: Jessica Kingsley Publishers.

References

BBC News (2003) *Mixed Reception for Disability Bill* Available at: http://news.bbc.co.uk/1/hi/uk/3288685.stm (Accessed 24 September 2022).

Boronski, T. and Hassan, N. (2015) *Sociology of Education.* London: Sage.

Campbell-Stephens, R. (2020) *Global Majority; Decolonising the language and reframing the conversation about race.* Available at: https://www.leedsbeckett.ac.uk/-/media/files/schools/school-of-education/final-leeds-beckett-1102-global-majority.pdf (Accessed 15 September 2022).

DfE (2019) *Relationships Education, Relationships and Sex Education (RSE) and Health Education.* London: Department for Education. Available at https://assets.publishing.service.gov.uk/government/uploads/system/uploads/attachment_data/file/1090195/Relationships_Education_RSE_and_Health_Education.pdf (Accessed 27 September 2022).

DfE (2015) *Special Educational Needs and Disability Code of Practice: 0 to 25 Years.* London: Department for Education. Available at https://assets.publishing.service.gov.uk/government/uploads/system/uploads/attachment_data/file/398815/SEND_Code_of_Practice_January_2015.pdf (Accessed 24 September 2022).

DWP (2021) *The Employment of Disabled People 2021.* London: Department for Work and Pensions. Available at https://www.gov.uk/government/statistics/the-employment-of-disabled-people-2021/the-employment-of-disabled-people-2021 (Accessed 24 September 2022).

Fryer, P. (1984) *Staying Power: The history of black people in Britain.* London: Pluto Press.

Hirji, Z. (2019) *Annual Leadership and Equity Symposium.* Toronto: University of Toronto Available at: https://people.utoronto.ca/news/second-annual-angela-hildyard-leadership-equity-symposium/ (Accessed 15 September 2022).

Gov.UK (2021) *G7 To Boost Girls' Education and Women's Employment in Recovery from COVID-19 Pandemic.* London: Gov.UK. Available at https://www.gov.uk/government/news/g7-to-boost-girls-education-and-womens-employment-in-recovery-from-covid-19-pandemic (Accessed 25 September 2022).

HM Government (1965) *Race Relations Act 1965*. Available at: https://www.legislation.gov.uk/ukpga/1965/73/enacted

HM Government (2010) *Equality Act 2020*. Available at: https://www.legislation.gov.uk/ukpga/2010/15/section/6 (Accessed 15 September 2022).

Inner London Education Authority (1986) *Girls into Mathematics*. Milton Keynes: Open University.

Millett-Gallant, A. (2017) Sculpting Body Ideals: *Alison Lapper Pregnant* and the Public Display of Disability. In J.L. Davis (Ed.) *The Disability Studies Reader* (5th Edition). Abingdon: Routledge.

O'Mallay, K. (2019) What is Upskirting and when did it become a Criminal Offence, *The Independent*, 12 April 2019. Available at: https://www.independent.co.uk/life-style/women/upskirting-illegal-definition-crime-uk-sexual-harassment-a8864636.html (Accessed 29 September 2022).

Ofsted (2021) *Review of Sexual Abuse in Schools and Colleges*. London: Ofsted. Available at: https://www.gov.uk/government/publications/review-of-sexual-abuse-in-schools-and-colleges/review-of-sexual-abuse-in-schools-and-colleges (Accessed 26 September 2022).

Olusoga, D. (2016) *Black and British: A forgotten history*. London: Macmillan.

Renold, E. (2006) Gendered Classroom Experiences. In C. Skelton, B. Francis and L. Smulyan (Eds.), *The Sage Handbook of Gender and Education*. London: Sage.

Rieser, R. (2012) The Struggle for Disability Equality. In M. Cole (Ed.) *Education, Equality and Human Rights* (3rd Edition). Abingdon: Routledge.

Times Educational Supplement (2019) *Police Report Upskirting of School Pupils* Available at: https://www.tes.com/magazine/archive/police-report-upskirting-school-pupils (Accessed 29 September 2022).

UK Parliament (2022) *A Short Introduction to Equality Law*. London: UK Parliament. Available at https://commonslibrary.parliament.uk/research-briefings/cbp-9448/ (Accessed 24 September 2022).

United Nations (2015) *Transforming Our World: The 2030 agenda for sustainable development*. New York, NY: United Nations. Available at https://sdgs.un.org/sites/default/files/publications/21252030%20Agenda%20for%20Sustainable%20Development%20web.pdf (Accessed 25 September 2022).

Webster, L. (2022) *Let's storm Parliament! The punks who risked their lives to fix ableist Britain*. The Guardian, 11 March 2022. Available at https://www.theguardian.com/tv-and-radio/2022/mar/11/then-barbara-met-alan-lets-storm-parliament-the-punks-who-risked-their-lives-to-fix-ableist-britain (Accessed 24 September 2022).

Witcher, S. (2015) *Inclusive Equality*. Bristol: Policy Press.

Yates, D. (2021) Untitled. In P. Sng (Ed.), *Invisible Britain This Separated Isle*. Bristol: Policy Press.

4 Resilience and Vitality as Necessary Leadership Traits

Mark T. Gibson

Introduction

This chapter will explore some early theories of leadership, including 'personality trait theory' and indicate how problematic this has become as a prescription for successful leadership. However, two personal traits, resilience and vitality, are suggested as required overarching traits in all leaders, irrespective of other traits or 'leadership styles'. Following a discussion of what 'resilience' is and its importance for school leadership, the chapter will look at how it can be developed in leaders and managers. It is of interest that, despite resilience perceived as being an 'essential' quality for school leaders, little has been written about it in this context (Day and Gu, 2013). The chapter will argue that resilience capacity among leaders is developed throughout their careers and continues within leadership; in so doing, it also draws upon the author's own published research own and the concept of 'vitality'. Finally, the notion of a *resilient school* is addressed.

Individual/group task

Before reading this chapter please consider the following:

You probably already have an understanding of the term 'resilience'– what do you think it is? Can you think of a situation in your life when you have been highly resilient?

The role of a school principal

School principals or headteachers (the more international term 'principal' will be used as it is becoming more frequently used in the UK too) have a varied but demanding role. It can be all-consuming and very demanding on an incumbent's time, spending long hours dealing with the different aspects of the post. Rhodes and Fletcher (2013), citing BBC work, provide a list of an account of one primary principal's day which illustrates not only the variety of roles expected of a principal, but also that they are 'presented in rapid, unpredictable succession:

- dealing with health and safety issues;
- dealing with school support staff;
- modelling the values of the school;
- meeting with parents;
- rewarding success by teachers and staff;

DOI: 10.4324/9781003321439-4

- implementing sanctions to combat misconduct;
- interacting with external agencies for pupil support;
- overseeing school finances and reporting to interested parties;
- overseeing school building and maintenance of school accommodation;
- contributing to the culture of enquiry with a view to improved practice; and
- interacting with local council officials to combat youth related problems' (Rhodes and Fletcher, 2013: 52).

The high expectations and accountability which go with this multiplicity of roles creates a post that is physically and mentally demanding and requires high resilience in order to survive and flourish.

Defining 'resilience'

The leadership of schools can be very rewarding, helping others, both staff and students fulfil their ambitions. It can involve deliberately developing an organisation's improvement either in part or as a whole. Having a vision and desire to improve an institution can bring significant rewards when an image is manifested. However, school leadership also has its own challenges, from reluctant staff to poor student behaviour or parental complaints. The daily role brings adversity and the practice of leadership is an emotional activity (Crawford, 2009). Leadership requires an ability to be able to endure such inherent difficulty. It is this area that resilience occupies.

The challenges that school principals face vary across sectors from early years to high school, from schools that serve economically disadvantaged communities to those that cater for the wealthy and elite; they all have their own difficulties. Globally such difficulties differ; however, they will always be present; any school will face different challenges in different phases of its history. Being able to cope with adversity is an important trait for a principal.

Resilience is to do with this ability to be able to cope in adversity and can be defined as 'the ability to overcome and "bounce back" from the extremes of adversity' (Day, 2014: 639). It is frequently perceived as a trait within individuals and research around it is normally within the field of psychology. Resiliency has the Latin root meaning 'to jump back' from the verb *resilire*, though some definitions go further than simply 'bouncing back' from adversity. There is a growing litera-ture on resiliency, which has parallels with those on well-being, which emphasises the positive nature of resiliency and its development. Day (2014) proposes the notion of 'everyday resilience', seeing it as 'an essential everyday quality because of the variety, intensity and complexity of the worlds which principals inhabit' (Day, 2014: 641); it is necessary to cope with the daily role. For Patterson and Kelleher (2005: 1), on the other hand, resilience is a 'multidimensional... construct', defined as

> using your energy productively to emerge from adversity stronger than ever... Three dimen-sions form a comprehensive resilience framework: the interpretation of current adversity and future possibility, the resilience capacity to tackle adversity, and the actions needed to become more resilient in the face of the adversity (Patterson and Kelleher, 2005: 3).

These definitions focus on an individual's traits and can be related to the trait theory of leadership.

Leadership and trait theory

According to Earley and Weindling (2004), leadership theory has developed chronologically under five headings, the earliest being trait theory, followed by styles then contingency theory (the coexistence of the person and context), power/influence, and finally back to trait theory. They were writing in 2004 and one could argue that leadership models and system leadership have been dominant theories in the intervening years. Trait theories, although still popular, have declined during this century. Trait theory attempts to portray the characteristics of successful leaders such as being inspiring, at ease with others, sufficiently forceful, and able to accept criticism. Managerial qualities such as effective communication, being decisive, an interest in colleagues and their work all follow (Earley and Weindling, 2004). The problem with personal trait theory is that of definitions of traits: what is 'inspirational' or 'sufficiently forceful' to one person may not be to another. Equally, the belief that certain people have the correct traits, could produce a situation whereby some people are deemed to be [natural?] leaders, i.e. those who hold the traits and others not so. This could result in restrictions in leadership development and access to employment opportunities.

Leadership styles and models have also been researched and promoted, each one containing their own advantages and challenges. Space does not allow for such discussion here, but the recommended reading list below has some references you may wish to follow up. However, it would appear fundamental to successful leadership that such a person would have a high level of resiliency, irrespective of what their preferred style is or individual traits they possess; without being able to cope with adversity they would find school leadership problematic.

It is interesting to question whether resilience is innate or learned: are some people innately more resilient? If resilience is important for anyone to become a leader, then it becomes important for us to know if it is innate or can be developed. Resilience theory and research have their roots in child development: for example, humans develop resilience in being able to walk, despite initially falling over and hurting themselves. Studies of resilience in children have been undertaken in a wide variety of conditions globally, the results of which point to a remarkable consistency in the conditions which promote higher resilience and that there are several key strategies to be used in intervention to help foster resilience (Masten and Coatsworth, 1998). It is no surprise, therefore, that resilience-building in children is a key element in early years curricula.

Research has also been conducted into novice teachers' success and resilience and the ability of adults to develop resilience over a career in different contexts and in times of change (Tait, 2008). As Day (2014) concludes, 'resilience in education, then, is not a quality that is innate. Rather, it is a construct that is relative, relational, developmental and dynamic' (Day, 2014: 641). Resilience, then, becomes part of career development for a leader; it can be developed in staff and is not a chance occurrence.

The importance of resilience in school leadership

In their seven strong claims about successful school leadership, Leithwood *et al.* (2008), in a frequently cited and important paper, refer to 'understanding and developing people' in which the 'primary aim is building not only the knowledge and skills that teachers and other staff need in order to accomplish organisational goals, but also the dispositions (commitment, capacity, and *resilience*) to persist in applying the knowledge and skills' (p. 30). Resilience becomes the heart of successful school leadership. Furthermore, they also state that 'most successful school leaders are open-minded and ready to learn from others. They are also flexible rather than dogmatic in their thinking within a system of core values, persistent (e.g. in pursuit of high expectations of staff motivation, commitment, learning and achievement for all), *resilient* and optimistic' (Leithwood *et al.*, 2008: 36 italics my emphasis).

Research on the work and lives of principals suggests that the process of leading successfully requires more than the ability to bounce back in adverse circumstances (Day and Gu, 2013). It requires them to have a '"hardiness", a resolute persistence, hope and commitment which is supported in these by strong core values over three or more decades' (Day, 2014: 642). Day's (2014) notion of 'everyday resilience' becomes an essential quality and a necessary capacity for leaders.

Patterson and Kelleher (2005) go further than this idea that leaders require resilience: they describe a type of leader that they name a 'resilient leader', one who, due to resilience being embedded in them and their practice, operates in a specific way. They then distil this analysis into what they term 'Six Strengths of Resilient Leaders' (Patterson and Kelleher, 2005: 147). These strengths are each worth considering describing:

1. 'Resilient leaders accurately assess past and current reality'. Earlier in this chapter, it was pointed out that Patterson and Kelleher use a three-dimensional construct to resilience, the first of which is the interpretation of current adversity and future possibility. So, in this first strength resilient leaders have an accurate sense of reality, they expect the world to be full of disruptions, and they develop a tolerance of ambiguity. Further to this, they are able to see reality from multiple perspectives, a point has links with emotional intelligence (EI) – see later in the chapter.

2. 'Resilient leaders are positive about future possibilities'. Such leaders are the glass half-full rather than half-empty person, they focus on opportunities not obstacles, maintain a positive outlook which affects others and believe that good things can happen despite adversity.

3. 'Resilient leaders remain true to personal values'. Such leaders know which values are important to them and have a clear value hierarchy. Their focus is *value-* rather than *event-*driven. They create opportunities for others to give feedback and align this with their value set; finally, they present a model for others leadership based around their personal core values.

4. 'Resilient leaders maintain a strong sense of personal efficacy'. Later in this chapter, we will look at self-efficacy and its role in leadership resilience, and it is not surprising that Patterson and Kelleher ensure its position in the six strengths. These leaders have a strong self-belief that they can achieve something and concentrate on small wins, celebrating them. They maintain a strong level of personal competence and recover quickly from setbacks. Resilient leaders maintain a base of caring and support for others and themselves.

5. 'Resilient leaders invest personal energy wisely'. Resilient leaders look after their own physical and mental health to allow for recovery. They retain mental focus and concentration in the face of adversity, and they develop self-awareness and emotional empathy, which also has links with EI covered later in the chapter.

6. 'Resilient leaders act on the courage of personal convictions'. Resilient leaders are clear about what matters and act accordingly, even when risks are high. They act decisively, based on their deepest values and remain resolute even when faced with strong opposition. Finally, they are reflective and learn from their mistakes, modifying actions accordingly.

Individual/group task

Discuss the following questions:

> What sort of challenges do school leaders, whether senior or middle leaders, face where their resilience would be important?
> How would a high level of resilience help them?

Resilience links with self-efficacy and emotional intelligence

Self-efficacy

The sense of efficacy is a 'belief about one's own ability (self-efficacy), or the ability of one's colleagues collectively (collective efficacy), to perform a task or achieve a goal. It is a belief about ability, not actual ability' (Leithwood and Jantzi, 2008: 497). Leaders tend to have high levels of self-efficacy. Self-efficacy differs from self-belief in that it is specific about roles and tasks, whilst self-belief is more general.

The main theorist on self-efficacy is Albert Bandura. In addition to his work on aggression and social cognitive theory, he researched self-efficacy. Efficacy can be influenced by the context and is part of Bandura's social cognitive theory of learning. School leaders face differing contexts with differing external and internal environmental pressures, so leadership as a practice becomes complex. Bandura (1997) asserts that:

> People make causal contributions to their own functioning through mechanisms of personal agency. Among the mechanisms of agency, none is more central or pervasive than peoples' beliefs about their capabilities to exercise control over their own level of functioning and over events that affect their lives (Bandura, 1997: 118).

For Patterson and Kelleher (2005), the role of self-efficacy in resilience is as a fuel, along with personal values and personal energy, to make up a leader's resilience capacity. Efficacy is a belief, you think you can do the task required; however, leaders will need to assess the situation to see if the environment hinders or assists in actioning the task.

Emotional intelligence

In recent years, the notion of EI has gained traction, even in the media, following the success of popular books by Daniel Goleman and others. The idea that some leaders appear to appreciate others' motivations and emotions is beneficial to their success. EI can be defined as, 'the capacity for recognising our own feelings and those of others, for motivating ourselves, and for managing emotions well in ourselves and in our relationships' (Goleman, 1998: 373). This skill would have many uses for everyone, but particularly leaders of any organisation. It would involve leaders' reining in their emotion when needed, to read others' feelings and in so doing handling relationships smoothly. For Goleman, this EI is an expanded view of what it is to be intelligent and includes self-control, persistence, and self-motivation (Goleman, 1995). It differs but is complementary to, academic intelligence, the cognitive capacity measured by IQ tests. The pervasiveness of Goleman's argument is that, for him, IQ is essentially hard-wired, but EI can be taught and improved. It would follow from Goleman's perspective that EI improvement should form part of leadership preparation and development programmes.

Without EI, high levels of resilience may become problematic for leaders in that they may become intolerant of a lack of resilience among others in the staff they lead: for example, being insensitive in dealing with a teacher who is distraught over their teaching experience. EI then becomes a counter to the 'hardiness' of leaders that Day (2014) refers to earlier. It would not be exaggerating to suggest that leaders have greater resilience than some of their staff, and it could be argued that it is that which is required in order to get to their leadership position. It would be important, though, for leaders to appreciate that they are potentially different to their staff in this regard, and to have an empathy for others' positions, which is all part of EI.

Self-efficacy and EI link with resilience. In order to be resilient you will need to feel you can do what is required of you, to have a level of self-efficacy. Equally, EI can reduce the hardiness of resilience to make leadership more humane.

Building resilience

Building resilience, whether planned or fortuitous, is an important part of leadership preparation and development for those in post; as Day (2014) states, 'it is both a product of personal and professional histories, exercised through professional dispositions and values' (Day, 2014: 641). The adversity that leaders face prior to leadership, and moreover overcoming this adversity helps build resilience capacity. However, much of the literature on school leaders' resilience focuses on the school leader's role rather than evaluating the formative influences on such individuals (Steward, 2014).

The research on resilience capacity building can be summarised as leaders developing healthy coping mechanism, such as a routine of exercise and healthy diet; accentuating the positive as a life view; a focus on one's own values and professional mission; spiritual renewal, and this may mean time away from the 'coalface'; to seek reward in being able to model resilience for others, and utilising supportive networks (Farmer, 2010). Lugg and Boyd (1993) also emphasise the importance of strong communication in the workplace and recommend that individuals create positive alliances and groups to establish a collaborative culture, minimise stress, and encourage resiliency in others.

In order to build resilience based on past experiences, Patterson and Kelleher (2005) posit a *Resilience Cycle*: (1) deteriorating, (2) adapting, (3) recovering, and (4) growing. This cycle will commence following a disruption to what they call 'normal conditions'. Such conditions will vary from context to context and may well, in some situations, involve conditions that will be adverse when compared with the norm; Day's (2014) work on principals of challenging schools is an example. The point that Patterson and Kelleher make is that irrespective of your conditions which are the norm for you, further adversity frequently occurs, and this is stage 1, deteriorating. This adverse event causes the individual significant emotional problems, either professional or in their home life. Initially, there may well be denial, anger, and grief, and this is an unhealthy stage to remain in for a prolonged period. Most school principals move to stage 2, adapting, where they reverse the trajectory of the downward trend by taking personal actions. Adapting this deterioration involves less anger, confronting any denial. This phase is seen as a necessary transition but is still not a healthy place, as long-term here will result in operating in survival mode. For those principals that continue on the upward curve, they address the issues through the recovering phase. Finally, and importantly, resilience is built not only by going through these experiences but also reflecting on them, making permanent changes to such skills as self-efficacy that allows phase 4 growth. Through repeated uses of this cycle, principals can develop high levels of resilience.

School leaders' resilience: Does coaching help?

There has been an increase in the use of coaching in school leaders' professional development in the last decade or so (Lofthouse and Whiteside, 2019; Rhodes and Fletcher, 2013). Coaching and mentoring are used frequently in different areas of school professional development, from induction of new entrants to teaching experienced staff, to staff gaining a new leadership role. 'Leaders need peers to enable them to develop a sense of what is possible to be achieved but need to implement action to validate a sense of their own self-efficacy' (Rhodes and Fletcher, 2013: 49).

Principals, in particular, can benefit from coaching that is external to the school; being non-judgmental and confidential, it gives them time out to reflect on their work (Steward, 2014). Evaluations of coaching schemes in England for principals have been highly positive. Lofthouse and Whiteside (2019) reporting that a coaching programme supported principals in developing and maintaining effective management practice had a positive impact on their self-belief and reduced resilience erosion. This view is supported by other research, Sardar and Galdames (2018) summarising that 'coaching is beneficial to increase resilience and confidence, cope with stressful situations, bounce back from obstacles and emotional detachment from practical perspective' (p. 57).

It appears then that resilience, which is an extremely important trait for successful school leadership, can be nurtured, developed, and increased. This is important for developing future talent and maintaining the quality of present post-holders.

Individual/group task

Discuss the following question:

In what ways can prospective school leaders build their resilience?

Resilience in extremis: Testing resilience of school leaders

Resilience, as we have seen, is important for school leaders as they face regular adverse conditions; their ability to 'bounce back' is crucial to success. Sometimes when looking at an issue, it is interesting to look at outliers, situations that are not the norm in order to gain greater knowledge. The following two situations, leading in the Covid-19 lockdown and involuntary job loss provide extreme situations where resilience is tested highly.

Resilience and the Covid-19 pandemic

During the Covid-19 pandemic many education systems globally closed for face-to-face teaching in 2020 and 2021, moving to remote learning as governments restricted people's movement in order to contain the spread of the virus. Teachers were required to upskill their teachers using online methods, and school principals also became remote leaders, leading staff, students, and parents in a world where frequently there was little guidance.

In a large survey of school leaders ($n = 1491$) conducted in April/May 2021 by Greany *et al.* (2021), most leaders were seen as coping with the challenges, but there were negative aspects such as lack of sleep, becoming overweight, drinking too much alcohol, hospitalised by catching the virus, put on medication for depression and, in some 40 per cent of cases, a desire to leave the profession. Managing staff and parental anxieties were indicated as the most stressful areas, with nearly half of participants indicating parent-related issues being the main stressor. However, Greany *et al.* (2021) note that 'success in meeting ongoing challenges gave most interviewees a profound sense of satisfaction in providing a worthwhile public service at a time of national crisis' (Greany *et al.*, 2021: 7) and that, in responding to the crisis, their staff had rapidly gained new skills and relationships and had developed stronger relationships in the staff and the communities they serve. Clearly, there were high levels of resilience operating which were recognised by other work: McLeod and Dulsky (2021) for example were impressed with the resilience and courage their principal participants showed in rising to the challenge. However, amongst these findings, there will be many principals who may have found the situation of the Covid-19 lockdown too much an adversity: the literature here also calls for external support such as mentoring or counselling services for principals too.

Resilience and involuntary job loss

I conducted work with a colleague, Sue Simon, from the University of the Sunshine Coast in Australia on school principal job loss (Gibson and Simon, 2020; Simon and Gibson, 2019). The participants in this study were all former school principals in England and Australia; all lost their job when they did not wish to lose it, referred to as 'involuntary occupation dissolution'. This became a situation in which their resilience was highly tested. It is important to note that none of the participants in the study was dismissed from their role, but rather specific individual contextual circumstances led to events where each one felt they had no choice but reluctantly to resign. We interviewed 10 participants. This job loss affected them personally and professionally, having effects on them and their families particularly economically.

There was a high level of congruence between data from the two countries, and key findings were effects on former principals' physical and emotional health, self-belief, professional identity, and finances, plus a sense of loss of power. The effects of these job losses were significant and long-lasting.

Health and well-being issues ranged from anxiety and depression to suicide ideation, to cardiac problems, through to social withdrawal. Several found counselling helpful. Two were prescribed antidepressants, two experienced significant weight loss, and one of those also experiencing physical skin rash and hair loss. In addition to this they spoke of a lack of self-esteem, one saying he was made to feel like a criminal, despite not doing anything wrong. There were also issues surrounding relationships with family members. It is unsurprising that this scenario tested their resilience. They referred in their interviews to previous levels of self-efficacy, making a point of how successful they had been. The fact that all these participants had 'got back on track' despite such an adverse circumstance points to high levels of resilience. Each participant gained employment again, despite long-lasting effects, some returning as school principals, others moving into other sectors, for example university lecturing.

Personal vitality

The participants in the study above talked of their self-efficacy in acknowledging that they felt confident and competent at being a school principal; in fact, for several of them the adverse condition of potential job loss (Stage 1 of Patterson and Kelleher's (2005) resilience model) came as a surprise, given that recent employer performance appraisal ratings had been high. In addition to this they talked passionately about what originally motivated them to teach and then to lead a school. In a second paper, Sue Simon and I concentrate on this passion (Simon and Gibson, 2019). They had a strong sense of belonging to a community, feelings of pride about such work. The use of this original motivation to teach we regard as personal vitality, defining it as 'the retention of the original passion for teaching and then leading a school' (Simon and Gibson, 2019: 710). Vitality emphasises the positive, and is developed over the course of a career, rather than just something one innately possesses. It is also developed in parallel with resilience; they are complementary. However, it differs from resilience in that it is a counter to the negative use of term 'resilience' in performative agenda – whereby the term 'resilient' is used as a deficit, 's/he has not got enough resilience' and resilience can be perceived as negative rather than the positive of 'vitality'.

Personal vitality – the ideas and drivers that first inspired leaders to work with youngsters and then to lead their schools – is challenged by the long hours and complex nature of their work and the sense of isolation that comes from being at the top. Leaders will need to 're-vitalise' their vitality; this is not the same as their well-being and mental health (though it would be part of that); it is returning to those original drivers. Simon *et al.* (2016) refer to participants in their study (all school principals) on a particular challenging day, engaging in such activities as going into classrooms and having conversations with young learners or even reading to small children under a tree. This sustenance of vitality was important to them.

According to Simon *et al.* (2016), there are seven interrelated but interconnecting themes of personal vitality and leadership development, although they also accept these are presently under researched. The seven themes are:

1. Motivational roots. This area is about the seeds of a leader's leadership, where their motivational has been generated and may even refer to their childhood and how this may produce durability.
2. Emotions. Leadership as an emotional activity has been explored by some (Crawford, 2009); here it is seen as at the core of personal vitality.
3. Self-efficacy. This concept has been explored earlier, but here it is noted that it can help in the sustainability of personal vitality.
4. View of role/leader efficacy. Efficacy here is not just about ability and confidence to be able to undertake a task, but links with a view of the principal's role and further motivation having effects on professional functioning of principals and their subsequent success in the role.
5. Reaction to stress. Despite a principal's role being to be able to manage stress in themselves and others, there is a lack of research in this area and maybe in a post-pandemic world we may see further action from employers on caring for the leader.
6. Coaching/mentoring – ways of topping up vitality levels. This theme has also been addressed earlier in the chapter, Simon *et al.* (2016) suggesting that such practices as coaching and mentoring will improve and sustain personal vitality.

7. The Vitality – Fragility Continuum. The final theme in developing personal vitality points to the polar opposite, fragility, and how these two operate on a continuum. Leadership constructs such as moral purpose, and self-sacrifice can curb the tendency to fragility. These aligned with EI and resilience help build personal vitality.

In further work, Simon *et al.* (2018) have developed a programme for serving principals in Australia to help develop vitality. The 'PIVOTAL' (Partnerships, Innovation, and Vitality – Opportunities for Thriving Academic Learning) model addresses the gap identified in recent research in the preparation and ongoing development of school leaders. The programme offers opportunities for educational leaders to address their own vitality and places an emphasis on coaching, peer mentoring, and activities which promote an understanding of factors contributing to personal vitality in complex leadership roles.

In writing this piece I am reminded of a relevant event from my own past. A few years ago, I was at one of my older brother's 40th birthday party where a friend of his, whom I had not met in about 15 years or so, talked to me. He said rather sarcastically, 'Well Mark you don't seem to have done it, I'm afraid'. 'Done what?' I replied. 'Changed the world', he said, 'changed the world through teaching and education'. He then proceeded to describe the young man I had maybe forgotten, the young man who was fired up and passionate about what education could achieve, how it could improve people and society as a whole, seemingly curing all ills. Although this brother's friend had initiated this conversation in a joking manner, he had reminded me of my vitality; there it was so real to me. I am acutely aware of the renewed verve and zeal with which I approached my professional work subsequently.

Resilient schools

In this chapter, resilience has essentially been about individual leader's resilience. However, it was acknowledged at the beginning that part of leadership is to not only building self-resilience but team and even school resilience. A resilient school will have high levels of resilience across the staff and students as a whole. For Day and Gu (2013), there is much to be learned about the resilience of leadership in challenging schools, the ones that serve disadvantaged communities. These leaders face 'a greater range of more persistent, intensive challenges than others' (Day and Gu, 2013: 113). They refer to the development of resilience through an ability to be able to take (calculated) risk, academic optimism, trust, and hope. The building of these dispositions leads to resilient schools. This model, though it still has a large emphasis on the individual principal, it is their (shared) dispositions. Aguilar (2016) on the other hand places the emphasis on team building via coaching to build a resilient school.

Aguilar's (2016) model commences with the principal having a high level of self-awareness and in particular a strong EI. The next step to build a strong team is to *intentionally* build a culture of trust that involves, for example, modelling behaviour that reinforces trustworthiness. The teams then need a clear purpose and product. Following trust as a norm being a foundation of the team, team EI can be developed. Other stages involve effective communication and being able to navigate conflict. The key here for Aguilar is the 'art of coaching' as a mechanism to build a resilient school.

Resilient schools, however, still need maintenance. Allison (2012) indicates five signals to leaders that their school's resilience is at risk: top leaders stop learning; people blame everything on the budget; leaders ignore critical indicators; too many initiatives drain people, and that success goes uncelebrated. It clearly falls to the leader of such a school to be able not only to recognise these signals where they occur but also to take action to ensure they are addressed; school resilience maintenance becomes part of the resilience of the school principal.

Conclusion

This chapter has explored the nature of resilience and vitality and how they are key traits for school leadership. Resilience, the ability to be able to 'bounce back' after adverse conditions, is built during a career following several situations that demand it. There is a resilience cycle where challenging conditions break the status quo and after initial denial, leaders will confront the event, and this 'conquer' will build further resilience (Patterson and Kelleher, 2005). Resilience has links with self-efficacy, belief that you can be competent at a task and EI. The latter is required to temper the hardiness built by resilience.

Resilience can be developed in staff during preparation for leadership and continually developed within leaders. Such techniques as quality coaching and mentoring have been shown to be beneficial, although financial constraints can hinder their use.

Schools, not just their leaders, can become resilient. This would enable staff and students alike to be able to sustain quality learning as they cope with the difficulties that working and learning brings; this would be the ultimate goal. Team development and trust appear key facets of resilient schools, building a collective efficacy.

In addition to resilience, the chapter has explored the nature of leader personal vitality, which is defined as that initial driver and value set that the leader possessed on entry into the profession and continued to motivate them. Time will need to be provided for leaders to re-vitalise themselves during leadership, to engage in being reflective, and acknowledge their own core beliefs and values.

An experienced leader develops leadership over time on different levels, those that are personal, system, and peer-based. On a personal level, this may involve reliable and trustworthy staff and familial relationships that are steadfast in difficult times. The personal level will also include their vitality, their inner drive that has been present from the onset of teaching. Equally, systemic alliances become important in times of challenge in building self-efficacy and providing collegial reassurance. Resilient leaders have a positive outlook on life and their professional role, and they possess longer-term views. They believe adversity makes them stronger and a better leader.

Resilience and vitality are core traits of school leadership and are mutually coexistent, and they are required irrespective of any leadership styles such as authoritative or laissez-faire, or models such as transformational leadership or distributed leadership (which are well documented). Without resilience or vitality school leaders would not be able to function competently and may not last long in post.

Summary points

- Resilience is an essential trait for school leadership and is defined as the 'the ability to overcome and 'bounce back' from the extremes of adversity'.
- Levels of resilience can be developed and improved throughout a teaching career.
- Resilience has links with EI and the notion of self-efficacy.

- Vitality, defined as 'the retention of the original passion for teaching and then leading a school', is also developed in parallel with resilience; they are complimentary. Vitality emphasises the positive and is seen as a core trait for successful school leadership.
- Resilient schools can be developed, ones where all adults and students have high levels of resilience.

Recommended reading

Arias, A. (2016) Build Your Grit: Fostering Resilience for Education Leaders. *Leadership* **45**(4), pp. 12–15.
Bristow, M., Ireson, G., and Coleman, A. (2007) *A Life in the Day of a Headteacher: A study of practice and well-being*. Nottingham: NCSL.
Bush, T. and Glover, D. (2014) School Leadership Models: What Do We Know? *School Leadership and Management* **34**(5), pp. 553–571.
Hilton, J. (2018) *Ten Traits of Resilience: Achieving positivity and purpose in school leadership*. London: Bloomsbury Publishing.

References

Aguilar, E. (2016) *The Art of Coaching Teams: Building resilient communities that transform schools*. San Francisco, CA: John Wiley and Sons.
Allison, E. (2012) The Resilient Leader. *Educational Leadership* **69**(4), pp. 79–82.
Bandura, A. (1997) *Self-Efficacy: The exercise of control*. New York, NY: W.H. Freeman.
Crawford, M. (2009) *Getting to the Heart of Leadership*. London: Sage.
Day, C. (2014) Resilient Principals in Challenging Schools: The Courage and Costs of Conviction. *Teachers and Teaching* **20**(5), pp. 638–654.
Day, C. and Gu, Q. (2013) *Resilient Teachers, Resilient Schools: Building and sustaining quality in testing times*. Abingdon: Routledge.
Earley, P. and Weindling, D. (2004) *Understanding School Leadership*. London: Paul Chapman Publishing.
Farmer, T. A. (2010). Overcoming Adversity: Resilience Development Strategies for Educational Leaders. *Georgia Educational Researcher* **8**(1), DOI: 10.20429/ger.22010.080101.
Gibson, M. T. and Simon, S. (2020) Losing Your Head: Are Principals Attached to Their School? *Educational Management Administration and Leadership* **48**(1), pp. 25–44.
Goleman, D. (1995) *Emotional Intelligence: Why it can matter more than IQ*. London: Bloomsbury Publishing.
Goleman, D. (1998) *Working with Emotional Intelligence*. New York, NY: Bantam Books.
Greany, T., Thomson, P., Martindale, N. and Cousin, S. (2021) *Leading in Lockdown Final Report*. Nottingham: University of Nottingham.
Leithwood, K., Harris, A. and Hopkins, D. (2008) Seven Strong Claims About Successful School Leadership. *School Leadership and Management* **28**(1), pp. 27–42.
Leithwood, K. and Jantzi, D. (2008) Linking Leadership to Student Learning: The Contributions of Leader Efficacy. *Educational Administration Quarterly* **44**(4), pp. 496–528.
Lofthouse, R. and Whiteside, R. (2019) *Sustaining a Vital Profession: Evaluation of a Headteacher Coaching Programme*: Project Report. Leeds: Leeds Beckett University. Available at https://eprints.leedsbeckett.ac.uk/id/eprint/6322/1/Sustaining%20A%20Vital%20Profession%20final.pdf. (Accessed 5 September 2022).
Lugg, C.A. and Boyd, W.L. (1993) Leadership for Collaboration: Reducing Risk and Fostering Resilience. *The Phi Delta Kappan* **75**(3), pp. 253–258.
Masten, A.S. and Coatsworth, J.D. (1998) The Development of Competence in Favorable and Unfavorable Environments: Lessons from Research on Successful Children. *American Psychologist* **53**(2), p. 205.
McLeod, S. and Dulsky, S. (2021) Resilience, Reorientation, and Reinvention: School Leadership During the Early Months of the COVID-19 Pandemic. *Frontiers in Education* **6**, 637075. doi: 10.3389/feduc.2021.637075
Patterson, J.L. and Kelleher, P. (2005) *Resilient School Leaders: Strategies for turning adversity into achievement*. Alexandria, VA: ASCD.
Rhodes, C. and Fletcher, S. (2013) Coaching and Mentoring for Self-Efficacious Leadership in Schools. *International Journal of Mentoring and Coaching in Education* **2**(1), pp. 47–63.
Sardar, H. and Galdames, S. (2018) School Leaders' Resilience: Does Coaching Help in Supporting Headteachers and Deputies? *Coaching: An International Journal of Theory, Research and Practice* **11**(1), pp. 46–59.

Simon, S., Christie, M., Graham, W. and Summers, J. (2016) The PIVOTAL Leadership Model: Improving School leaders' Professional Capacity and Personal Vitality Through Innovative Postgraduate Course Design. *The International Journal of Educational Organization and Leadership* **23**(3), pp. 1–16.

Simon, S., Christie, M., Heck, D., Graham, W. and Call, K. (2018) Making Headway: Developing principals' Leadership Skills Through Innovative Postgraduate Programs. *Australian Journal of Teacher Education* **43**(2), pp. 76–99.

Simon, S. and Gibson, M. T. (2019) Principal Resilience and Vitality in Extremis: The Scenario of Involuntary Occupational Dissolution. *International Journal of Educational Management* **33**(4), pp. 709–720.

Steward, J. (2014) Sustaining Emotional Resilience for School Leadership. *School Leadership and Management* **34**(1), pp. 52–68.

Tait, M. (2008) Resilience as a Contributor to Novice Teacher Success, Commitment, and Retention. *Teacher Education Quarterly* **35**(4), pp. 57–75.

5 Effective School Management: Leadership Capacity of the School Principal

Pinar Ayyildiz and Adem Yilmaz

The debate on effective school management and on the role of the school principal as the manager and leader is ongoing. To capture the zeitgeist of the new millennium, it is deemed essential to revisit the theoretical discussions and cast (more) light on current insights. This chapter intends to shed light on these areas by examining salient aspects: school culture, processes that come into play whilst practising effective school management and leadership, as well as prominent theories of leadership.

Creating and maintaining an effective school culture

Schools are amongst the organisations today that are still highly influential at individual and societal levels (Kafalı, 2022; Karadağ and Özdemir, 2015). They affect the society they are in and take an active role in the constant renewal of the culture. Culture, on the other hand, is vital for the development of groups and communities and can be expressed as the total of all the material and spiritual values that societies own (Aas *et al.*, 2020; Köse *et al.*, 2001). Yet, the concept of organisational culture was first referred to in the 1920s (Roethlisberger and Dickson, 1939; Wanburg, 2012). This line of thought suggests that organisational culture can also be expressed as the collective sum of its members' beliefs, feelings, and philosophies (Deal and Kennedy, 1984; Mullins, 1996; Schein, 2011). The organisation of societies and those of organisational cultures compose a micro-macro sort of construction, or 'cosmos'; hence the existence of the organisation in society and the formation of organisational culture can directly and indirectly benefit the community. This reformation of the(ir) identity contributes to the reformation of values, norms, and goals and to the overall progress; individuals become aware that they are a part of a larger society and learn about their responsibilities and value judgments in a formal and informal fashion (Robbins, 1991).

Schools are unique in that they are institutions with their own rules, boundaries, values, and common living principles (Schein, 2004). In relation to organisational culture, stakeholder traditions, rituals, and myths make up the school (Colley, 1999; Stolp and Smith, 1994). Creating a culture in schools that desirable and sustainable is crucial (Sergiovanni, 2001). Such an understanding towards modus operandi is necessary for schools to be(come) successful, offer quality education, and be trusted. Also, schools have a dynamic structure and a school culture is, and actually needs to be, constantly changed and renewed. A sole individual or a single direction cannot build a school culture. To bring into being an effective school culture and maintain it, all the members of the organisation should interact and behave in a harmonious manner. At this point, it

DOI: 10.4324/9781003321439-5

is necessary indispensable to establish ordinary value judgments and have regulatory and guiding rules. School culture acts as a guide and takes over the role of a facilitator in this process (Hinde, 2004). When a school culture is built on weak foundations its outcomes will inevitably be ineffective (Hollins, 1996).

In schools with a strong organisational culture, teachers, students, parents, and members of the management work collaboratively and cooperatively, and decisions are made in a joint way (Hargreaves, 1997). In organisations with a strong school culture, job satisfaction and, accordingly, organisational belonging and motivation levels are relatively higher, and academic performance is satisfactory (Demirtaş, 2010; Stolp, 2002). Strong school culture is attained thanks to an effective leader who can manage all the operations well and add value to them (Hoy and Miskel, 1996; Sepuru and Mohlakwana, 2020). An effective school administrator should also have the ability to manage the school culture and be the key player in the alignment of the school culture (Newman and Ford, 2021). School managers are the agents creating the school culture and examine and fulfil the expectations, wishes, needs of the members (Bengtson *et al.*, 2013). The sustainability of effective school culture is vital (Barth, 2002). This is because a sustainable school culture ensures success. There are factors impacting effective and sustainable school culture: short-term, medium, and long-term goals of the school, the socioeconomic background of the members and the demographics of the society, the facilities available, and the education system (Karadağ and Özdemir, 2015).

A robust school culture offers educational services efficiently (Mangla, 2021). In an effective school culture that is sustainable, each individual who is a part of the organisation can contribute to the school using their skills, abilities, and intellect. The school manager coordinates the characteristics that account for the school culture, defining the appropriate and inappropriate behaviours of the members, and the sustainable school culture practices (Bush and Anderson, 2003). Assembling viable communication channels, two-way contact, and intercommunication, laying the foundations of synergies and strong bonds between subordinates and superiors, and transparent and accountable management processes are among the arrangements in question. The efforts of the members of the organisation towards a common aim, moving with the accepted value judgments, and making attempts to keep the organisational culture 'alive', are all closely related to the leadership capacity and qualities of the leader as manager (Akpolat, 2020).

However, the knowledge and skills of the school leader alone are not sufficient for the sustainability of an effective school culture (McCarley *et al.*, 2016). School culture should be considered as a whole entity with its members' sense of belonging to the school, the affirmed unity around a shared purpose, and the leadership qualities of the school principal as the manager (Timperley, 2005). School cultures created merely for short-term needs carry the potential to deteriorate in the longer run, yielding failure in fulfilling essential tasks (Balcı, 2002).

Fundamental concepts of effective school management

It is helpful now to consider the idea of management. Management is a phenomenon that has taken shape in various forms since the first ages of human existence (Keskinkılıç, 2011).

Schools today renew themselves by taking into account the expectations of society, the specific needs of individuals and those of the age, and they strive to keep up with change. The expectations of society undoubtedly impact the structure and quality of schools. To create effective management for schools as social 'organisms' through the school culture, chief conceptualisations should be integrated (De Grauwe, 2005; Shibuya, 2020). These are listed below.

System: This is the constituent that is made up of the combination of components that influence and support each other regularly (Bursalıoğlu, 2000). Additionally, a system refers to a complexity affected by the properties of the elements that comprise a unit and can have new properties later. However, each holistic structure formed cannot be expressed as a system. For a structure to be a system, it needs to have certain qualities (Duverger, 1982; Keskinkılıç, 2011):

- All elements should be inter-related and complement each other.
- The system should be able to react as a whole to any situation that might come from outside.

Once school management is accepted as a system, three explanations for the system approach become visible: open system, semi-open system and closed system. In open systems, there is a mechanism in the form of input, process, output, and feedback. Semi-open systems have inputs, processes, and outputs. There are not enough inputs or outputs in closed systems, and they may lose their activity in a shorter time and disappear (Bertalanffy, 1971).

Management

This is striving systematically to reach the previously determined goals in an organisation and to arrive at a typical result (Koçel, 2001). Derived from this definition, school management can be expressed as the systematic management of educational processes aligned with the goals and coordinating legal regulations, social norms, and curricula for a consolidated objective.

School culture

Represents the ingredients of the ethos that come together to build the 'character' and 'personality' of a school. Norms, rules, values, symbols, rituals, and beliefs make the school culture. There are written rules that make up the school culture alongside unwritten ones like developing a positive attitude and creating a sense of belonging.

Leadership

The concept of a leader is depicted as an individual who can draw people after them (Drucker, 2000). Leaders head a group or an organisation. In modern school structures, which are often called 'new generation schools', the concepts of leader, administrator, and school principal are often blended. Principals are the people who manage the school and are paramount in the successful creation of an effective school culture. To exhibit effective leadership behaviours in school management, problems are handled realistically and resolved by taking a reasonable stance (Ilgar, 2005). The managers with a say in school management display behaviours that differ from those of leaders. Bennis (2009) describes these as differences in the use of authority, influence, and control.

Responsibility

Responsibility is an essential feature of effective school management. Responsibility can generally be the ability of individuals who are part of the school management to accomplish successfully the tasks and duties assigned to them. That said, 'mistakes' by superiors can lead to severe problems and trigger negative consequences (Pfeffer and Salancik, 1978).

Vision

For effectively enacted school management, the most current snapshot of a situation is first determined, and a status report is prepared. In the next stage where the school wants to be in the near future is identified. The mirror symmetry of this signals a lack of vision in schools, which means plans for the future are not being made. Having a vision is closely related to schools being open to advancement (Durna and Eren, 2002).

School management schemes

To guarantee in an optimal way that education services are provided for all, school management processes must be well organised and human resources and fiscal features planned well. There are theories in the literature on school management processes. According to Henri Fayol (1841–1925), a pioneering name of Classical Management Theory, these are divided into five types: planning, organising, giving orders, coordination, and control (Özdemir, 2015; Shafritz et al., 1992). Gulick classified these as planning, staffing, directing, coordination, reporting, and budgeting (Gulick, 1937). It will be wise to further scrutinise the characteristics of these processes to better understand the entire process.

Decision-making: Decision-making is truly the cornerstone of management processes. It is essential that the management makes decisions and intervene in the processes in the face of actions, events, and situations that they come across. In the decision-making process, the decision needs to be made that serves the purpose most appropriately. Often, and unavoidably, managers cannot make a decision that will satisfy all the stakeholders.

Simon (1987) states that managers want to make the best decisions, but usually this cannot be realised for good reasons such as the limited processing capacity of the human memory, inadequate knowledge and experience of the managers, sudden occurrence of undesired events and the need to make decisions quickly. To demonstrate effective decision-making behaviour in the school management process, there exist stages to be followed carefully (Lunenburg and Ornstein, 1991)

Keskinkılıç (2011) highlights internal elements consisting of administrative aids, teachers, non-teaching staff, students, and financial resources, whereas external factors consist of senior management, local administrations, parents, environmental groups, non-governmental organisations, unions, and geographical structure. There are multiple dimensions that the school manager should consider during any decision-making process (Hanson, 1991), and the school management can take decisions collectively or individually (Scheerie, 1997).

Planning: In accomplishing educational goals, deciding on the ways to conduct the work and operations and on the methods to utilise are made possible by planning. Discerning alternative methods for managing the processes and deciding on the steps to take are some of the activities to be completed as part of the planning process (Lunenburg, 1995). School management should consider material, physical and geographical components at the planning stage and should be able to efficiently invite human resources to the processes (Şişman, 2019).

Organising: An organisation can be depicted as a community of individuals serving the same purpose. At the same time, organising can be portrayed as spotting the requisite actions and taking action to realise a common goal (Eren, 2021). Organisations can be modelled in differing ways as vertical, horizontal or a combination of the two. There is a hierarchical system in the vertical model, and more meaning is attributed to disciplinary processes. A smoother hierarchy and cooperation processes come to the fore in the horizontal model.

Communication: Communication is the activity of sharing information within the organisational culture and developing relations for the same purpose (White, 2007). Communication is the kernel for the continuity of an organisation and members working in harmony when they come together (Gül, 2018), although communication in school management should not be one-sided. This hints at the fact that, in the communication process, there should be a mutual and dynamic interplay between the school management and all the pieces that make up the school culture. Communication in school management is necessary to achieve consensus, find alternative solutions and get feedback (Bolman and Deal, 1993).

Influence: For the organisation's members to work efficiently as part of school management processes, they must first be influenced, and their expectations for a shared purpose must be met. This can be achieved through in-service training, holding short meetings, writing up evaluation reports, and exchanging ideas (Paullay *et al.*, 1994). School management-influencing processes should tend towards the highest level starting from the lowest level (Koç, 2009).

Coordination: Coordination in the school management process can be pointed out as combining the physical sources and human resources of the organisation around the same goal and harmoniously using them to achieve that goal. Traditions and customs, moral norms, laws and regulations, field-specific internal and external standards, and inspection mechanisms are all influential in coordination within and of the school management processes.

Evaluation (audit): The last stage of the school management process includes evaluation or supervision. Evaluation is the stage where the effects and consequences of all actions and interventions taken while managing the school are discussed. It is fundamental for the school manager to be competent in the field, to have the experience in and knowledge of, or the wisdom, in measurement and evaluation, and to bring a novel perspective to the events taking place (Aydın, 2005). In general, the evaluation process encompasses four stages including measurement, comparison and correction (Başaran and Çınkır, 2011).

School management theories

To be able to talk about a thorough analysis of an effective school management, it is worth taking a closer look at the theories with a scientific perspective. School management can be considered in two ways: for those who manage and for those who are organised. These dimensions interact with each other and create a mutual development process (Kuru Çetin, 2021). The literature presents the theories of school management in three categories.

Classical management theories

Classical or Traditional Management Theories emerged in the early eighteenth century. In this theory, the need to operate the system mechanically and to set specific rules are the basis for the management processes. The increase in mechanisation with the industrial revolution across the world made it necessary to establish large-scale factories rather than small-scale workshops, to construct systematic management, and to set specific standards (Hatch, 1997). Four different approaches are found under the heading Classical Management Theories. The first is 'Scientific Management' developed by Taylor (Hatch, 1997). In this theory, the basic principles for managing large-scale industrial establishments are determined.

Another Classical Management Theory was developed by Fayol (Çalıkoğlu, 2013). While determining the management processes, Fayol attempted to look from the eyes of the managers and emphasised that management 'science' is universal and certain principles should be addressed in a versatile way (Çalıkoğlu, 2013). According to Fayol, management processes are gathered into five groups: planning, organising, commanding, coordinating, and controlling (Cole, 2004).

Yet another critical approach in Classical Management Theory is the Bureaucracy Theory developed by Weber (Koçel, 2005). According to Weber, an ideally designed bureaucracy systematises management operations and helps the organisation work (Koçel, 2005).

The last of the theories is the Management Approach by Gulick and Urwick (Bursalıoğlu, 2022). This contrasts with Fayol's view: his five-stage management process is transformed into a seven-stage process constituting the acronym POSDCORB: planning, organising, personnel management, directing, coordination, reporting, and budgeting.

Neo-classical management theories

The main feature of these theories is the human factor, and the interaction with the internal and external environment of the organisation is pivotal (Karip, 2005). Neo-classical thinkers are scholars who are interested in the fields of sociology, psychology, and anthropology (Bursalıoğlu, 2022). Neo-Classical Management Theories focus on human factors such as the interaction between social and technical systems, individual peace and group harmony, leadership, motivation, job satisfaction, and conflict of interest (Ross and Murdick, 1977). Mayo is an important name in neo-classical management theories.

New management theories

After the 1970s, the increase in the need for fresh perspectives and innovative management methods brought new ways of organising individuals and work. These new approaches can be termed 'the System Approach', 'Contingency Approach', 'Total Quality Management', and 'Strategic Management' (Kuru Çetin, 2021). The Systems Approach is also known as 'the Modern Organisation Theory'. The systems approach can be expressed as synthesising classical and neoclassical theories (Memduhoğlu, 2013) and taking an eclectic route. In the Systems Approach, emphasis is placed on the organisation/management and on the people. The Contingency Approach first emerged in organisational research in England in the 1960s along similar lines of thought.

In the Contingency Approach, instead of the principles of the organisation, the internal and external characteristics of the environment, technology, and the related infrastructure owned, and size of the organisation are considered as the context. When new and different situations arise, alternative methods are adopted to understand and solve these novel situations. It was appreciated that no leadership role or behaviour can be embraced automatically. Managers can and should take on varying types of leadership (Balcı, 2003).

As a systematic approach, Total Quality Management emerged in the 1990s. The most crucial aspect of Total Quality Management is that it can be applied and recognised in all kinds of institutions (Özevren, 1997). When it comes to school management, Total Quality Management is the responsibility of educators, managers, families, students, the school itself, and physical buildings since components together form a whole (Doğan, 2002). Also, in line with the Strategic Management Approach, strategic steps are taken, and the organisation's purpose, vision, target, policy, action plans, resource measurements, and performance indicators are specified (Bryson, 1995).

The case of leadership in the education management process

Towards the end of the nineteenth century, educational management began to be accepted as a science and a field of expertise (Oplatka, 2008). Educational management started to develop with the steps taken in the USA and gradually spread worldwide (Gümüş, 2021). Educational management is indeed a process that includes management of the school in general (Murphy, 1998), whereas Classical and Neo-Classical Management approaches were dominant in educational management until the 1970s, new methods began to be adopted with advances in science and technology, and this challenged the managers through the behaviours expected from them (Comte, 2011). Instead of a mere management system, management that works in cooperation and puts the human factor in the foreground was embraced (Tschannen-Moran and Gareis, 2005).

After the 2000s, the roles of school managers began to change, and new concepts emerged. One of the increasingly emphasised concepts is undoubtedly leadership. The notion of a manager has been replaced by school leader, education leader and programme leader. That is, the concept of 'the manager' gives way to that of 'the leader', and the two have started to be used through a blended approach. In fact, in the twenty-first century, it is well-known that the school manager should act like a leader, to keep up with the requirements of the era and to manage effectively (Gül, 2020). This brings us to the last part of this chapter which will illustrate modern theories.

Contemporary leadership approaches

There is a collection of situations and components in educational management. It is expected that school managers have different identities and exhibit dissimilar leadership behaviours towards situations in which they have to act as leaders. There are two classifications of leadership traits in the literature: traditional and contemporary. In this section, Contemporary Leadership Approaches will be discussed within the framework of educational management.

Instructional leadership

The foremost function of schools is to ensure that teaching and learning activities are properly carried out. Instructional leadership gives responsibilities to managers in three different roles. These responsibilities include determining the school's mission, managing the curriculum within the framework of the regulations, and assuring a positive school climate (Hallinger, 2005). Managers of a school consider it their duty to find solutions to any problem that affects the teaching process within the scope of teaching leadership (Kılınç, 2021).

Teacher leadership

School managers are expected to take full responsibility for incidents within the school and to deal with any problems on their own. The concept of 'teacher leadership' assumes that leadership is not an authority that should be sought only in managers: leadership can be shared by all the members of the school when appropriate, and teachers should help managers carry out the processes that are pertinent to managing (Leithwood and Jantzi, 2000).

Distributed leadership

In the management of schools, modern management processes have lately been adopted, and human factors and more democratic management styles have come to the fore (Özer and Beycioğlu, 2013). Distributed leadership is based on the idea that each member of the school can display their leadership skills and contribute directly or indirectly to the school leadership (Spillane *et al.*, 2003) (see Chapter 2).

Visionary leadership

Having visionary managers in the school is indeed an advantage for the members of the organisation. Today, there is a greater need for leaders who can analyse the needs of the age, bring innovative suggestions to the school culture, and draw a progressive vision for management (Doğan, 2021).

Transformational leadership

Changing environmental conditions and an ever-increasing level of knowledge and technology point to changes in the leadership phenomenon. Transformational leaders at this point act as agents inspiring change within and beyond their organisation (Eraslan, 2006). Their main purpose is to ensure that the organisation adapts to changing conditions without experiencing serious problems (Eisenbach *et al.*, 1999).

Servant leadership

The purpose of servant leadership is basically to serve (Greenleaf, 1977). Leadership behaviours are later included in the process. These leaders primarily observe the needs and expectations of the members of the organisation they are affiliated with (Spears, 2010). In Servant Leadership, the concept of 'we' is adopted to the highest extent instead of the 'self' (Drury, 2004).

Spiritual leadership

Spiritual leadership mainly deals with issues such as honesty, justice, independence, and ethical values (Fry, 2003). In the school management process, spiritual leaders try to cater to the inner worlds of the members of the organisation and motivate them. Ensuring the members' sense of belonging to the school culture, self-confidence, and positive attitudes are among the main goals of spiritual leaders (Doohan, 2007).

Competencies that an effective school manager should possess

Recalling that in contemporary management processes, people and organisational culture come to the fore rather than rules and management, the focus is now on the working process rather than the result of the operating system, and at this point, humans become central. It is found that managers who use contemporary management processes to assure effective school management should possess several traits: technical, conceptual, and human (social) competencies (Eren, 2021). School manager qualifications and sub-features are shared in Figure 5.1.

The competencies that come to the fore are now: being a guide and mentor (Ada and Baysal, 2012), being entrepreneurial and brave, using resources effectively (Erdem, 2005), thinking critically and creatively (Ayyıldız and Yılmaz, 2021), and having the skills pertaining to questioning, effective time management, innovative thinking (Tierney, 2015), owning ethical values, managing stress, and having multi-criteria decision-making skills.

Conclusion

One cannot be fully sure about what the future will bring for the area of school management. Nonetheless, it is still possible to make projections saying that things will be even more complex, requiring managers to stay humane and be innovative.

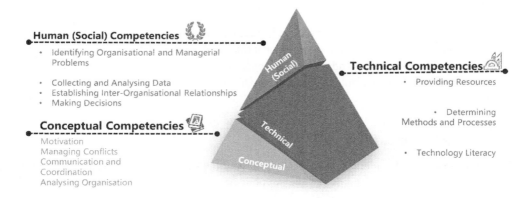

Figure 5.1 School Management and Sub-characteristics

Learning tasks

Try to contact two school principals working in different districts. Talk to them to see how
  their roles regarding management differ in line with the profiles of their schools.
Ask these principals if they would define themselves as leaders and why.
Describe what twenty-first-century school leadership and management will be like for various
  contexts around the globe.

Summary points

- Effective school management is related to effective school culture.
- Effective school culture is inclusive for all members.
- Effective school managers today are those with leadership qualities.
- A changing world entails changes to the understanding of school management.
- Contemporary leadership theories are expected to further evolve in the theoretical and practical pillars of the area.

Recommended reading

Fullan, M. The *principal 2.0: Three keys to maximizing impact*. (In press).
Shibuya, K. (2022). *Community Participation in School Management: Relational trust and educational outcomes.*
  Abingdon: Routledge.
Ubben, G.C., Hughes, L.W. and Norris, C.J. (2021) *The Principal: creative leadership for excellence in schools*
  (8th Ed.). London: Pearson.

References

Aas, M., Andersen, F.C. and Vennebo, K.F. (2020) How can School Leaders Gain Role Clarity and Grow Their
  Leadership Identity? *Research in Educational Administration & Leadership* **5**(2), pp. 18–551.
Ada, S. and Baysal, Z.N. (2012). *Türk eğitim sistemi ve etkili okul yönetimi* (2nd Ed.). Ankara: Pegem Akademi.
Akpolat, E.K. (2020). *Primary school teacher's percepions of school culture and value system.* Master Thesis.
  Fırat University, Institute of Educational Science.
Aydın, İ. (2005) *Öğretimde Denetim.* Ankara: Pegem Akademi.
Ayyıldız, P. and Yılmaz, A. (2021) Moving the kaleidoscope' to See the Effect of Creative Personality Traits
  on Creative Thinking Dispositions of Preservice Teachers: The Mediating Effect of Creative Learning
  Environments and Teachers' Creativity-Fostering Behavior. *Thinking Skills and Creativity* **41**, pp. 1–10.
Balcı, A. (2002) *Etkili okul geliştirme: Kuram uygulama ve araştırma.* Ankara: Pegem Akademi.
Balcı, A. (2003) Eğitim örgütlerine yeni bakış açıları: Kuram araştırma ilişkisi II. *Kuram ve Uygulamada Eğitim
  Yönetimi Dergisi* **9**(1), pp. 26–61.
Barth, R. (2002) The Culture Builder. *Educational Leadership* **59**(8), pp. 6–11.
Başaran, İ.E. and Çınkır, Ş. (2011) *Türk eğitim sistemi ve okul yönetimi.* İstanbul: Ekinoks Yayınları.
Bengtson, E., Zepeda, S.J. and Partlo, O. (2013) School systems' Practices of Controlling Socialization During
  Principal Succession: Looking Through the Lens of an Organisational Socialization Theory. *Educational
  Management Administration and Leadership* **41**(2), pp. 143–164.
Bennis, W. (2009) *On Becoming a Leader* (4th. Ed.). New York, NY: Basic Books.
Bertalanffy, L.V. (1971) *General System Theory: Foundations, development, applications.* London: Penguin.
Bolman, L. and Deal, T. (1993) *The Path to School Leadership: A portable mentor.* Thousand Oaks, CA: Corwin
  Press, Inc.
Bryson, J. (1995) *Strategic Planning for Public and non-Profit Organizations.* Hoboken, NJ: John Wiley and Sons.
Bursalıoğlu, Z. (2000) *Okul yönetiminde yeni yapı ve davranış.* Ankara: Pegem Akademi.

Bursalıoğlu, Z. (2022) *Eğitim yönetiminde teori ve uygulama* (16th Ed.). Ankara: Pegem Akademi.

Bush, T. and Anderson, L. (2003) Organisational Culture. In M. Thurlow, T. Bush and M. Coleman (Eds.), *Leadership and Strategic Management in South African Schools*. London: Commonwealth Secretariat.

Çalıkoğlu, A. (2013) *Genel ve endüstriyel yönetim* (H. Fayol). Istambul: Adres Yayınları.

Cole, G.A.(2004) *Management Theory and Practice* (6th ed.). London: Thomson Learning.

Colley, K.M. (1999) *Coming to know a school culture*. Doctoral Thesis. Faculty of the Virginia Polytechnic Institute and State University.

Comte, A. (2011) *General View of Positivism*. Cambridge: Cambridge University Press.

De Grauwe, A. (2005) Improving the Quality of Education Through School-Based Management: Learning from International Experiences. *International Review of Education* **51**(4), pp. 269–287.

Deal, T. and Kennedy, A. (1984) *Corporate Cultures: The rites and rituals of corporate life*. Reading, MA: Addison-Wesley.

Demirtaş, Z. (2010) The Relationship in High Schools between School Culture and Student Achievement. *Mustafa Kemal University Journal of Social Sciences Institute* **7**(3), pp. 208–223.

Doğan, E. (2002) *Eğitimde toplam kalite yönetimi*. Istanbul: Academyplus.

Doğan, S. (2021) *Çağdaş liderlik yaklaşımları*. In N. Güçlü and S. Koşar (Eds.), *Eğitim yönetiminde liderlik: Teori, araştırma ve uygulama* (7th Ed.). Ankara: Pegem Akademi.

Doohan, L. (2007) *Spiritual Leadership: The quest for integrity*. Mahwah, NJ: Paulist Press.

Drucker, P.F. (2000) The Change Leader. *National Productivity Review* **19**(2), pp. 13–20.

Drury, S. (2004) Employee Perceptions of Servant Leadership: Comparisons by Level and With Job Satisfaction and Organizational Commitment. *Dissertation Abstracts International* **65**(9), pp. 314–324.

Durna, U. and Eren, V. (2002) Kamu sektöründe stratejik yönetim. *Amme İdaresi Dergisi* **35**(1), pp. 55–75.

Duverger, M. (1982) *Political Sociology*. Chicago, IL: Ariel.

Eisenbach, R., Watson, K. and Pillai, R. (1999) Transformational Leadership in the Context of Organizational Change. *Journal of Organizational Change Management* **12**(2), pp. 80–89.

Eraslan, L. (2006) liderlikte post-modern bir paradigma: Dönüşümcü liderlik. *International Journal of Human Sciences* **1**(1), pp. 1–30.

Erdem, A.R. (2005) *Etkili ve verimli (nitelikli) eğitim*. Ankara: Anı Yayıncılık.

Eren, Z. (2021). *Okul örgütü ve yönetimi*. In U. Akın (Ed.), *Türk eğitim sistemi ve okul yönetimi* (5th Ed.) (pp. 177–233). Ankara: Pegem Akademi.

Fry, L.W. (2003) Toward a Theory of Spiritual Leadership. *The Leadership Quarterly* **14**(6), pp. 693–727.

Greenleaf, R.K. (1977) *Servant leadership: A journey into the natüre of legitimate power and greatness*. Online. Available at: https://www.greenleaf.org/products-page/servant-leadership-a-journey-into-the-nature-of-legitimate-power-and-greatness/ (Accessed 23 October 2022).

Gül, İ. (2018) *Türk eğitim sistemi ve okul yönetimi*. Ankara: Pegem Akademi.

Gül, İ. (2020) *Türk eğitim sistemi ve okul yönetimi* (2nd Ed.). Ankara: Pegem Akademi.

Gulick, Luther (1937) Notes on the Theory of Organization. In L. Urwick Luther Gulick ve (Ed.), *Papers on The Science of Administration*. Dublin: Institute of Public Administration.

Gümüş, E. (2021) Eğitim yönetimi programlarında liderlik. In N. Güçlü and S. Koşar (Eds.), *Eğitim yönetiminde liderlik: Teori, araştırma ve uygulama* (7th Ed.). Ankara: Pegem Akademi.

Hallinger, P. (2005) Instructional Leadership and the School Principal: A Passing Fancy That Refuses to Fade Away. *Leadership and Policy in Schools* **4**(3), pp. 221–239.

Hanson, E.M. (1991) *Educational Administration and Organizational Behavior*. Bostoon, MA: Allyn and Bacon.

Hargreaves, A. (1997) *Rethinking Educational Change: Going deeper and wider in the quest for success*. Alexandria, VI: Association for Supervision and Curriculum Development.

Hatch, M.J. (1997) *Organization Theory: Modern, symbolic, and postmodern perspective*. Oxford: Oxford University Press.

Hinde, E.R. (2004) School Culture and Change: An Examination of the Effects of School Culture on the Process of Change. *Essays in Education*, **11**.

Hollins, E.R. (1996) *Culture in School Learning: Revealing the deep meaning*. Abingdon: Routledge.

Hoy, W.K. and Miskel, C.G. (1996) *Educational Administration: Theory, research, and practice* (5th ed.). New York, NY: McGraw-Hill.

Ilgar, L. (2005) *Eğitim yönetimi, okul yönetimi, sınıf yönetimi*. Istambul: Beta Basım Yayım.

Kafalı, U. (2022) The Role of School Managers in Creating School Culture. *Balkan and Near Eastern Journal of Social Sciences* **8**(1), pp. 48–56.

Karadağ, N. and Özdemir, S. (2015) School principals' Opinions Regarding Creation and Development of School Culture. *International Journal of Science Culture and Sport*, Special Issue 4, pp. 259–273.

Karip, E. (2005) Yönetim biliminin alanı ve kapsamı. In Y. Özden (Ed.) *Eğitim ve okul yöneticiliği* (2nd Ed.) Ankara: Pegem Akademi.

Keskinkılıç, K. (2011) Yönetim ve okul yönetimi ile ilgili temel kavramlar. In K. Keskinkılıç (Ed.), *Türk eğitim sistemi ve okul yönetimi.* Ankara: Pegem Akademi.

Kılınç, A.Ç. (2021) Çağdaş liderlik yaklaşımları. In N. Güçlü and S. Koşar (Eds.) *Eğitim yönetiminde liderlik: Teori, araştırma ve uygulama* (7th Ed.). Ankara: Pegem Akademi.

Koç, U. (2009) Örgütsel öğrenme: Tanımı, yakın terimler arasındaki kavramsal ayrımlar ve davranışsal yaklaşım. *Afyon Kocatepe Üniversitesi, İ.İ.B.F. Dergisi,* **10**(1), pp. 151–165.

Koçel, T. (2001) *İşletme yöneticiliği ve organizasyonlarda davranış.* Istambul: Beta Basım Yayım.

Koçel, T. (2005) *İşletme yöneticiliği: Bürokrasi yaklaşımı* (10th Ed.). Ankara: Arıkan Yayınevi.

Köse, S., Tetik, S. and Ercan, C. (2001) Factors Forming Organizational Culture. *Journal of Management and Economics* **8**(1), pp. 219–242.

Kuru Çetin, S. (2021) Yönetim ve yönetim kuramları. In U. Akın (Edt, 5th Ed.) *Türk eğitim sistemi ve okul yönetimi.* Pegem Akademi.

Leithwood, K. and Jantzi, D. (2000) Principal and Teacher Leadership Effects: A Replication. *School Leadership and Management* **20**(4), pp. 415–434.

Lunenburg, F.C. (1995) *The Principalship.* Hoboken, NJ: Prentice-Hall.

Lunenburg, F.C. and Ornstein, A.C. (1991) *Educational Administration.* Belmont, CA: Wadsworth Publishing Company.

Mangla, N. (2021) Working in Pandemic and Post-Pandemic Periode-Cultural Intelligence Is the Key. *International Journal of Cross Cultural Management* **21**(1), pp. 53–69.

McCarley, T. A., Peters, M. L. and Decman, J. M. (2016) Transformational Leadership Related to School Climate: A Multilevel Analysis. *Educational Management Administration and Leadership,* **44**(2).

Memduhoğlu, H.B. (2013) Yönetim düşüncesinin evrimi ve yönetimi. In H.B. Memduhoğlu and K. Yılmaz (Eds.), *Yönetimde yeni yaklaşımlar* (2nd Ed.). Ankara: Pegem Akademi.

Mullins, L.J. (1996). *Management and Organisational Behaviour* (4th Ed.). London: Pitman Publishing.

Murphy, J. (1998) Preparation for the School Principalship: The United States' Story. *School Leadership and Management* **18**(3), pp. 359–372.

Newman, S. A. and Ford, R. C. (2021) Five Steps to Leading Your Team in the Virtual COVID-19 Workplace. *Organizational Dynamics,* **50**(1).

Oplatka, I. (2008) The Field of Educational Management: Some Intellectual Insights from the 2007 BELMAS Conference. *Management in Education* **22**(3), pp. 4–10.

Özdemir, M. (2015) Yönetim süreçleri. In U. Akın (Ed.), *Türk eğitim sistemi ve okul yönetimi.* Ankara: Pegem Akademi.

Özer, N. and Beycioğlu, K. (2013) Paylaşılan liderlik ölçeğinin geliştirilmesi: Geçerlik ve güvenirlik çalışmaları. *İlköğretim Online* **12**(1), pp. 77–86.

Özevren, M. (1997) *Toplam kalite yönetimi: Temel kavramlar ve uygulamalar.* Istambul: Alfa Yayınları.

Paullay, I., George, M.A. and Eugene, F.S.R. (1994) Construct Validation of Two Instruments Designed to Measure Job Involvement and Work Centrality. *Journal of Applied Psychology* **79**(2), pp. 210–224.

Pfeffer, J. and Salancik, G.G. (1978) *The External Control of Organizations: A resource dependence perspective.* New York, NY: Harper and Row.

Robbins, P.S. (1991) *Organizational Behavior Concepts, Contreversies and Applications.* Hoboken, NJ: Prentice Hall.

Roethlisberger, F.J. and Dickson, W.J. (1939) *Management and the Worker.* Cambridge, MA: Harvard University Press.

Ross, F. and Murdick, R. (1977) People, Productivity and Organizational Structure. In F. Luthans (Ed.), *Contemporary Readings in Organizational Behavior.* New York, NY: McGraw Hill.

Scheerie, E.L. (1997) Shared Decision Making in Schools: Effect on Teacher Efficacy. *Education* **118**(1), pp. 1–4.

Schein, E.H. (2004) *Organizational Culture and Leadership* (2nd Ed.). San Francisco: CA: Jossey-Bass.

Schein, E.H. (2011) *Leadership and Organizational Culture.* New York, NY: Wiley.

Sepuru, M.G. and Mohlakwana, M.A. (2020) The Perspectives of Beginner Principals on Their New Roles in School Leadership and Management: A South African Case Study. *South African Journal of Education* **40**(2), pp. 1–11.

Sergiovanni, T. (2001) *The Principals: A reflective practice perspective.* Boston, MA: Allyn and Bacon.

Shafritz, J.M., Ott, J.S. and Jang, Y.S. (1992) *Classic of Organization Theory.* Boston, MA: Brooks/Cole Publishing Company.

Shibuya, K. (2020) Community Participation in School Management from the Viewpoint of Relational Trust: A Case from the Akatsi South District, Ghana. *International Journal of Educational Development* **76**, pp. 1–7.

Simon, H. (1987) Decision Making and Organizational Design. In H. Simon (Ed.), *Organization Theory, Selected Readings*. London: Penguin Books.

Spears, C.L. (2010) Character and Servant Leadership: Ten Characteristics of Effective, Caring Leaders. *The Journal of Virtues and Leadership* **1**(1), pp. 25–30.

Spillane, J.P., Diamond, J.B. and Jita, L. (2003) Leading Instruction: The Distribution of Leadership for Instruction. *Journal of Curriculum Studies* **35**(5), pp. 533–543.

Stolp, S. (2002) *Leadership for school culture*. ERIC Clearinghouse on Educational Management Eugene OR (ED370198).

Stolp, S. and Smith, S.C. (1994) *School Culture and Climate: The role of the leader*. OSSC Bulletin. Eugene: Oregon School Study Council.

Tierney, W.G. (2015). *Barriers to Innovation and Creativity in Higher Education*. 1.Uluslararası Yükseköğretim Çalışmaları Konferansı. Boğaziçi Üniversitesi, 14–16 Ekim.

Timperley, H.S. (2005) Distributed Leadership: Developing Theory from Practice. *Journal of Curriculum Studies* **37**(4), pp. 395–420.

Tschannen-Moran, M. and Gareis, C.R. (2005) Cultivating principals' sense of efficacy: Support that matters. Paper presented at the annual meeting of the University Council for Educational Administration, November 10–13, 2005.

Wanburg, C. (2012) *The Oxford Handbook of Organizational Socialization*. Oxford: Oxford University Press.

White, D. (2007) *Management and Communication Skills*. London: University of London Press.

6 Observations of Classroom Management and School Leadership in the COVID-19

Purvi (Vi) Gandhi

Introduction

The academic year 2020 to 2021 was characterised by school lockdowns and a partial return to school following the COVID-19 pandemic. The disruptions resulted in various challenges for educators in managing behaviour for learning. When students were not in school and instruction was pivoted to online (remote instruction), teachers faced a variety of difficulties. When students finally returned fully to school, they had to stay in their teaching groups (bubbled lessons), so new complications emerged. Finally, when school started in 2021, a 'new normal' phase of schooling began as activities cautiously began to run more as they had been before the pandemic hit, and classroom management continued to be a focus for many school leaders.

Classroom management is defined here as any teachers' actions, including lesson planning, organising, and delivery for their students that contribute to create a healthy, caring classroom culture where all students, and teachers can thrive (Bennett and Smilanich, 2012). The terms 'classroom management', 'behaviour management', and 'creating a positive learning environment' are all used interchangeably in the chapter. The chapter aims to focus on the challenges faced by teachers and school leaders in classroom management as they reacted and responded to the COVID-19 pandemic. We will discuss some factors that impacted the delivery of effective behaviour management in the context of the three phases of 'remote' instruction, 'bubbled' lessons, and the 'new normal'. The various leadership styles that were used to develop the resources needed to meet the unique challenges, and how the lessons learned might inform future behaviour policies, and practices will also be discussed.

There is very little empirical evidence available for this relatively short-term event, so much of the discussion is based on the author's observations in one secondary school in the East Midlands. However, where possible, it is framed in the context of previously published work.

Remote learning

When the school gates in England closed on Monday, 20 March 2020, school leaders were not sure when they would reopen. Teachers had to develop a new way of educating their students. Most were taught online remotely (Greenhow et al., 2021). Teachers and students faced challenges such as lack of preparedness, absence of sufficient IT technology, and unfamiliarity with technological pedagogy. Coping with a crisis of this scale was not something that many in schools had trained for or experienced.

DOI: 10.4324/9781003321439-6

A key factor that determines competence is knowledge. The need to introduce remote learning revealed a skills gap for many teachers who were unfamiliar with computer technology and the delivery of online education. This lack of knowledge and familiarity caused increased levels of stress for many teachers. The combined effects of increased stress and unfamiliarity with the new online teaching modality had a detrimental impact on teachers' ability to properly manage disruptive behaviours. For example, the behaviour management strategies, such as asking students to move seats that worked in the classroom, were no longer available in the online classroom. A vicious circle developed where disruptive behaviour further increased teacher stress and feelings of incompetence and further inhibited their ability to deal with disruptive behaviour. Therefore, upskilling teachers in online behaviour management was an important area of attention for school leaders during remote learning.

Social psychologists such as Milgram (1963) suggest that factors such as 'proximity' and 'legitimacy of authority' affect levels of obedience, applied here as following the instructions of an authority figure such as a teacher. In the context of a classroom, the 'proximity' of a teacher to a student and the student's confidence that their teacher has 'legitimate authority' is important when thinking about behaviour management. Whilst recognising that blind obedience is completely undesirable, some obedience is necessary in ensuring effective classroom management because it creates accountability, predictability, and order. During remote instruction, teachers not only had to deal with the increased distance from their students and limited non-verbal feedback from their students, but they were also in a situation where they were perceived to have less experience with the technology compared to their students. These factors contributed to decreasing the legitimacy of their authority and making establishing classroom expectations and routines more challenging. Structures and systems for ensuring accountability for student behaviour were not fit for purpose – for example, sanctions such as detentions were no longer available to teachers – which meant that teachers had to think differently about how they would manage behaviour of their students.

Questions for discussion

How could student behaviour be assessed remotely?
How would the effectiveness of any behaviour management strategy be assessed?

Leadership for remote learning

Leadership is a process of influencing, motivating, and encouraging people to act to achieve collective goals and shared aspirations (Leithwood *et al.*, 1999). The unique challenges that the pandemic presented called for strong leadership from the senior leadership team and from the ground up (teacher leadership) like never before. Three characteristics of educational leadership during the pandemic include:

1 Leadership is guided by values

Harris and Jones (2020) assert that leaders during these disruptive times were 'defined by their determination, their hope, and their unshakable belief that, whatever happens, whatever the cost, whatever the scale of the challenge, they will continue to do everything in their power to safeguard the learning of all young people'. School leaders were faced with the school closures at short notice, without much information, no previous experience to draw from, and no how-to guide to help them. Leadership requires quick decision-making, flexibility, open-mindedness, and courage. Effective leadership when facing challenging times, such as the pandemic, is characterised by a value system that embraces a moral purpose (Harris and Chapman, 2002). For example, values in the author's school were captured in the statements made by the headteacher during his regular briefings such as 'we must keep providing a good quality education for all students' and 'making sure that we connect with every student every day' (Penty, 2020). These ideals acted as a compass that guided action and provided balance. Leaders inspired and influenced staff to set high expectations of themselves and their students amid so much uncertainty and unfamiliarity, setting the tone for remote lessons and expected standards of behaviour. Teachers were role models and students turned to them to provide familiarity, structure, and reassurance. Similarly, effective leaders were role models that provided direction, encouragement, and support for their teams. Values-driven approaches from leadership influenced teachers to respond to the pandemic in a way that enhanced relationships, empathy, and collaboration (McLeod and Dulsky, 2021).

Questions for discussion

Talk to teachers you may know. How were the core values that unite a school expressed during online learning?
How did these values guide staff and student behaviour?

---

2 Leadership is distributed

Distributed leadership is where leadership is shared between multiple leaders to bring about the process of improvement by learning, sharing and networking (Azorín *et al.*, 2020). During the pandemic, making quick decisions with considered deliberations of outcomes, balancing equity with accountability and addressing both human needs and organisational outcomes were among the many tensions faced by educational leaders (Netolicky, 2020). Distributed leadership was one way the demands of the crisis were addressed.

Many teachers (with or without formal leadership positions) shared the responsibility of leadership during the pandemic. According to Fairman and MacKenzie (2012), teacher leadership, an example of distributed leadership, is described as a practice in which teachers engage in their learning by experimenting, reflecting, and sharing their ideas with other teachers. They work collaboratively to bring about improvement within the school community and beyond. Some spheres in which individual teachers' leaders can exercise leadership and influence others include:

- Experimenting and reflecting on their practice.
- Sharing their ideas with other teachers.
- Collaborating and reflecting together on collective work.
- Engaging in collective school-wide improvement.
- Engaging with the wider school community and parents.

An example of teacher leadership from the author's experience was when individual teachers experimented using different online platforms to teach. If they found that it was useful, they provided training sessions to other interested colleagues. The training sessions ran one evening a week and influenced the provision of remote education to those who attended. Training included managing classroom behaviours on platforms such as MSTeams, and Google Classrooms, monitoring student participation, and assessing learning with software such as Seneca, Microsoft forms, and Nearpod. Teachers collaborated to plan and share resources that aided the creation of positive online learning environments. A by-product of these sessions was the opportunities to work together to problem solve. For example, during one of these sessions, teachers discussed the ethics of requiring all students to have their cameras on and the etiquette of online learning. They shared what had and had not been successful in their lessons and worked together to draw up some guidance on what acceptable behaviour should be like in an online lesson. These were then fed back to the senior leaders, who evaluated and communicated them to all staff, students, and parents resulting in consistent classroom expectations across the school. Such a collaborative leadership approach enhanced the quality of teaching and learning.

Teacher leadership builds competency, provides opportunities for autonomy, and increases levels of relatedness within the school. Therefore, teacher leadership contributes to levels of resilience in schools.

Questions for discussion

What do you understand teacher leadership to be?
Suggest some examples of teacher leadership in practice.

3 Leadership is more progressive with technology

The pandemic has brought significant changes to education, most obviously via information technology (IT). According to Bennet (2008), IT specialists can develop leadership roles within schools and influence classroom policy and school practice. The challenges of remote instruction highlighted such opportunities. During the pandemic, technological leadership involved readying staff and students for working online quickly and safely. There were no guidelines on how to achieve this task: leaders had to lead, and they had to make decisions that would influence how teaching and learning occurred at their schools. Leaders had to analyse the suitability of online platforms such as MSTeams, Google Classrooms, and Zoom and decide which ones to invest in for their schools. Decisions about how student work would be stored, shared, and tracked had to be made. School leaders were also responsible for ensuring that the staff and students were equipped with knowledge about online safety and the safe storage of confidential data. In many schools, leaders allocated resources for equipment such as laptops, graphics pads, or even internet connections for their staff and students to allow remote learning to take place. Without technological leadership, remote education would have been virtually impossible for many students and teachers.

Questions for discussion

Has COVID-19 highlighted a need to prioritise technology in the curriculum and staff CPD?
In what ways does IT enhance (or not) classroom management?

Return to school: A change in expectations

School closures negatively impacted students' learning and their physical and mental health (Garbe *et al.*, 2020; Lee, 2020). Moreover, there was a concern for students who lacked access to technology and a worry about the increase in the widening of the knowledge gap between the advantaged and the disadvantaged students (Bayrakdar and Guveli, 2020). In response to this situation, the government announced the reopening of schools in September 2020. However, schools had to ensure that staff and students engaged in risk-reduction behaviour. Key actions that were almost universally implemented were: the teaching of students in 'bubbles', ensuring social distancing, the wearing of masks, testing, enhanced cleaning, and sanitising (DfE, 2020). To ensure that new behaviours were managed effectively, new policies and procedures had to be put in place.

Classes taught in 'Bubbles': groups of students were allocated to a classroom/area of the school. They were required to stay within their groups or 'bubbles' during the school day to reduce the risk of 'contaminating' others. A positive test result in one bubble meant that members could isolate without triggering a shutdown of the entire school. The 'bubbled' lessons meant that the same groups of students had to remain in the same classroom for the entire school day, every day. Between lessons, students were unsupervised and 'misbehaviour' during this time was also a concern, as was the potential of students' interpersonal difficulties within their bubbles. Teachers needed to walk into the 'students' spaces' and had to work quickly and purposefully to set the tone for their lessons. If a student was upset because of an earlier event, it was difficult for him/her/them to 'switch gears' and refocus because their environment was still the same. Students' inability to focus could be seen as poor behaviour for learning. Teachers had to manage these behaviours without the use of tools such as asking students to move seats, using group work to enhance engagement, or setting detentions. They had to be more creative and empathetic in their approach: for example, by allowing students more time before the lesson to get settled and keeping classroom routines consistent, and putting an even bigger emphasis on differentiation during the planning and delivery of the lessons.

Social distancing: Two-metre distancing between teachers and students was required (DfE, 2020). Lunch times were staggered; so too were arrival and leaving, and schools had one-way systems. Some teachers had screens between their desks and the class, whilst others had a physical line drawn on the classroom floor to mark 'teacher space'. Teaching styles changed from moving around the classroom to teaching from the front all the time. Assemblies were reduced and/or delivered online.

Rules on social distancing posed challenges for teachers and school leaders. They were difficult to enforce due to crowding and made conversations with students about their behaviour difficult. Lessons were less interactive so students with additional needs possibly struggled more because teachers were unable to closely (physically) support them, and many schools removed 'safe spaces' for students who found it difficult to cope in lessons. For example, staff worried that the most vulnerable students might not fully understand the need for personal space and social distancing (Anna, SENCO in Lorenc *et al.*, 2021) and so comply with the new rules or withdraw from lessons. One way that leaders managed these behaviours was by using a combination of education about the importance of the new rules and encouragement of a culture of collective responsibility underpinned by clear and consistent messaging.

Masks: Government rules on wearing face coverings varied during this time, but secondary students were advised to wear masks in the corridors and/or in lessons. For some students, the mask symbolised impending danger, resulting in anxious behaviour that could have been detrimental to learning. As social distancing increased physical distance, masks increased the psychological distance between teachers and students making communication in the classroom more difficult and increasing the likelihood of disruptive behaviour. 'Deindividuation', where students engage in seemingly impulsive and deviant behaviour as they believe they cannot be personally identified, increased the likelihood of misbehaviour from students inclined to disrupt lessons. On the other hand, because groups of students were allocated to the same physical space, behaviour management became easier in some ways. Teachers and pastoral staff knew exactly where to find the students if they needed to speak with them and intervene if inappropriate behaviour was noticed. Either way, the necessity to reduce infection rates whilst taking into consideration students' psychology called for adaptations to behaviour policies that were compassionate and focused on building support for the students.

Leadership for returning to school

Leadership during the pandemic had to be context-responsive (Harris and Jones, 2020), so in the context of 'bubbled' lessons, schools needed to revise their policies and practices so that they were fit for purpose. Schools are social and interactive places where relationships are built and nurtured. The restrictions in place to reduce the spread of the virus made that difficult. The challenge for leaders was supporting their students and staff to create an environment where effective learning can take place despite the obstacles created by the new regulations.

Two examples of leadership characteristics during this period are given below.

1 Leadership is logistical

Besides ensuring that students and staff comply with the new behaviours expected of them, school leaders were also expected to organise regular COVID-19 testing on-site and hand out home-testing kits. The lack of concrete government guidelines coupled with the fast pace of change over this period meant school leaders had to develop their own plans for implementing the new protection measures in schools. Leaders had to ensure that schools were equipped and prepared for 'bubbled' lessons. Teamwork was required to make logistical decisions like revised timetables, developing one-way systems, organising how the 'bubbles' would be allocated and whether there was enough space available for social distancing, plus ensuring availability of resources (sanitiser/soap, bathroom cleanliness, cleaning equipment for teachers, etc.). Students were expected to stay in their bubbles, socially distance, and teachers were expected to manage these new behaviours. However, unless school leaders had the logistical infrastructure set up and clearly communicated, behaviour management would have been impossible for teachers.

2 Leadership is instructional

Instructional coaching is another example of teacher leadership. Teachers showed leadership by supporting each other to develop new coping strategies to deal with the difficulties presented by the new restriction. Teacher leaders collaborated with each other to reset expectations, re-establish classroom routines, and rethink consequences when students fail to meet expectations. The process of instructional coaching is as follows: goals are set (for example, establishing a routine for the start of a 'bubbled' lesson); feedback is given following lesson observations; coaches/leaders model or direct coaches towards specific improvements (such as setting up lessons while the students are already in the classroom and, when ready, the use of non-verbal cues to indicate the start of lesson). The new techniques are then rehearsed (Sims *et al.*, 2021). Such leadership, if done well, has the potential to strengthen collegial relationships and increase levels of autonomy and competence.

However, it is worth noting that to enable colleagues with work difficulties (such as behaviour management), strong relationships are needed; therefore, leaders are advised to increase formal (e.g., professional collaboration on CPD) and informal staff interaction (e.g., social events) (Beltman *et al.*, 2011). Peer coaching, where two peers engage in a dialogue about reflection, refinement, and development of their skills, can also be beneficial in strengthening professional relationships because the equity in such relationships allows teachers to be open in a non-judgemental space (Jordan-Daus and Austin, 2021). During the pandemic, many teachers engaged in peer coaching, sharing ideas and experiences with each other through the challenges of COVID-19. Formal collaboration such as co-planning schemes of work and informal interactions, such as online social activities such as online crossword clubs or discussing bakes-of-the-week, also took place. When leaders cultivate strong relationships by listening, providing support, and communicating well, well-being is positively enhanced (Ofsted, 2019). This in turn results in teachers being more receptive to interventions such as instructional coaching.

It takes time (repeated sessions) for coaching to yield significant results (Reddy *et al.*, 2021). However, it could be argued that, during the pandemic, when school leaders were time-poor, and there was a need to socially distance, coaching meetings and lesson observations were more difficult to organise. An interesting solution to this could be video technology such as IRIS Connect, an innovative tool that allows teachers to record their lessons, reflect on them and collaborate with colleagues. Using the tool involves teachers setting up recording devices and microphones that they then upload, edit, and analyse. Such technology, if used effectively, could allow teachers to engage in coaching conversations without physically having to be in the classroom.

Questions for discussion

How are positive interactions nurtured in your school/university?
What might be some advantages and some disadvantages of using videos to do lesson
   observations?

New normal

When schools recommenced in September 2021, they entered the 'new normal' phase. Lessons were taking place without the risk-reduction measures of the previous academic year, and 'bubbles' were a thing of the past. However, not everything has returned as they were during the pre-Covid era. There was still uncertainty about the public exams for Year 11 and 13 students, both staff and students were still catching COVID-19 and intermittently missing school, and the learning gap persisted. Rules, routines, and expectations changed yet again and so behaviour management needed to be rev+isited.

When teachers considered their approach to behaviour management, there was a new variable they had to account for during the 'new normal phase': the learning gap. In England, 98 per cent of teachers reported that their students were behind where they would normally expect them to be in their curriculum learning at the end of the 2019/20 school year (Sharp *et al.*, 2020). So, in 2021, teachers and school leaders worked to bridge the gap. The approach to do this varied and had implications for classroom learning environments.

+Teachers' approaches to bridging the gap could be categorised in two ways: the 'making up' and the 'building up'. The 'making up' approach saw the year as a chance to make up for missed learning and to get students to where they 'should' be compared to their counterparts during the pre-Covid era by teaching the content intensely. Teachers with this view were more focused on the structure and content of the lessons to cover the curriculum. Disruptive behaviour was seen as a barrier to learning. Rewards and punishments used were aimed at getting the students to behave so that the class could make academic progress fast. Teachers examined teaching practices, and when they found something that could be used to close the learning gap, they influenced others to use it. For example, tools such as knowledge organisers, low-stakes testing, and quizzing have been supported by research to improve recall (Smailes, 2018). In the author's observations, some teachers experimented with knowledge organisers, evaluated them, and worked in groups to improve them and make them relevant for each subject area. They were then shared with students and their parents centrally. Some teachers prioritised getting their students 'exam ready' and making up for the lost learning. However, there was a danger that such an approach overwhelmed the students, damaging the learning environment.

In contrast, the 'building on' view saw the year as a chance to assess students' knowledge and help them build on their learning without any fixed endpoint. When teachers used this approach, they spent the time building rapport with their classes and getting to know what they had learned (or not) during remote learning and bubbled learning. For example, in the author's school, some teachers trialed 'mindfulness for learning' sessions to support their students emotionally. Lessons were planned carefully so that they were well differentiated. However, teachers were not concerned about making sure that the entire syllabus was taught. Teachers prioritised the 'basic skills' over teaching the content in order to narrow the learning gap in the short term. By taking this approach, perhaps students would be better able to catch up in the longer term. One downside to this approach, though, was the risk of students going into the exam hall not having been fully prepared to take high-stakes examinations, resulting in repercussions for their future pathways and widening the gap further.

The teachers' approaches to bridging the learning gap depended not only on their behaviour-management styles but also on the classes' circumstances. For example, a teacher might have had a 'building up' approach with Year 8 students, but a 'making up' approach for a Year 11 class because Year 11 had to be prepared for their GCSE exams. Exam boards did not release any information about what the exams were going to be like until February 2022. This uncertainty influenced how teachers decided to teach their lessons and manage the learning environment within them. The consequences of this lack of information cannot be overstated. It was a key contributing factor in the 'making up' mentality, particularly for Year 11 and Year 13 teachers.

Questions for discussion

How can we truly measure the learning gap?
Besides exams, are there alternative ways of assessing learning?
What role does school leadership have here?

Leadership for the new normal

School leaders and teachers recognised the need to bridge the learning gap quickly because not doing so would have long-term consequences on the students' lives. However, this had to balance with students' emotional, social, and cognitive needs. While some teacher leadership focused on developing differentiation in lessons, using strategies such as knowledge organisers to help students to catch up, others aimed at improving the well-being of students.

Recovery from a crisis involves evaluation and organisational learning (Bundy *et al.*, 2017). As educators reflected on what their students needed, they evaluated their priorities and learned their lessons. There were differing and opposing views about how to move forwards. In the middle of this were the students who needed not just consistency, predictability, and structure but also flexibility and support for their individual needs. So, school leaders had to work collaboratively to come up with strategies that were balanced and consistent, yet flexible and applied equally to all, yet taking additional needs highlighted by the pandemic into account. Schools were entering new territory with new tensions and challenges. It will take time for leaders to reflect on the COVID-19 journey, identify priorities, and develop strategies.

Questions for discussion

What role do educational leaders have in addressing the equity issues highlighted by the pandemic?
How can teacher leaders address the challenge of closing the learning gap?
What is crisis leadership and what role does it have in the future of educational leadership?

Conclusion

2020 to 2022 brought seismic changes to school life across the globe. In the UK, this resulted in learning taking place online remotely during periods of lockdown. When schools reopened, they did so under strict restrictions to reduce the spread of the virus, and students were taught in groups/bubbles. Finally, when schools returned with some resemblance of normality in 2021, the 'new normal' phase of reflection and recovery had begun. Students and teachers faced different difficulties during each of these phases. The chapter discussed these challenges and the characteristics of educational leadership that helped to overcome them.

Many factors affected behaviour management during this time such as the physical and psychological distance between teachers and their students, the challenges of unfamiliarity with new technology, rules and routines, and the lack of clarity on high-stakes exams. Teachers showed resilience in managing classroom behaviours by upskilling themselves, building collaborative relationships with students, parents, and colleagues, and developing differentiated lessons to support their students. Teachers showed leadership by working together to research, trial, and share new ways of creating positive learning environments. They were helped by courageous school leaders who were guided by strong values. Leaders who embraced change and were agile in their responses, worked closely with others to provide resources ranging from timely CPD to laptops, to cleaning products, so that good teaching and learning could be facilitated.

Although COVID-19 brought a colossal amount of change, the crisis also provided an opportunity to reflect and take stock. Many silver linings resulted from the pandemic including advancement of technological knowledge, more collegial approach to leadership and more flexible and inclusive work practices (Jones *et al.*, 2021). On the other hand, the pandemic exposed some deficits that need to be analysed closely. For instance, the learning gap is widest among students with special needs, mental health difficulties, underserved communities, and students who speak English as an additional language (Sharp *et al.*, 2020). School leaders must ask themselves if these students were provided with adequate support. By answering this question objectively, leaders can inform their policies and procedures to ensure that they meet the needs of all their students. It is difficult to know the true impact of the pandemic on students currently because there is a paucity of empirical research. However, school leaders should be proactive in gathering data from their schools so that they can monitor and evaluate progress.

School leadership evolved during the pandemic. Firstly, there was a greater need for collaborative relationships. Distributed leadership became necessary for institutions to cope. Leaders relied on the collective wisdom of their teams and their networks to navigate through the many challenges posed by the pandemic. The relationships established between students, parents, and the school community were also essential in ensuring that schools continued to educate. Moving forwards, these partnerships should be maintained and enhanced to allow recovery from the loss of learning resulting from the disruption (Harris and Jones, 2020). Secondly, the role of information technology in schools is more crucial than ever before. The pandemic created opportunities for teachers and students to learn IT skills that have been beneficial in creating new skill sets (McLeod and Dulsky, 2021). Leaders should aim to capitalise on this new knowledge and not let it decay. Thirdly, responsive and context-driven crisis and change management are now part of the job description of senior leaders (Harris and Jones, 2020). School leaders have a lot to learn from the pandemic with more work to be done. Flexible, pragmatic, and ethical leadership now will be required to harness the opportunities for the creation of genuine and lasting improvements in education (Outhwaite, 2022). Only time will tell how the education community will reflect on and respond to the long-lasting impact of these years of disruption.

Summary points

- The challenges to behaviour management varied during each phase of the crisis.
- Although there are some positives that have resulted from the pandemic, a negative conse-quence of the disruption is the widening of the learning gap. As leaders try to bridge this gap, there is no clear indication of what approach will work yet. There is an opportunity now for educational leaders to reflect honestly on the effectiveness of their response to the demands of the pandemic and to develop ambitious strategies for long-lasting improvements. in their settings and beyond. Such leadership will require courage – which they have shown they have plenty of.
- To overcome these challenges, educational leaders, which include teacher leaders and those with formal leadership positions, had to step up to the plate. Leadership had the following characteristics:
    - It was values-driven.
    - It was distributed and collaborative.

- ○ It was progressive with technology.
- ○ It was logistical. A focus on the mechanics of operating the schools in line with rules of social distancing and enhanced hygiene procedures allowed leaders to keep their students and staff safe.
- ○ It was instructional. Timely and relevant CPD in which teachers supported each other to effectively develop their practice for teaching despite the restrictions on distance and movement enabled teachers to upskill themselves and support their students.
- ○ It depended on strong, positive relationships.
- • Although there are some positives that have resulted from the pandemic, a negative consequence of the disruption is the widening of the learning gap. As leaders try to bridge this gap, there is no clear indication of what approach will work yet. There is an opportunity now for educational leaders to reflect honestly on the effectiveness of their response to the demands of the pandemic and to develop ambitious strategies for long-lasting improvements in their settings and beyond. Such leadership will require courage - which they have shown they have plenty of.

Recommended reading

Harris, A. and Jones, M. (2020) COVID-19: School Leadership in Disruptive Times. *School Leadership and Management*, **40**(4), pp. 243–247.

Brown, B. (2018) *Dare to Lead: Brave work. Tough conversations. whole hearts.* London: Random House.

DeWitt, P.M. (2020) *Instructional Leadership: Creating practice out of theory.* Thousand Oaks, CA: Corwin Press.

References

Azorín, C., Harris, A. and Jones, M. (2020) Taking a Distributed Perspective on Leading Professional Learning Networks. *School Leadership & Management* **40**(2–3), pp. 111–127.

Bayrakdar, S. and Guveli, A. (2020) *Inequalities in Home Learning and Schools' Provision of Distance Teaching During School Closure of COVID-19 Lockdown in the UK.* Colchester: Institute for Social and Economic Research. Available at: https://repository.essex.ac.uk/27995/ (Accessed 11 September 2022).

Beltman, S., Mansfield, C. and Price, A. (2011) Thriving Not Just Surviving: A Review of Research on Teacher Resilience. *Educational Research Review* **6**(3), pp. 185–207.

Bennett, N. (2008) Distributed Leadership and IT. In J. Voogt and G. Knezek, (Eds.), *Spinger International Handbook of Information Technology in Primary and Secondary Education.* 20. Boston, MA: Springer. https://link.springer.com/chapter/10.1007/978-0-387-73315-9_35

Bennett, B. and Smilanich, P. (2012) *Power Plays: Moving from coping to cooperation in your classroom.* Saskatoon: Pearson Education

Bundy, J., Pfarrer, M., Short, C. and Coombs, W. (2017) Crises and Crisis Management: Integration, Interpretation, and Research Development. *Journal of Management* **43**(6), pp. 1661–1692.

Garbe, A., Ogurlu, U. and Logan, N. (2020) COVID-19 and Remote Learning: Experiences of Parents With Children During the Pandemic. *American Journal of Qualitative Research* **4**, pp. 45–65.

Greenhow, C., Lewin, C. and Staudt Willet, K.B. (2021) The Educational Response to COVID-19 Across Two Countries: A Critical Examination of Initial Digital Pedagogy Adoption. *Technology, Pedagogy and Education* **30**(1), pp. 7–25.

Harris, A. and Chapman, C. (2002) Leadership in Schools Facing Challenging Circumstances. *Management in Education* **16**(1), pp. 10–13.

Harris, A. and Jones, M. (2020) COVID 19 – School Leadership in Disruptive Times. *School Leadership and Management*, **40**(4), pp. 243–247. Available at: https://www.tandfonline.com/doi/full/10.1080/13632434.2020.1811479 (Accessed 18 August 2022)

Jones, A., Cominos, N. and Rissel, N. (2021) COVID-19 Disruption can Have a Silver Lining. *Management in Education* **35**(3), pp. 149–152.

Jordan-Daus, K. and Austin, L. (2021) Not on Our Own: Peer Coaching Our Way through COVID-19. *Management in Education* **35**(3), pp. 146–148.

Lee, J. (2020) Mental Health Effects of School Closures During COVID-19. *Rapid Review Lancet* **395**, pp. 912–920. Available at: Mental health effects of school closures during COVID-19 (thelancet.com) (Accessed 18 August 2022).

Leithwood, K., Jantzi, D. and Steinbach, R. (1999) *Changing Leadership for Changing Times.* Buckingham: Open University Press.

Lorenc, A., Kesten, J., Kidger, J., Langford, R. and Horwood, J. (2021) Reducing COVID-19 Risk in Schools: A Qualitative Examination of Secondary School Staff and Family Views and Concerns in the South West of England. *BMJ Paediatrics Open* **5**. Available at: https://www.ncbi.nlm.nih.gov/pmc/articles/PMC7948157/pdf/bmjpo-2020-000987.pdf (Accessed 18 August 2022).

Fairman, J. and MacKenzie, S. (2012) Spheres of Teacher Leadership Action for Learning. *Professional Development in Education* **38**(2), pp. 229–246.

Milgram, S. (1963) Behavioral Study of Obedience. *The Journal of Abnormal and Social Psychology* **67**(4), p. 371.

Netolicky, D. (2020) School Leadership During a Pandemic: Navigating Tensions. *Journal of Professional Capital and Community.* Available at: https://www.emerald.com/insight/publication/issn/2056-9548#earlycite (Accessed 18 August 2022).

Ofsted (2019) Teacher well-being at work in schools and further education providers. Available at: https://www.voced.edu.au/content/ngv:89756 (Accessed 18 August 2022).

Outhwaite, D. (2022) School leadership in a time of Covid: Learning to cope with the system changes. *British Educational Research Association.* Available at: https://www.bera.ac.uk/blog/school-leadership-in-a-time-of-Covid-learning-to-cope-with-the-system-changes (Accessed 11 September 2022).

Penty, W. (2020) *Weekly Staff Briefings.* Nottingham: Trent College.

Reddy, L.A., Shernoff, E. and Lekwa, A. (2021) A Randomized Controlled Trial of Instructional Coaching in High-Poverty Urban Schools: Examining Teacher Practices and Student Outcomes. *Journal of School Psychology* **86**, pp. 151–168.

Sharp, C., Nelson, J., Lucas, M., Julius, J., McCrone, T. and Sims, D. (2020) *Schools' Responses to COVID-19: The challenges facing schools and pupils in September.* National Foundation for Educational Research. Available at: https://files.eric.ed.gov/fulltext/ED608738.pdf (Accessed 18 August 2022).

Sims, S., Fletcher-Wood, H., O'Mara-Eves, A., Cottingham, S., Stansfield, C., Van Herwegen, J. and Anders, J. (2021) *What Are the Characteristics of Effective Teacher Professional Development? A Systematic Review and Meta-Analysis.* Education Endowment Foundation. Available at: https://files.eric.ed.gov/fulltext/ED615914.pdf (Accessed 18 August 2022).

Smailes, N. (2018) A critical analysis of how Knowledge Organisers and Recall Practice can be used to facilitate learning. An Action Research project of Year 7 pupils studying cells and organisation. Available at: https://www.repository.cam.ac.uk/bitstream/handle/1810/336764/141-190-smailesn.pdf?sequence=3 (Accessed 10 September 2022).

7 Pedagogical Leadership in Early Childhood Education and Care: What Is It, Why Do We Need It, and How Do You Do It

Mona Sakr

Introduction

The aim of this chapter is to introduce you to pedagogical leadership in ECEC, so that you have a strong understanding of what it is, why it matters and how it can be developed. You will first learn about three key characteristics of pedagogical leadership: (1) the contribution it makes to positive organisational culture, (2) distributed leadership and power of 'invisible leadership', and (3) the role of advocacy and action in pedagogical leadership. You will then explore the contribution that pedagogical leadership makes to quality in ECEC and conditions across the sector. Finally, we will look at some global initiatives designed to improve pedagogical leadership. In particular, we will consider a Chilean programme that aimed to develop skills of continuous quality improvement among ECEC teachers, an action research project in Australia, and finally, a US community of practice that put oral inquiry at the heart of developing pedagogical leadership in ECEC. In our discussion at the end of the chapter, you will be prompted to consider examples of pedagogical leadership that you see around you and the impact it has, as well as starting to think about your own pedagogical leadership and how it might be developed through small practical steps you can take now.

What is pedagogical leadership?

Pedagogy is how we think about learning and teaching and the actions we take in relation to these beliefs about learning and teaching. For example, in ECEC play-based pedagogies subscribe to the understanding that play is the primary vehicle through which young children learn and that the role of the teacher is to enable an effective play-based learning environment. Whether or not a pedagogical approach is committed to explicitly, or whether it is enacted without a full and conscious understanding, pedagogy is an essential aspect of ECEC provision (Stephen, 2010). Pedagogy will shape every single interaction that happens in the context of ECEC learning and teaching, whether it's a moment with parents at the beginning of the day, a conversation with a child or an exchange between staff. How we engage in these micro-interactions depends on pedagogy.

Pedagogical leadership is made up of actions that articulate, support, encourage and align the pedagogy of an ECEC setting. Pedagogy and pedagogical leadership are relevant to all stages of education, but they tend to be the subject of many more conversations in ECEC because of the unusual structures and training and qualification routes that characterise the sector. There has traditionally been a divide between those who manage ECEC settings, such as a nursery manager, and those who provide pedagogical leadership within a setting, such as a teacher or practitioner within

DOI: 10.4324/9781003321439-7

the setting who develops pedagogy, even though they have no line management responsibilities. Because of this distinction, ECEC is characterised by a commitment to pedagogical leadership as something that can be developed across all practitioners whether or not they have formal leadership and management responsibilities. To put it another way, pedagogical leadership sidesteps hierarchies, and everyone has the potential to be a pedagogical leader in ECEC.

What does pedagogical leadership involve? Below we consider three aspects of pedagogical leadership that have identified by researchers as essential. These are:

1. Positive contributions to organisational culture through modelling, coaching, and mentoring.
2. Supporting the emergence of distributed leadership or even invisible leadership (we will come back to these terms later for a fuller explanation), so that everyone in an organisation thinks of themselves as a leader and takes responsibility for improving practice.
3. Envisioning and promoting a brighter future for ECEC through advocacy and activism whereby pedagogical leaders spread the word about the importance of ECEC and the urgent need for greater investment and understanding across society.

Questions for discussion

Have you met any pedagogical leaders in your experience so far? Can you think of individuals you have met in practice that meet some of the criteria in the chapter without having a position of formal responsibility? Your example does not need to be grand; it might be something as simple as someone who helped you on your first day of placement to find your way around the setting, or praised you for one of your ideas and encouraged you to take it forward.

Contributions to organisational culture

Pedagogical leadership involves supporting a positive organisational culture to flourish. Organisational culture is made up of the everyday interactions that occur in an organisation, including the way that staff members say hello to one another, how they work with parents and – of course – interactions with children. Leaders know that no matter how clear your vision for the organisation is on paper, if the organisational culture is not aligned with this vision, it will be impossible to achieve it. While culture is vital for the success of any organisation, including educational institutions, it is problematic to identify exactly what culture is and understand how to develop it effectively.

These difficulties are outlined in the classic business manual *Organisational Culture and Leadership* by Edgar Schein. Schein (2017) offers an insight into several 'embedding mechanisms' for organisational culture, which are ways in which leaders can influence the organisational culture and help it to align with the vision. Some of these embedding mechanisms are about saying the right things (e.g. codes of conduct in the organisation, policy documents, email communications), but the most important mechanisms are those that involve *doing* the right thing. Most importantly, organisational culture must be modelled by leaders across the organisation – and for ECEC, it means that pedagogical leaders play an essential role in modelling behaviours and interactions aligned to the pedagogical approach of the setting.

Some examples of this influence on organisational culture might include when pedagogical leaders:

- Offer a warm welcome to new staff in the organisation, helping them to settle in by showing them practical details such as where to drop their bag or where the nearest facilities are.
- Introduce themselves to the parents of children, speak to siblings of the children in their setting, and say hello to families when they see them 'out and about'.
- Maintain a gentle tone even in stressful circumstances and are able to model, not only to children but to other staff, how to stay calm and avoid reactive behaviours in challenging moments of practice.

Modelling can easily develop into peer coaching and mentoring. In the examples above, the staff member that makes a point of welcoming new staff might begin to have conversations with that new member of staff about what they like to do and what they most enjoy doing with the children. They might then use this information to encourage a new member of staff to engage in particular activities and use their skills and passions in ways that are of pedagogical benefit to the setting. They might hear that the new staff member enjoys arts and crafts, for example, and encourage that individual to think of some ways to share this passion with the children and other staff. They might say something like: 'It's so great you're into crafts. Our crafts table is looking a little tired at the moment and I've noticed that the children aren't heading that way as much as they used to. I wonder if you have any ideas about breathing new life into it?'

Murray and McDowall Clark (2013) describe this as 'catalytic leadership' and argue it is the key contribution of pedagogical leaders in ECEC. This form of leadership is catalytic in that the individual is supporting the emergence of interests, passions and responsibilities that exist in an early form but need to be recognised and developed. Pedagogical leaders might not have the power to introduce brand-new initiatives, but they can support a stronger pedagogical environment by identifying the strengths around them and suggesting ways to build on these.

Distributed leadership and investing in others' leadership

Research on pedagogical leadership has tended to emphasise its distributed nature. Distributed leadership is when there is an understanding that leadership responsibilities and practices are distributed throughout a setting rather than being reliant on a single authoritative leader (Heikka *et al.*, 2013). In this empowering vision of leadership, it does not matter where you sit in a formal organisational hierarchy – whether you are an apprentice or a nursery manager – as long as you have the passion and capacity to make positive changes that support children's learning and well-being. Advocates of distributed leadership are clear that this is not just about delegating responsibilities so that particular actions are ticked off by different individuals. Instead, distributed leadership works on the basis that there is a shared sense of commitment and purpose, which generates action and change across the workforce. Without this shared sense of purpose, attempts at distributed leadership can lead to feelings of irritation and frustration when individuals feel that they have more to do, but without the underlying drive and vision to guide them (Heikka *et al.*, 2013).

When distributed leadership is developed to a high level, it can even grow into what Hickman and Sorenson (2014) identify as 'invisible leadership'. This is the idea that if there is a clear enough vision and purpose in an organisation, this itself works to organise everyone and to prompt actions that are aligned with this purpose. That is, the purpose becomes the leader rather than any one individual or group of individuals taking up this position. In the case of ECEC, it would mean that if all staff had a clear sense of the setting's social purpose and pedagogy, absolutely anyone could take action to support the advancement of this purpose and pedagogy.

Pedagogical leaders support distributed leadership by investing in others' leadership capacity and helping everyone to believe that they can lead the changes they want to see (O'Sullivan and Sakr, 2022). Pedagogical leaders do this by speaking the language of leadership with everyone. In the example of peer coaching above, where a pedagogical leader encourages a new member of staff to re-invigorate the arts and crafts table for the children, the language of leadership could be made even more explicit by asking: 'Could you lead on this?'. Using this language is an important way to help everyone understand that they have the potential to lead (O'Sullivan, 2015).

Pedagogical leaders can also look for opportunities to give leadership away in practical ways. In a conversation with Nichole Leigh Mosty, former head teacher of Osp Playschool in Reykjavik, Iceland (documented in detail in O'Sullivan and Sakr, 2022), Leigh Mosty described the practical opportunities she created for everyone working in the playschool to take the lead in particular spaces and activities. The more she engaged with staff members' passions and interests, the more she organised the children's movement and timetables for learning around these aspects. Eventually, rather than the teachers moving around the setting to join the children for different activities, the teachers began to lead on particular facets of provision (e.g. the clay table, the outdoor growing space, the book corner), and it was the children who would move around. Staff led the parts of provision that got them most excited, and in doing so, their passion supported children's learning and engagement to flourish.

Advocacy and activism

Models of pedagogical leadership in ECEC recognise that ECEC is not a fair sector. The sector is rife with inequalities, in terms of the provision for children and families and the inconsistency of this provision, but also in the mistreatment of the ECEC workforce, who tend to be underpaid, under-valued, and under-supported when it comes to professional development. Pedagogical leadership happens from a place of optimism but simultaneously recognises and grapples with the inequalities of the sector (O'Sullivan and Sakr, 2022). Being able to remain optimistic while determined to see social change depends on a particular set of advocacy and activism skills. In defining pedagogical skills, some have particularly emphasised these aspects of the role and the need for pedagogical leaders to speak up on behalf of the sector.

Woodrow and Busch (2008), for example, put advocacy and activism at the heart of their model of pedagogical leadership in ECEC. In their model of leadership, leaders are those committed to speaking up on behalf of the ECEC workforce and mobilising the sector. Pedagogical leaders might be able to do this through social media, engaging with dialogues across the workforce that break down barriers between different types of ECEC provision (e.g. private and voluntary provision, state-maintained nurseries, and childminders. for example) in order to find and strengthen the united cause and front. Pedagogical leaders might also carry out this kind of advocacy work in their day-to-day interactions with parents or other members of the local community when they explain and stress that what they do is not 'just' childcare but something of huge social importance.

Pedagogical leaders therefore bring a level of determination, resilience, and confidence to their work in ECEC, which can change – even transform – the attitudes of those around them in thinking about the contribution that ECEC makes to society.

Questions for discussion

If you imagine a spectrum from positional leadership to distributed leadership to invisible leadership, what do you think about some of the placement experiences you have had so far? Can you position these placements on this spectrum? What is the evidence that you use to make these judgments?

Why does pedagogical leadership matter?

Pedagogical leadership matters because it improves children's outcomes. It does this in three ways.

Firstly, Douglass's (2019) model of leadership in ECEC suggests that improvements in organisational culture are fundamental for improving the quality of the learning environment and child-adult interactions. In turn, these impact positively on children's learning. If we see pedagogical leadership as a facet of organisational culture, it follows that improving pedagogical leadership will lead to improvements in children's learning.

Secondly, the emphasis on distributed leadership when we focus on pedagogical leadership can improve outcomes across sectors. This is the argument made by Hickman and Sorenson (2014) in their business manual on the power of 'invisible leadership'. When everyone is motivated by the same goal and feels empowered to act, and to lead, with this goal in mind, then improvements in performance will follow. Applied in an ECEC context, this means that encouraging pedagogical leadership across the organisation – regardless of formal hierarchies – will lead to improvements in the performance of the organisation (in this case, children's learning and well-being).

Finally, pedagogical leadership improves outcomes in a broader sense by improving the conditions and profile of the sector. With its focus on advocacy and activism, pedagogical leadership can support a better understanding across society of the importance of ECEC. Over time this can lead to changes in the policy conditions of the sector and urgently needed improvements in the conditions for those working in the sector. With better pay, conditions and opportunities for professional development, the chances of attracting more qualified and experienced practitioners to the sector increase, and this in turn has a positive impact on quality of children's experiences. In the UK, for example, advocacy across the sector has led to the first Department for Education funded and approved qualification in leadership that is freely available to all ECEC leaders, including those working in private settings (the National Professional Qualification in Early Years Leadership). This is a drop in the ocean but demonstrates a policy development that can occur as a result of consistent advocacy and activism across the sector.

How is pedagogical leadership developed?

Pedagogical leadership has been developed in different ways around the globe. We will showcase three particular initiatives taken in Chile, Australia and the US: training in continuous development, action research and communities of practice.

Training in continuous improvement, Chile

To begin with, researchers Arbour *et al.* (2016) were interested in the potential of professional development focused on children's language and literacy outcomes in ECEC. They offered intensive professional development to practitioners focusing on ways to support children's language and literacy. The initiative was known as '*Un Buen Comienzo*', which translates as 'A Good Start'. To see whether the intervention was successful, Arbour *et al.* (2016) measured classroom interaction quality through the CLASS measure as well as tracking children's language and literacy. The researchers were surprised to see that, after the first iteration of the intervention, the improvements in environment quality and children's outcomes were not as robust as they had anticipated. At this point, they wanted to see what would happen if more of an emphasis was placed on pedagogical leadership in the context of the intervention. What they did was to continue with the professional development programme focused on language and literacy, but alongside the standard programme, participants were trained in applying the approach of continuous quality improvement (CQI). CQI is an approach whereby participants are encouraged to collaboratively and iteratively identify issues in practice for themselves and work out ways to address them. CQI can be seen as a facet of pedagogical leadership since it supports practitioners, regardless of formal hierarchies, to take the lead in identifying potential improvements and working out how to implement them. The emphasis is on cycles of reflection and action so that practitioners develop an attitude of looking for ways to constantly improve what they are doing and the learning environment for the children. When *Un Buen Comienzo* was applied alongside the training in CQI, Arbour *et al.* (2016) found significantly better outcomes in both the classroom interaction quality and the children's language and literacy outcomes.

Action research, Australia

Several initiatives to develop pedagogical leadership have used action research as a means to help orientate individuals working in ECEC towards collaborative reflective practice and to use it as a starting point for thinking about and improving organisational culture, environment quality, interactions and conditions for those working in the sector. Action research involves collaborative cycles of observing, planning, implementing changes and reviewing the impact of changes made; it is a research process conducted for the purpose of improving practice. For example, Henderson's (2017) evaluation of action research projects developed by ECEC teachers in Australia suggests that the model of action research can encourage practitioners to develop their own powerful vision of practice. This can then guide them in developing not just ideas for day-to-day improvements but integrating this with advocacy for the entire sector over a longer period of time. Through before-and-after interviews, Henderson found that action research was a powerful way to develop pedagogical leadership across practitioners and had a special role to play in helping practitioners in ECEC to grow in confidence and a positive collaborative working culture.

Communities of practice, US

What Henderson ultimately finds out through her research on action research is that reflective dialogues really matter. Through authentic reflective dialogues, all members of the workforce can come together to share their understanding, perceptions, experiences, and ideas. They can develop plans together for improvement that feel grounded in reality, rather than top-down initiatives put together by a management team that feel detached from day-to-day experiences. This is at the heart of pedagogical leadership – building the capacity for bottom-up change in every ECEC setting. Nicholson and Maniates (2015) take this further in exploring the potential for communities of practice to emerge among ECEC practitioners. Communities of practice can take different forms but ultimately enable practitioners to come together in a flexible but regular way to share their problems and experiences. Some structures and routines may be used to help support the community of practice to flourish, but ultimately everyone in the community of practice is empowered to use the community as a vehicle for their professional and personal development. This is an in-depth development of pedagogical leadership in that it focuses on changing the self-perception of practitioners so that they really see themselves as capable of leading change. Nicholson and Maniates (2015), particularly, explore how using structured oral inquiry can be used in the context of a community of practice to help professionals to develop their leadership through a focus on critical reflection and dealing with the complexity of practice. Together, the practitioners in this study explored the complex problems that they faced day to day in their work. Together they used the inquiry as a way to look more closely at the uncertainty and ambiguity of particular situations and develop nuanced pedagogical leadership skills to maintain hope and design and implement actions to address the issues they faced.

Questions for discussion

We've talked about some of the ways that you can develop pedagogical leadership (continuous improvement, action research, communities of practice). Which of these most excited you and why? Can you see small ways in which these initiatives may begin to influence your own practice?

Developing your own pedagogical leadership

Taking inspiration from these global initiatives, there are ways in which individuals working in ECEC – in whatever position and at whatever level – can begin to develop their own pedagogical leadership.

Critical reflection lies in the centre of pedagogical leadership (Daly *et al.*, 2017). Critical reflection depends on developing regular, ideally daily, habits of reflection with a willingness to challenge what we see around us and ask questions about what we see (Brock, 2014). Keeping a daily journal is a great way for an ECEC practitioner to grow the skill of critical reflection. It can be difficult to find the time and energy to do this at the end of a long day working in an ECEC setting, but having a notebook available at lunchtime or breaks can encourage us to jot down questions or ideas as they occur to us. For example, during a morning spent inside you might notice that more of the children seem to be bored or not in such a good mood. This might prompt you to ask the question of what is impacting on mood in the room, or whether the atmosphere would be the same if everyone was outside. You might find yourself writing down questions like:

- Why is everyone so grumpy today?
- What would happen if we went outside?

- Is there a way to get outside more?
- How did my mood affect the children?
- How does my mood change when I'm outside?
- Are our interactions different when we're outside?
- What are conversations like when we're outside vs. inside?
- And so on…

If you are fortunate to find yourself in a supportive setting, these questions might emerge through conversations between the team. Social media can also be a way to start conversations and dialogues that go beyond a particular setting. Asking these kinds of questions on social media does require care though to ensure that conversations embody critical reflection and not just criticism, disappointment or despair.

Critical reflection is a starting point for pedagogical leadership, but it needs to be joined by a willingness to try new things, take actions, and inspire others with an idea for change. Already, some of the questions above are starting to suggest further explorations and avenues of action to take. For example, the question 'Are our interactions different when we're outside?' suggests that there may be a small action research project to develop within the setting. Of course, anyone can begin to observe and note down the nature of conversations inside versus outside. Ideally, though, it would have the greatest impact to develop an interest in this question across the setting and find a way to explore it together as a community of practice. There may be a chance to raise this question as part of a team meeting: 'I noticed on Tuesday morning that the children seemed fairly grumpy, and we were in the whole morning. Did anyone else notice this? I wonder whether it would have been different if we were outside. What do you think? I know it was raining, but could it be worth trying to get outside anyway and seeing what effect this has on everyone?' Whether you can ask questions like this and have a genuine conversation about the possibilities will depend a lot on organisational culture, and in particular, whether there is a culture of collaborative innovation in the organisation (O'Sullivan and Sakr, 2022). Regardless of the reception your questions and ideas get, taking the first step at starting these kinds of conversation demonstrates the bravery that ultimately characterises pedagogical leadership in ECEC. Reflecting on the responses of others to your questions and suggestions is a way to continue the explorations. Instead of taking responses personally, try to see them as embodiments of the organisational culture and think like a leader – how can I improve things with the resources I have available? How can I work within this organisational culture to have a positive influence on children's learning and well-being?

Questions for discussion

When you think about developing your pedagogical leadership, do particular barriers come to mind? Jot these down and explore them. Are they a result of organisational culture, for example, the response you'll get from colleagues when sharing new ideas? Or are they more personal, such as your willingness to put new ideas forward? Registering these barriers and beginning to explore them is a starting point to thinking about how you might take a step forward nonetheless, but don't feel that you need to race past the barriers. Exploring the barriers to action is such an important part of pedagogical leadership. Give yourself credit for reflecting on what you see around you and in your own practice.

Conclusion

This chapter has explored the concept of pedagogical leadership in early childhood education and care (ECEC). We have discussed key components of pedagogical leadership, most notably (1) contributions to organisational culture, (2) the potential of distributed leadership and ideally 'invisible leadership', and (3) the urgent need for advocacy and activism across the sector. Focusing on these components of pedagogical leadership, we have examined the potential positive impact of pedagogical leadership on organisational culture, children's outcomes, and even the conditions of those working in the sector. Finally, we have considered three types of initiatives that have been designed and implemented across the globe to develop pedagogical leadership across those working in ECEC. We looked at training in continuous improvement in Chile, action research in Australia and communities of practice and structured oral inquiry in the US.

Summary points

- Pedagogical leadership in ECEC can be contrasted with positional leadership; pedagogical leadership is based on the capacity to influence positive change, regardless of formal position within an organisation.
- Pedagogical leadership involves supporting the emergence and sustenance of a positive organisational culture which can enable improvement; as well as supporting others' leadership within the model of distributed leadership; and finally embracing advocacy and activism as a way to question the current role of ECEC in society and co-construct alternative visions of ECEC for the future.
- Pedagogical leadership has been developed in different ways around the world. We have looked in this chapter at three approaches: training in continuous quality improvement (CQI), action research and communities of practice making use of structured oral inquiry.
- You can begin to develop your own pedagogical leadership through daily practices of critical reflection (e.g. journaling, conversations with colleagues, conversations on social media) and opening up questions and dialogues among teams that in turn can lead to further action and exploration of an issue. The response you get to your questions and ideas will depend on the organisational culture of the setting, but considering this itself in your critical reflection is fundamental for advancing pedagogical leadership further.

Recommended reading

Sakr, M. and O'Sullivan, J. (2022) *Pedagogical Leadership in Early Childhood Education: Conversations from across the world*. London: Bloomsbury.

O'Sullivan, J. and Sakr, M. (2022) *Social Leadership in Early Childhood Education and Care: An introduction*. London: Bloomsbury.

Douglass, A. (2019) *Leadership for Quality in Early Childhood Education and Care*. OECD Working Paper No. 211. Available at https://www.oecd-ilibrary.org/education/leadership-for-quality-early-childhood-education-and-care_6e563bae-en (Accessed 13 July 2021).

References

Arbour, M., Yoshikawa, H., Atwood, S., Duran Mellado, F.R., Godoy Ossa, F., Trevino Villareal, E. and Snow, C.E. (2016) *Improving Quality and Child Outcomes in Early Childhood Education by Redefining the Role Afforded to Teachers in Professional Development: A continuous quality improvement learning collaborative among public preschools in Chile*. Evanston, IL: Society for Research on Educational Effectiveness.

Brock, A. (2014) *The Early Years Reflective Practice Handbook*. London: Taylor and Francis.

Daly, J., Hayes, C., Whitehouse, A., Gill, R. and Duncan, M. (2017) *Developing as a Reflective Early Years Professional: A thematic approach*. St Albans: Critical Publishing.

Douglass, A. (2019) *Leadership for Quality in Early Childhood Education and Care*. OECD Working Paper No. 211. Available at https://www.oecd-ilibrary.org/education/leadership-for-quality-early-childhood-education-and-care_6e563bae-en (Accessed 13 July 2021).

Heikka, J., Waniganayake, M. and Hujala, E. (2013) Contextualizing Distributed Leadership within Early Childhood Education: Current Understandings, Research Evidence and Future Challenges. *Educational Management Administration and Leadership* **41**(1), pp. 30–44.

Henderson, L. (2017) Someone Had to Have Faith in Them as Professionals': An Evaluation of an Action Research Project to Develop Educational Leadership Across the Early Years. *Educational Action Research* **25**(3), pp. 387–401.

Hickman, G.R. and Sorenson, G.J. (2014) *The Power of Invisible Leadership: How a compelling common purpose inspires exceptional leadership*. London: Sage.

Murray, J. and McDowall Clark, R. (2013) Reframing Leadership as a Participative Pedagogy: The Working Theories of Early Years Professionals. *Early Years* **33**(3), pp. 289–301.

Nicholson, J. and Maniates, H. (2015) Recognising Postmodern Intersectional Identities in Leadership for Early Childhood. *Early Years* **36**(1), pp. 66–80.

O'Sullivan, J. (2015) *Successful Leadership in the Early Years* (2nd Ed.). London: Featherstone.

O'Sullivan, J. and Sakr, M. (2022) *Social Leadership in Early Childhood Education and Care: An introduction*. London: Bloomsbury.

Schein, E. H. (2017) *Organisational Culture and Leadership* (5th Ed.). Hoboken, NJ: Wiley.

Stephen, C. (2010) Pedagogy: The Silent Partner in Early Years Learning. *Early Years* **30**(10), pp. 15–28.

Woodrow, C. and Busch, G. (2008) Repositioning Early Childhood Leadership as Action and Activism. *European Early Childhood Education Research Journal* **16**(1), pp. 83–93.

8 The Role of Primary Headteachers within School Trusts: English Landscape Divergence in a Post-Pandemic World

Megan Crawford and Deborah Outhwaite

Introduction

In this chapter, we encourage you to take a critical or questioning stance. A critical stance is when you ask yourself questions about what is behind the ideas you are being asked to consider by colleagues, policymakers, or other interested stakeholders in your particular educational setting. Looking behind what is right in front of you, can often give clearer insights into the context and arguments underlying policy. The history of why we have arrived where we are is also very important. Readers may draw upon their own values and a sense of purpose to begin to understand what is happening in the educational world, and where it may be going. This chapter could be seen as a starting point to the huge area that is leadership policy and practice in primary education. Ideas will be given at the end of the chapter to enable you to follow up particular areas of interest.

Since the Education Reform Act of 1988, there has been constant change in the English school system, sometimes slowly, but at a quickened pace since the Conservative coalition government of 2010. The s government energetically pursued a programme to create a school system of 'independent publicly funded schools' (DfE 2010; Woods and Simkins, 2014), or academies, often within larger trusts. With the most recent White Paper (2022), it is even clearer than before that the government's intention is for most schools to become academies – schools which operate under direct funding agreements with central government and freeing them from local authority (LA) control. There is currently an acceleration of school trusts with the UK government aim that all English schools are in trusts by 2025.

The school system has become the subject of an experiment in marketisation where schools have, on the one hand, been given more autonomy (budgets, internal organisation, and appointment of staff), while being rigorously held to account (curricula, high stakes testing and rigorous Ofsted inspections). This has led to dilemmas for those in the primary school sector, whether it is to their benefit to become part of a larger rust.

These changes may be hard to understand and difficult to follow. This chapter paints in the background of these changes to examine how primary school leadership has and is changing even more rapidly since the Covid-19 pandemic. We will look at the role of the primary headteacher, how the role has evolved in the last decade and how the role of headteacher has been framed in the system. The chapter also gives a short overview of systemic changes, including ways that theory can be used to examine what is happening in the system now and in the future. Finally, it draws some conclusions across the education system within England and summarises the key issues, whilst also giving some questions for discussion.

DOI: 10.4324/9781003321439-8

Questions for discussion

Start to question how the current school system works.
What is your own experience of headteachers in terms of age, and gender? What are the sizes of the schools that you are thinking about? Does this differ between primary and secondary schools?

Overview

To simply explain the changes over the last 20 plus years is a challenge. Secondary school 'Academies' were introduced in 2000 by the New Labour Government. They were generously funded by central government and by May 2010 they comprised six per cent of the English secondary school landscape in challenging areas and that needed extra support. In Scotland, Wales, and Northern Ireland their regions govern education policy, and they have quite different systems without academies.

The Conservative-led Coalition Government in 2010 and the 2015 Conservative Government and since have sought to convert every state school, both primary and secondary, into an academy, originally with a financial bonus for converting. This 'school-led' (Chapman, 2015) system expanded rapidly and by 2017 there were over 6500 academies (DfE, 2017). As a result, the role of the LA was much reduced, and the government continued to move towards a fully-academised system. Once academies were established, the government moved to consolidate its preferred model: grouping schools into formally constituted 'multi-academy trusts' (MATs), currently referred to as 'School Trusts', or just 'Trusts'. Initially these could be led by a high-performing school and varied in size with the aim of school improvement (SI), support, and challenge. These School Trusts vary in character: some are very large and operate nationally as branded chains, some are regional, and some are small and based on organic groupings of local schools.

The role of Regional Schools Commissioner (RSC) was created in 2014, appointed in each of eight regions in England to oversee these chains of academies. The title changed from RSC to Regional Director (RDs) in 2021. RDs are widely believed to be powerful and instrumental in implementing the government's preferred model, and this continues to develop at the time of writing. Covid-19 has played a part in these changes as the Department for Education (DfE) coordinates through the RDs to Trusts LAs are now being encouraged to directly academise their remaining schools. Overall, there has been a major reorganisation of schools in England in which state schools have been passed to alternative groupings, with 125-year leases of education buildings (DfE, 2022). Management structure, often known as the individual School Trusts 'Central Team', has been created to replace the Las. They provide the recruitment, finance, and SI functions across groups of schools.

For this chapter, our focus is on how primary schools are responding to the changes outlined above in terms of their leadership, and how this is affected by past history. Currently, only a third of primary schools but more than 80 per cent of secondary schools are Academies. One of us has written previously how well-positioned headteachers have strong influence in shaping local and national policy (Coldron *et al.*, 2014). Primary schools are very different from secondary schools with characteristic educational and institutional practices (Coldron *et al.*, 2015). The role of the primary headteacher is a demanding one and, as in many countries around the world, the expectations of the headteacher, are increasing all the time.

The primary headteacher role demands time, energy and expertise, and fewer people are interested in taking on primary headship. There are many reasons for this, including multiple (and often conflicting) accountabilities, increased demands and heightened expectations by parents and society about the purposes of education, and how it should be delivered. Primary heads have had to deal with ever-changing government policies and priorities, yet are expected to forward plan in a strategic manner. Administration has also increased in terms of bureaucracy, and yet the whole system in England has seen diminishing resources and, we argue, little genuine autonomy for a primary head in managing their school.

Questions for discussion

Building on your answer to the first question, see if you can find out where in the policy landscape the schools you attended are now in terms of Trusts and academisation. Do you notice any difference between the primary and secondary schools? If you are a student who didn't go to school in England, look up the closest schools near to where you live/study.

What's the difference?

Historically, there have been many differences in pedagogic practice between primary and secondary schools, with, in practice, a distinct primary school ethos, drawing on various historical events such as the Plowden Report (1967). Looking at these differences can help with an understanding of the relationship of primary to secondary education and how primary heads have always been subordinately positioned in relation to secondary school heads and have had less power within the system. Drawing on Coldron *et al.* (2015), we will examine the consequences of the difference in the typical size of primary and secondary schools, and how the idea of capital can be used to examine the role of the primary head. Finally, we will briefly look at pedagogical identities, the role of the fast-developing 'all-through' school and how gender is a key part of the story of the primary headteacher.

Differences with primary headship

Primary schools have always varied in size, from village schools of twenty students to those of over four hundred, with an average of around two hundred pupils. The average secondary is over one thousand students. This variation on pupil numbers affects funding which is based on size: technically on what is referred to as pupil number on roll (NOR). This number, or size of school, creates the sets of relationships that can form between staff and other staff and the students themselves, and the relative levels of formality. Primary heads of smaller schools often have a large teaching load as well as administrative responsibilities. Another effect of size is on the reward and career opportunities for teachers. In the secondary sector there have always been more opportunities for career advancement. The more favourable funding of secondary schools is a sign of how successive governments have viewed the importance, or otherwise of the primary school. These economic issues encompass the whole background of the relative importance of a primary head as they work within a system which has not historically valued primary schooling as much as secondary, and further change in the system have put them in an even weaker position.

The consequence of this lack of parity in funding between primary and secondary sectors in England is that primary headteachers have repeatedly been regarded by government as bringing less to the table in terms of their knowledge of finance, HR management, and even policy knowledge. These are all types of capital: economic, material; social; and professional capital. There is a great deal of work in education drawing on Bourdieu's relational concepts of symbolic and material capital (Bourdieu, 1990), and Maroy and Van Zanten (2009) offer a helpful relational analysis of the different capitals possessed by schools, which is very relevant to the ways in which primary and secondary schools are placed within the system. Economically, primary heads are paid less than secondary. Historically, the salary of a head has been fixed in proportion to the number of pupils, thus primary head teachers are paid less than secondary head teachers, and resourcing is less generous. Put simply, in a capitalist society, being paid more signals greater prestige. Similarly, the historic legacy of secondary and primary means that secondary teachers have often been viewed as curriculum experts who have a great deal to 'give' to the primary sector, a point emphasised by many recent curricular reforms in England, evidenced with the current focus on the 'knowledge-rich' curriculum. The caring aspect of primary teaching, which could be very useful in the systemic wellbeing crisis post-Covid, seems to hold little weight for those who make policy.

The role of the trust in framing how the curriculum works, and the development of all-through schools from nursery to sixth form, means there is more opportunity for the vision of the trust leader (CEO) to be particularly important. Many of the current CEOs are from a secondary background, in part at least because the secondary sector has been academised in England to a greater extent. This basis of subject expertise in the secondary school aligns closely with current policy frameworks in England and emphasises the importance of subjects means that primary heads are viewed as less competent to drive change. Some examples of where primary heads are marginalised are the fact that the PGCE bursary has been scrapped but still exists in key shortage secondary subjects. Teaching Assistants (TAs) and Higher-Level Teaching Assistants (HLTAs) can now teach even specialised content in both primary and secondary sectors, as promoted by the DfE's use of resources through Oak (DfE, 2022).

In terms of individual teacher identity, the history of the English education system has been to position primary as weaker than secondary. The process of MATs has only exacerbated this positioning further, as trusts made up of primary schools go to secondary trusts for their subject-knowledge expertise. As secondary schools academised faster in the last decade, primary schools have been left behind in this policy agenda and are either more likely not yet to be academised, or to be in smaller trust groupings. This division has reinforced long-standing dichotomies in English schooling, where primary schools and their staff are regarded as generalists/interested in the

---

Questions for discussion

Does this difference between primary and secondary schools match the experience that you have? Have you come across the idea of different capitals before (cultural, economic, social, professional, etc.)?

How could these terms be useful to you in examining the similarities and differences in the roles of the primary and secondary heads? Can you see the sense in having 'mixed' School Trusts (i.e. primary and secondary, sometimes with SEND schools, PRUs, and all-through schools, 3–18s)?

domestic/relationship-orientated/pastoral responsibilities, whilst secondary schools and staff are regarded as subject experts/business focussed/task orientated/academic. This is a complex combination of capitals, especially if there are primary-led Trusts, which want to add secondary schools to their trust to give additional status.

As part of this changing schooling landscape, headteacher roles themselves appear to be decreasing in significance as trusts create different roles. This may be linked to the many expectations of the primary head, which we mentioned earlier, and the very difficult situations they often have to manage from a smaller resource base than their secondary colleagues. Some examples are:

- Head of School
- Deputy Head (Primary) in all-through schools
- Executive Headteachers
- Primary Lead across a Trust
- Director of Education roles (School Improvement)

Such roles are a boon for those in charge of primary schools because they provide support to the administrative and perhaps strategic responsibilities for headship. However, the influence on pedagogic practice by the subordination of the primary head's role may not be a bargain that many want to make. In summary, primary roles currently are still paid less, with less independence in post, another being not always, or wholly, responsible for SI. Another historically subordinate role is becoming even more so, as the implications of policy changes since 2010.

Over the years the role of a primary teacher, and the primary head teacher, has grown vastly more complex. Many of the issues that were secondary-only issues, are now commonplace in primary schools, and the nature of social media and parental expectations, has certainly changed the demands on primary heads.

Questions for discussion

Why do the Critical Education Policy groups argue that academisation is un-democratic? What are the tenets of democratic education? How has this changed over the last few decades? Where does accountability now lie? Has this improved the system?

Talk to a primary headteacher you know. How do they describe their role? Do they feel secondary headteachers have more power and influence in the education system? Why, why not?

Gender and primary headship

As has been outlined above, the structure of schooling in England has changed. The creation of school trusts has led to the creation of new central teams, and these are currently have more male than female CEOs (Staufenberg, 2018). Most nursery and primary headteachers are women, and almost two-thirds of secondary head teachers are men. The education workforce is 80 per cent plus female, but secondary headship rates were only 38 per cent female in 2016 (Fuller and Harford, 2016). Coldron *et al.* (2015) has argued that this discussion is replete with assumptions around the role of women and men in society, and that primary teachers are subject to discourses of care and mothering, and perhaps even a sense in society that working with young children is not as prestigious, or tough as working with near adults in the secondary sector. The majority female workforce for primary children strengthens the perception that teaching and caring for younger children is 'women's work'. Gender research in this area has also looked at the role of men in the Early Years and Primary sector (Wright and Brownhill, 2018). There is progress being made with some effort going in to support the careers of women as heads, but although the DfE have shown some interest in this (DfE, 2018) much of the work here has again been voluntary and unpaid, largely through the WomenEd movement: www.WomenEd.org. The voluntary nature of this work reinforces the idea that women's careers are less important. The all-female National Professional Qualification for Headship (NPQH) cohort, was brought about by the leaders of WomenEd working with the NPQH providers, believing that this creation of space, and opportunities for networking were important (Featherstone and Porritt, 2021).

In the primary headship context it must be remembered that primary schools are everywhere, and often very small, very rural, and coastal, as well as larger and inner-city, but they are also everything in between. The multiple roles that headteachers of smaller schools hold – serving the lunches as well as doing the accounts – may well lack both status and gravitas. Recent research shows us that there is a crisis in staffing of rural and coastal schools (Ovenden-Hope and Passy, 2020). There are organisations such as the Church of England, responsible for around 4500 primary schools, whose leadership training focuses on how to manage multiple and varied headteacher roles rather than focusing on what prospective headteachers may like to do with their leadership (CEFEL, 2022). The reality of primary headship, therefore, is quite unlike any perceived expectations of it, which may also contribute to some of the gender imbalance associated with it.

Questions for discussion

Had you already come across the grassroots organisation WomenEd? Why did such an organisation need to be established in 2015? What are its aims? What do you think of this movement, and the need for it? What do you understand by the term systemic gender inequality? There are many other organisations like this in education now; see the links at the end of the chapter.

Conduct an audit of your local primary and secondary schools. Do the primary schools have female head teachers? Are they in school trusts? Do the local secondary schools have male or female head teachers? Is the CEO of the school trust male or female? Why does this matter?

Conclusion

There is a great deal of change in the schooling system in England, as this chapter has outlined with the move from local authorities to MATs (now often referred to as school trusts or just trusts), these policy changes are affecting the role of the primary head in many ways. Further academisation is planned by the current Conservative Government; a move to mass academisation of the primary sector will undoubtedly change the educational landscape even further over the next ten years. Anticipated new titles for the role of primary headteacher, such as 'Head of Primary', may or may not be the same in terms of autonomy and power; the Trust and the CEO's own attitude to primary practice and the practice of primary pedagogy may also be different. This is a changing space to watch, and the policy implications of it are not yet fully known or understood, as practice changes on the ground in schools.

Summary points

- Systemic change is gathering pace, and this has resulted in new views of how the primary head role is conceptualised.
- Different titles for the role are now used within trusts, although they do not always reflect the role that individuals play within a school.
- Many historic issues, such as the gendered pay gap between secondary and primary Heads, may well be exacerbated by the move to Trusts.
- The idea of capital – economic, material, social, and professional – can be explored further to understand the way the school system is configured and headship is understood in England.

Recommended reading

Coldron, J., Crawford, M. and Simkins, T. (2014) The Restructuring of Schooling in England: The Responses of Well Positioned Headteachers. *Education Management Administration and Leadership*, **42**(3), pp. 387–403.

Crawford, M., Outhwaite, D. and Crawford, M. (2021) Unlocking Creative Leadership in the Primary School. In P. Burnard and M. Loughrey (Eds.), *Sculpting New Creativities in Primary Education*. Cambridge: Cambridge University Press.

Gibson, M. and Outhwaite, D. (2021) MATification: Plurality, Turbulence and Effective School Governance in England at Times of Crises. *Management in Education, Special Edition in Governance and Governing*: https://doi.org/10.1177/08920206211051473

Maguire, M. Braun, A. (2019) Headship as Policy Narration: Generating Metaphors of Leading in the English Primary School. *Journal of Educational Administration and History*, **51**(2), pp. 103–116, DOI: 10.1080/00220620.2018.1563531

References

Bourdieu, P. (1990) *The Logic of Practice* (Trans R. Nice). Stanford, CA: Stanford University Press.

Chapman, C. (2015) From One School to Many: Reflections on the Impact and Nature of School Federations and Chains in England. *Educational Management Administration and Leadership* **43**(1), pp. 46–60.

Church of England Foundation for Educational Leadership (cefel.org.uk), (2022). National Professional Qualification pathways, Online. Available at: https://www.cefel.org.uk/

Coldron, J., Crawford, M., Jones, S. and Simkins, T. (2015) The Positions of Primary and Secondary Schools in the English School Field: A Case of Durable Inequality. *Journal of Education Policy*, **30** (5), pp. 671–687, DOI: 10.1080/02680939.2014.972989

Coldron, J., Crawford, M. and Simkins, T. (2014) The Restructuring of Schooling in England: The Responses of Well Positioned Headteachers. *Education Management Administration and Leadership* **42**(3), pp. 387–403.

Department for Education (DfE) (2010) *The Importance of Teaching: The schools white paper*. London: DfE.

Department for Education (DfE) (2017) *Open Academies and Academy Projects in Development*. London: DfE.

Department for Education (DfE) (2018) *Diversity of the Teaching Workforce: Statement of intent*. London: DfE.

Department for Education (DfE) (2022) *Making Significant Changes to an Open Academy*. London: DfE.

White Paper (2022). HM Government: Opportunity for all: strong schools with great teachers for your child. Printed in the UK by HH Associates Ltd. on behalf of the Controller of Her Majesty's Stationery Office.

Featherstone, K. and Porritt, V. (2021) *Being 10% Braver*. London: SAGE.

Fuller, K. and Harford, J. (2016) *Gender and Leadership in Education: Women achieving against the odds*. Oxford: Peter Lang.

Maroy, C. and van Zanten, A. (2009) Regulation and Competition Among Schools in Six European Localities. *Sociologie De Travail* **51**, pp. e57–e79.

Ovenden-Hope, T. and Passy, R. (2020) Understanding the Challenges of Teacher Recruitment and Retention for 'educationally isolated' Schools in England. In T. Ovenden-Hope and R. Passy (Eds.), *Exploring Teacher Recruitment and Retention: Contextual challenges and international perspectives.* Abingdon: Routledge.

Plowden, B. (1967) Children and Their Primary Schools. *Report of the Central Advisory Council for Education (England).* London: HMSO.

Staufenberg, J. (2018) Revealed: the lack of diversity in education leadership roles. School's Week. Online. Available at: https://schoolsweek.co.uk/revealed-the-lack-of-diversity-in-education-leadership-roles/

Woods, P. and Simkins, T. (2014) Understanding the Local: Themes and Issues in the Experience of Structural Reform in England. *Educational Management Administration and Leadership* **42**(3), pp. 324–340.

Wright, D. and Brownhill, S. (2018) *'Men in Early Years Settings: Building a Mixed Gender Workforce'.* London: Jessica Kingsley Publishers.

9 Crisis Leadership in English Secondary Schools: Its Effects on School Leaders' Long-Term Visions of Education

Jacqueline Baxter and Alan Floyd

Introduction

Compulsory education in England is rarely free of policy initiatives, societal challenges, and 'wicked' issues, such as the achievement gap between socially and economically deprived pupils and their peers. In addition, since the Education Reform act of 1988 and subsequent policy initiatives, it has become one of the most marketised systems in the world. When the country was hit by the Covid-19 global pandemic with the ensuing restrictions on face-to-face education provision, the stresses, and cracks in a system suffering from innovation overload were brought to light as never before. Pupils from more affluent backgrounds transferred adeptly to online learning, while their less advantaged peers were held back by a lack of parental support, a lack of connectivity and hardware, and low skills in manipulating the digital environment. However, in common with other world-changing events, there have been some positive elements to emerge, particularly in relation to digital innovation. These key issues form the focus of this chapter.

Background to digital learning

Whilst integrating digital learning into classroom practice has been on the policy agenda in the UK since the early 1980s, it was not until the mid-1990s, with the emergence of the concept of a global information society, that it gained momentum (Younie, 2006). The first national assessment of the impact of ICT was conducted in 1993. This report highlighted a need for in-service training in ICT, as well as other recommendations, which were reiterated by the Stevenson report of 1997 (Stevenson, 1997). This independent inquiry into the 'issues and opportunities' with ICT concluded that, 'the state of ICT in UK schools was primitive and it was a public priority to increase its use'. However, since then, adoption of digital practices has not been as consistent or widespread as early advocates hoped.

Eickelmann (2011: 93) identifies eight characteristics of schools that have succeeded in sustainable digital integration:

1. Their leaders possess strong leadership skills and a sound understanding of the potential of ICT to enhance learning.
2. They have established cooperation with external partners to raise funding.
3. They realise intra-school cooperation, which is integrated into school concepts and culture. This way, digital and pedagogical knowledge of staff is improved.

DOI: 10.4324/9781003321439-9

4. Leaders developed strategies to cope with new digital trends, for example, the implementation of new staff development schemes.
5. They use their internal processes to deal with problems and challenges regarding digital integration and do not externalise problems.
6. They disseminate the idea of digital learning to improve learning outcomes throughout the school.
7. They link digital learning to existing and prospective pedagogical aims, and design an infrastructure with these in mind.
8. They integrate digital learning by embedding it into core curricula.

In other words, there needs to be an effective digital strategy in place in order for digital integration to occur.

However, a recent Department for Education report undertaken by Cooper Gibson Consultancy in 2021 (Department for Education, 2021) revealed that just 54 per cent of secondary schools have a digital strategy in place and that academies were more likely to have one than local authority (LA) maintained schools. In addition, there were clear geographical disparities: 'Schools in London (52 per cent) and the North East (54 per cent) were most likely to have a strategy in place, whilst schools in the South East (34 per cent), South West (36 per cent), and East Midlands (38 per cent) were least likely' (p. 76). The same report indicated that 84 per cent of secondary schools indicated that their school had increased or upgraded technology in the previous 12 months and that 64 per cent of these headteachers indicated that the upgrade was due to the pandemic. A minority of just seven per cent stated that they had already planned such changes before the pandemic.

The purpose of this chapter is to explore some of these headline findings in more detail by drawing on a UKRI-funded research project which involved 50 narrative interviews with school leaders undertaken during the Covid-19 restrictions to explore whether there is evidence that their digital strategic planning reflects a 'strategy as learning' approach, and if so, what the implications are for digital learning in schools going forward. There follows a description of our theoretical framework before moving on to describe our methods and sample, discussion, and conclusions.

Questions for discussion

Why have schools been so reluctant to embrace digital learning?
What do you think are the real sticking points for them?

Theoretical overview

Strategy as learning

Amongst the many conceptualisations of strategy, there is a considerable literature that views strategy as practice and, as part of this, strategy as a learning activity. In so doing, the work of researchers such as Goldman and Casey (2010) and Chia and Holt (20067) explores the micro-processes and activities that are activated during strategising processes. Chia and Holt's work is particularly relevant in the research presented here as they view strategy as, 'a practical coping mechanism' and a sensemaking activity in which, 'events, entities and meaning help compose one another' (Chia and Holt, 2006: 640). Thus, it is perceived as an activity during which individuals constantly modify their behaviour and actions in relation to shared practices and understandings.

Our previous research into strategy making in multi-academy trusts (Baxter and Floyd, 2019) supported the idea of strategy as an emergent phenomenon, whilst also emphasising the sense-making, practical coping actions that appear as a recurring theme in Chia and Holt's (2006) work. It challenges Bourgeois' distinction between what strategy *is* (success and failure of various strategies) and *how* a particular strategy emerges (Bourgeois III, 1980) arguing that, as a learning activity, the two are inextricably interwoven. Casey and Goldman's (2010) work looked to resolve what they viewed as the dichotomous nature of the ways in which strategy-making and strategic planning is conceptualised, arguing that the term 'strategic thinking' is often used interchangeably with strategy (p. 168). They reconciled this by conceptualising strategic thinking, together with strategy formulation, as 'strategic thinking in action' (STA) (p. 168). As this view brings together three literatures of strategy, learning and cognition, in our previous work on strategy making in education we successfully developed and tested a model that brings together these facets, (Baxter and Floyd, 2019; Baxter and John, 2021). This model is discussed later in the chapter (see Figure 9.1). Our conceptual model also incorporates Casey and Goldman's strategy as learning approach in acknowledging that it is:

- Conceptual – develops concepts that can then be applied to different situations;
- Systems orientated – involves not just the organisation but the system in which it is situated;
- Directional – aims for a desired future state;
- And finally, is opportunistic and a learning activity (*ibid*: 172).

Our previous empirical work adds to this by identifying a strong requirement for leader metacognition when crafting strategy (Baxter and Floyd, 2019; Baxter and John, 2021).

Questions for discussion

Think about how you developed your strategy for coming to university. What did you do, and how much did you learn in the process?

Imagine you are advising a friend on how to go about choosing and applying for university, what steps would you include in your advice?

Strategic thinking in crisis situations

In relation to strategy-making in crisis situations, the work of Weick has been highly influential on the field (Weick, 1988; Weick, 1993). His work describes how sensemaking – the integration of stimuli (information) into sensemaking frameworks or schema – aids individuals and organisations in making sense of an unfolding crisis in relation to their work. This approach connects with constructivist and social theories of learning. Constructivism is based on the idea that knowledge and learning are socially constructed, and that learning depends on individual and collective agency to critically question environmental cues and reflect on these in relation to their own knowledge (Amineh and

Asl, 2015). The term 'constructivism' derives from Piaget (1947) as well as from Bruner's work on dis-covery learning (Bruner, 1996). In this sense the learning is deep and transformative in relation to the individual, as it changes the perspective of the learner in such a way that it also infuses and develops their identity. Mezirow (1991: 14) explains the integration of new learning as: 'the process of becom-ing critically aware of how and why our presuppositions have come to constrain the way we perceive, understand, and feel about our world; of reformulating these, …'. This thinking, in essence, is the basis of the metacognitive element of strategy that we identify elsewhere (Baxter and John, 2021).

Other work on strategic thinking in times of crisis, also drawing on Weick, empirically investigates the ways in which effective leaders use strategising as a sensemaking activity in which schema is constantly adapted to integrate new information (Boin and Renaud, 2013; Thürmer *et al.*, 2020). Maitlis and Sonenshein (2010), in their work on sensemaking in crisis and change, draw on the work of Balogun to emphasise the key role of middle management in the sensemaking activities of senior management (Balogun, 2007: in Maitlis and Sonenshein, 2010: 559; Balogun and Johnson, 2004). They point out that, whilst senior management normally initiate change, middle managers are key to the process as they are the individuals who interpret and enact this change. They also point out that, during a crisis situation, sensemaking becomes a shared identity, 'which provides a vital anchor around which collectives construct meaning and understand their experiences…' (Maitlis and Sonenshein, 2010: 563). Additionally, they highlight the need to consider power and politics alongside 'visceral feelings as cues and frames', to the sensemaking process (ibid: 571).

Question for discussion

How important are middle-leaders in relation to strategy in your organisation who lead without a leadership title?

This, and our own empirical work, has added to the theory on strategy as learning. It extends Casey and Goldman's idea of STA and employing schema theory to examine strategy as a learning activ-ity, one in which metacognitive ability is key to the adaptation of existing schemas. Combining this with a socio-cognitive, constructivist view of learning also examines the different communities of practice and socio-material influences upon STA and identifies the need for future research to adopt a critical identity perspective (Black and Warhurst, 2019). Such an approach is necessary in order to examine how the development of capabilities relating to strategic thinking in action affects both individual feelings of capacity and agency. In this chapter, we explore whether there is evidence of such strategy as learning and sensemaking in a crisis situation by examining the narratives of school leaders during the period when restrictions were in place due to Covid-19, analysed accord-ing to our theoretical framework described in Figure 9.1.

As Figure 9.1 indicates, we will consider the narratives in relation to five key areas:

1. Evidence of metacognition – do leaders recognise or understand that they are learning?
2. Person schemas – perceptions of how the strategy will be, or is being, received.
3. Organisation schemas – the culture of the organisation in relation to strategy.
4. Object concept schemas – articulated through websites and strategic plans.
5. Event schemas – meetings and communications with stakeholders.

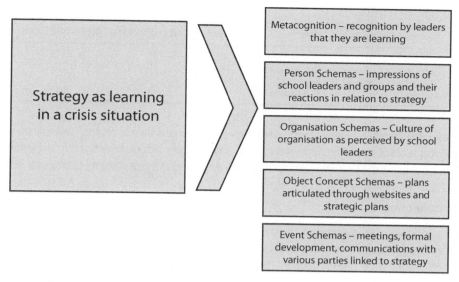

Figure 9.1 Strategy as Learning Theoretical Framework

Source: Adapted From Baxter and John (2021)

Questions for discussion

How effective are strategy inset days in relation to the overall direction of the organisation? Talk to a teacher in a placement school or a lecturer to gain an understanding.

How influential are school leaders' perceptions of how staff will relate to certain strategic directives?

What could the effect of these perceptions be on the overall organisational strategy?

In the next section, we outline our sample and methods.

Sample and methods

Sample and interview schedule

The sample is illustrated in Table 9.1. It should be noted that we refer to 'organisations' throughout the chapter when we wish to capture results from individual schools and multi-academy trusts (MATs).

In order to provide a full picture, our interviews drawn from 50 schools, 40 per cent of which are located in areas of high socioeconomic deprivation and chosen due to their above-average number of students receiving free school meals (FSM). The other 60 per cent of the sample derives from schools with average or below average on the FSM indicator. This allowed us to examine whether there were any differences between schools based on socioeconomic status. Participants were self-selecting and reached through various channels: through our three school support project partners (Schools North East, Derbyshire Teaching Alliance, and The Key for school leaders), and direct approaches via social media. The interview schedule was developed using themes that emanated

Table 9.1 Sample

Type of organisation	Role	Number	Number of schools	Abbreviation used
Multi-academy Trusts	Headteacher	4	31	CEO
Local Authority Schools	Headteacher	19	19	CS
Stand-alone Academy	Headteacher	20		SAT
Special Schools	Headteacher	2	2	SS

from an initial literature review. These were then peer-reviewed by our project partners (all senior educational leaders or researchers) and piloted. It was a very difficult time to carry out interviews, and we are grateful to those who gave up their time during this most challenging of times for schools.

Data collection

Ethics permissions were obtained from all participating universities, in line with BERA protocols, which included a consent form and information about the project. Online interviews, carried out via Microsoft Teams, were semi-structured, lasted between one and 1.5 hours and took place between March and October 2021. The school leaders interviewed included both heads of single schools and CEOs of MATs (groups of schools with one executive headteacher along with individual school heads). In total, there were four CEOs interviewed, representing a total of 31 schools in total, 21 of these in areas of high SED. A pilot was carried out in January 2021 and a code book derived from the researchers, each coding a sample of three scripts within the pilot. This involved all researchers reading and coding each transcript individually, then discussing, merging, and reflecting on the codes to form larger categories and emerging conceptual themes, then further analysing the themes by comparing and contrasting them across data sets and to the study's conceptual framework.

Narrative analysis

Narrative approaches are widely used as a method to study organisations and educational establishments (Clough, 2002). This is largely due to the links between a narrative and sensemaking approach (Elliot, 2005). In relation to strategy as learning they are useful in revealing the cognitive structures – the schema – that help individuals and groups to cope with the complexities of their worlds (Patterson, 2002). They are not only useful in identifying strategic thinking, but often become the basis of a written strategy, telling the future story of the organisation (Baxter and Floyd, 2019), as communication, as repositories of knowledge to be transmitted and re-enacted (Boudes and Laroche, 2009) as well as the foundation of meanings that become guidance for subsequent action and interpretation (May and Fleming, 1997). In line with our previous research, we adopt a narrative approach to data analysis. In what follows, we outline our findings and discuss them.

Questions for discussion

Think about a school or workplace you know. How effective are stories and overall 'narratives' within the organisation?
Do you think they help or hinder strategic planning? Why?

Findings and discussion

In common with previous approaches to this topic, we combine our findings with our discussion under several broad headings. Overall, we found evidence for all five categories within the study and discussed these in what follows.

Category 1: Metacognition

The narratives revealed considerable evidence of leader metacognition both during and after the period following restrictions (July 2021). Thirty-eight out of fifty reflected on all three lockdown periods as progressive learning events, describing, for example, how:

> *...it was a bit like ready, fire, aim. We had to adjust it in flight. In the second lockdown we were really well prepped and that was more about getting the chasing up better.* (CEO-6)

There was also evidence that the pandemic had considerably changed leaders' attitudes and thinking with regard to digital education, and this in turn was affecting the way that they conceptualised the future of their schools or, in the case of CEOs, their organisations. One of the most interesting aspects of this metacognition was their growing awareness that practices which occurred during lockdown had opened up new understandings of how best to reach pupils who had generally not been thought of as participative in lessons. In 20 organisations, leaders mentioned how introvert pupils had benefitted from online teaching:

> *Online learning isn't for everyone, but we've certainly seen quieter pupils see the benefits from working in a quieter environment and have time to provide a considered response to questions.* (Head-22)

In all 50 interviews, leaders acknowledged that their thinking around digital learning had advanced. Their awareness of its potential had increased, and their own learning advanced. In some cases, all schools in areas of multiple deprivation, leaders admitted that they had hardly embraced online education at all before the pandemic. This was largely due to constraints such as lack of pupil learning space at home, lack of parental support, and funding constraints. But during the pandemic, they explained how the crisis had broken down barriers, creating new levels of trust between staff and pupils/staff and leaders, as this head in an area of high SED explains:

> *We've learned a lot about the importance of student voice. One student said to me that they felt great respect that teachers had thought to ask and involve them and then acted upon their suggestions.* (Head-45)

Heads and CEOs from organisations that had already been considering digital learning in their strategies for some time had advanced their strategies, some of them bringing forward digital plans that had '*not been expected to be operationalised until 2025*' (CEO-15).

In the case of one large multi-academy trust, the CEO explained, '*We are bringing our whole curriculum online*' CEO-15 (18 schools). A detailed breakdown of where schools were in their digital strategic planning before, during, and post lockdown period, is discussed in a further paper from this project (Baxter *et al.*, under review).

Category 2: Person schemas and category 3: Organisation schemas

These two aspects are considered together in our findings, as the two are so closely interlinked. Although ample evidence relating to this category emerged, the evidence presented a mixed picture. Some school leaders felt that because teachers and leaders had learned so much in relation to digital learning during Covid, that their schools would never go back to '*business as usual*'. However, although this was articulated within the narratives, it was far from clear how this realisation would change the culture of the organisation, or how strategic plans would address this, as this head reports:

> *And I think while we started the system, this process, with this awful sense of a deficit and gaps in learning and knowledge, we're now thinking, actually, what it's shown us is that education and schooling is about far more than gaps in knowledge.* (Head-35)

This raises the question of how much of the learning would actually be implemented in the future, and how the major culture change that clearly occurred in 70 per cent of the schools in the sample, during Covid, would become the new normal. However, a number of leaders did explain how their new thinking would inform strategic change, in very practical terms, as this head reports:

> *So I want to have the situation where our children have... There's an expression in local primary school users, a computer is part of their pencil case, and I think that's a really great concept.* (Head-3).

Another head talked at some length about new tracking and monitoring and how it would change the way that teachers monitor learning:

> *The introduction of data analytics has supported staff supporting pupils. Clear information has led to targeted interventions and we've been supporting learners at risk of under-achieving. Tracking information has also been used to report to parents. Teachers and support staff have worked together to analyse attainment information to evaluate and revise accordingly. Pupils benefit from tracking discussions with staff which places the pupil at the centre.* (Head-9)

This shift would clearly make a big impact on the culture of the school and its modus operandi.

However, although there was much positivity within the narratives, there was also a concerning trend, particularly amongst struggling schools (either due to high SED or due to low Ofsted ratings), for heads to take a negative view of the culture of the school and how it could be changed. Whilst they acknowledged that they had learned during lockdown, and that some of the digital learning had been very effective, the practical and perceptual constraints on their organisations, since then, had been such that they anticipated a full return to the way they operated before Covid, as this head explains:

> *We don't want to script the children for failure, but inevitably some children have come back and we... They've gone away with a positive mindset, they've come back with an, I can't, it's not*

my fault I've missed it, you didn't teach me, and that's been a challenge. Again, having spoken to a number of my head teacher colleagues with a similar school, so a school with a similar demographic, it's mirrored. (Head-16)

Since the end of restrictions in 2021 schools have continued to suffer in relation to pupil and staff mental health issues, lack of funding, and staff absence due to subsequent waves of the omicron variant of the virus. In some cases, although the vision is there and it has clearly changed due to Covid, the appetite for change has been blunted by these issues, as this CEO pointed out:

During Covid it's been used significantly as a way for collaborative agency and to support children at risk during lockdown. Looking forward it requires innovation and transformation, but there's been a big emotional impact from 2020, all my staff have been personally impacted. Their wellbeing has been affected and they are exhausted. There's an element of trauma in my workforce and in the community. For all I'd like to develop online learning and not lose the momentum, there's a fine line because staff when they return will look for comfort, they'll want things to go back to how they were because it's a safety net and reassuring. I'm not sure they have the energy for transformation. Everyone is shattered. I question also if I am I a good enough leader when the appetite for risk taking is low. Do I have the right skills to inspire staff to continue with online learning? Some worry about online and how it could take their jobs. There's definitely been incubating of different types of provision such as differentiating learning (CEO-4).

From a strategy as learning perspective, the learning that takes place during a crisis is very often tempered within the post-crisis period, as the literature supports (Boudes and Laroche, 2009; Watkins and Walker, 2021). This is particularly true in relation to post-crisis inquiry reports that very often re-framed narratives in order to retrospectively justify particular policies and practices, and re-establish old patterns of sensemaking. As Boudes and Laroche report, in the case of the heatwave in the summer of 2003 in France, the health system was unable to anticipate the event in time, or to react appropriately. They analyse, through seven official reports, how narrative choices which, 'transform the chaotic events of a crisis into an ordered and official story made for reports' (Boudes and Laroche, 2009: 378). These narratives subsequently inform action. How leaders narrate their actions and thoughts in post-crisis reflection is key to their future actions. It appears in this sample that, if they perceive that the climate is not right for change, then no matter what learning has taken place, future digital strategy will be constrained by that thinking and post-action narrative. This is an important finding in relation to the strategy as learning approach.

Category 4: Event schemas and category 5: External schemas

Again, there is ample evidence of strategy as learning in relation to our theme 4, Event Schemas. The evidence in relation to this reveals that a variety of events, impromptu and planned, have helped to colour strategic thinking for digital education in the future.

This head teacher explains how they will take their learning forward:

So we have a working party set up that's actually meeting at lunchtime today around, what were the key things that really benefitted the children during lockdown and how can we build that into school, so we've got some tools and techniques that have been developed through that. Our digital strategy is ongoing and I need to pay attention back to that because what I want it to become more of is, what the research said was schools that had a clear digital usage in school were more successful during lockdown. So it was just a mirrored thing, you do this in school, you do exactly the same at home. (Head-12)

Whilst another head explains how their planning is being prompted by the opportunity to feed into policy for the whole area:

We've actually got a meeting with Nick Gibb coming week after next to talk about what we are trying to achieve here in the county and how collaboration between schools can bring about real change. So that's a really exciting time for us. (Head-17)

Trust and collaborative working again feature in the narratives, with leaders reporting new collaborations between staff and leaders due to the removal of norms of practice. This removal of norms of practice and relationships between staff features in much of the literature on crisis, for example, the positive relationships that emerged as a result of Hurricane Katrina (Beabout, 2007). This head describes how this worked in their own organisation:

I think trust has increased between staff because we were all inexperienced, a bit naïve when it came to online learning, but we trusted staff anyway because that's what they do. They will work things out, they work together and we together we found solutions and a way forward. (Head-45)

However, some heads did comment on the ways in which corporate interests had been allowed to run unchecked through the education system, winning contracts and gaining influence in schools that would have been impossible in a normal situation.

And I think there has been a lot of leveraging from a back door as a result of the pandemic of all sorts of nonsense which is going to take years for all of us to firstly see and find...(CEO-15).

Again, this appears as a recurring theme in the literature on crisis but has not been considered to any great degree in the literature on strategy as learning in crisis situations. As the effects of this and changes in power structures within schools, and with the external environment are likely to affect strategic planning, it is an important finding in relation to strategy as learning. Particularly as, whilst some leaders will be aware of this fact and preoccupied by the further and unchecked incursion of business interests in education, others are likely either not to be aware of it, or be unconcerned by it. An important element to consider in further research on this topic is the reaction of the school governors to this element of practice, planning and policy.

In relation to other external considerations, 50 per cent of school leaders said that they had worked far more closely with other schools and external organisations during the pandemic than they had previously. This had informed their strategy by offering a wider perspective than just their own organisational one, as this head reports:

> *It's been a real privilege to remotely join together with other schools for support. We've formed a collegiate group that will continue beyond covid. It's great to share aspirations and learn from each other. We share good practice and inspiration. This duality we have to hold on to. Share insights. The energy from the group fills me with optimism to carry on, build the most digitally enriched place in the universe. (Head -45)*

This positive finding also emerged in relation to multi-academy trusts, not a set of organisations where external collaboration has featured a great deal in previous research. Largely due to the marketised climate within English education, and the fact that due to their size and scale, many are now extremely isomorphic in their practices (Baxter and Cornforth, 2021). This element of collaboration will undoubtedly influence strategic practices and digital strategy if this collaboration continues for the foreseeable future. Whilst this head told us, *'There's opportunity to build upon the collaborative working we've done with other schools, to co-teach, continue buddy schemes and co-deliver curriculum...'* (Head-24). They were imprecise as to the way that this may continue and whether operational plans were in place. Concerningly, this aligned with the fact that only 45 per cent of organisations were willing to share their strategic plans for digital learning with us. This situation is perhaps unsurprising given the earlier statistics from the DfE study in Section 1.

Questions for discussion

What advantages has viewing strategy as a learning activity, for leaders of education?
How does this approach fit in a world wracked by climate change?

Conclusion

The research outlined in this chapter set out to investigate whether there was evidence of strategy as learning (as conceptualised by our theoretical model in section Background to digital learning) in a crisis situation. The work has revealed that there is ample evidence to support a 'strategy as learning approach' and that this aligns well with a view of strategy as a sensemaking activity. However, it has also revealed that building on learning done during a crisis, learning which would, in theory, change future digital strategy, is constrained by negative perceptions of staff attitude, practical issues (such as ongoing staff absence) and mental ill health amongst staff and students. It is also coloured and conditioned by the context in which the strategy is taking place; in areas of high deprivation with multiple social problems, aspirations are curtailed by real issues of both digital poverty and lack of parental support. Another key finding relates to the policy and political context of the strategy. If school leaders feel that their work is being highjacked by unchecked business interests, allowed to occur with seemingly little accountability during the crisis, then this will undoubtably influence the extent to which they allow their schools to develop digital learning. In this respect, the study points out the need to investigate power and policy and the feelings towards these in relation to future research in this area.

Summary points

- Strategy as learning is present during a crisis situation.
- Leaders learn and change their thinking as a result of strategy as learning during a crisis.
- Future strategy is constrained through ethical and practical concerns: for example, unchecked influence of business through digital platforms, staff illness, staff, and student mental ill health.
- Future strategy is also constrained by leaders' own appetite for change.
- Strategy as learning is closely linked to narrative and sensemaking approaches.

Recommended reading

Baxter, J. and Floyd, A. (2019) Strategic Narrative in Multi-Academy Trusts in England: Principal Drivers for Expansion. *British Educational Research Journal* **45**, pp. 1050–1071.
Baxter, J. and John, A. (2021) Strategy as Learning in Multi-Academy Trusts in England: Strategic Thinking in Action. *School Leadership & Management* **4**(4–5), pp. 290–310.
Goldman, E.F. and Casey A. (2010) Building a Culture that Encourages Strategic Thinking. *Journal of Leadership & Organizational Studies* **17**, pp. 119–128.

References

Amineh, R.J. and Asl, H.D. (2015) Review of Constructivism and Social Constructivism. *Journal of Social Sciences, Literature and Languages* **1**, pp. 9–16.
Balogun, J. (2007) The Practice of Organizational Restructuring: From Design to Reality. *European Management Journal* **25**, pp. 81–91.
Balogun, J. and Johnson, G. (2004) Organizational Restructuring and Middle Manager Sensemaking. *Academy of Management Journal* **47**, pp. 523–549.
Baxter, J.A. and Cornforth, C. (2021) Governing Collaborations: How Boards Engage with Their Communities in Multi-Academy Trusts in England. *Public Management Review* **23**, pp. 567–589.
Baxter, J. and Floyd, A. (2019) Strategic Narrative in Multi-Academy Trusts in England: Principal Drivers for Expansion. *British Educational Research Journal* **45**, pp. 1050–1071.
Baxter, J., Floyd, A. and Jewett, K. (under review) Pandemic, a catalyst for change: Strategic planning for digital education in English Secondary Schools before, during, and post covid.
Baxter, J. and John, A. (2021) Strategy as Learning in Multi-Academy Trusts in England: Strategic Thinking in Action. *School Leadership & Management* **41**, pp. 290–310.
Beabout, B. (2007) Stakeholder Organizations: Hurricane Katrina and the New Orleans Public Schools. *Multicultural Education* **15**, pp. 43–49.
Black, K. and Warhurst, R.P. (2019) Career Transition as Identity Learning: An Autoethnographic Understanding of Human Resource Development. *Human Resource Development International* **22**, pp. 25–43.
Boin, A. and Renaud, C. (2013) Orchestrating Joint Sensemaking Across Government Levels: Challenges and Requirements for Crisis Leadership. *Journal of Leadership Studies* **7**, pp. 41–46.
Boudes, T. and Laroche, H. (2009) Taking off the Heat: Narrative Sensemaking in Post-Crisis Inquiry Reports. *Organization Studies* **30**, pp. 377–396.
Bourgeois, L.J. III (1980) Performance and Consensus. *Strategic Management Journal* **1**, pp. 227–248.
Bruner, J.S. (1996) *The Culture of Education.* Cambridge, MA: Harvard University Press.
Casey, A.J. and Goldman, E.F. (2010) Enhancing the Ability to Think Strategically: A Learning Model. *Management Learning* **41**(2), pp. 167–185.
Chia, R. and Holt, R. (2006) Strategy as Practical Coping: A Heideggerian Perspective. *Organization Studies* **27**, pp. 635–655.
Clough, P. (2002) *Narratives and Fictions in Educational Research.* Buckingham: Open University Press.

Department for Education (2021) Education Technology Survey 2020–21, Cooper Gibson Research, (https://www.gov.uk/government/publications/education-technology-edtech-survey-2020-to-2021)

Eickelmann, B. (2011) Supportive and Hindering Factors to a Sustainable Implementation of ICT in Schools. *Journal for Educational Research Online* **3**(1), pp. 75–103.

Elliot, J. (2005) *Using Narrative in Social Research*. London: Sage.

Goldman, E.F. and Casey, A. (2010) Building a Culture That Encourages Strategic Thinking. *Journal of Leadership & Organizational Studies* **17**(2), pp. 119–128.

Maitlis, S. and Sonenshein, S. (2010) Sensemaking in Crisis and Change: Inspiration and Insights from Weick (1988). *Journal of Management Studies* **47**, pp. 551–580.

May, C. and Fleming, C. (1997) The Professional Imagination: Narrative and the Symbolic Boundaries between Medicine and Nursing. *Journal of Advanced Nursing* **25**, pp. 1094–1100.

Mezirow, J. (1991) *Transformative Dimensions of Adult Learning*. San Francisco, CA: Jossey-Bass.

Patterson, W. (2002) *Strategic Narrative. New Perspectives in the Power of Personal and Cultural Stories*. Oxford: Lexington.

Piaget, J. (1947) *The Psychology of Intelligence*. London: Routledge.

Stevenson, D. (1997) *Information and Communications Technology in UK Schools: An independent inquiry*. London: Independent ICT in Schools Commission.

Thürmer, J.L., Wieber, F. and Gollwitzer, P.M. (2020) Management in Times of Crisis: Can Collective Plans Prepare Teams to Make and Implement Good Decisions? *Management Decision*, 58(10), pp. 2155–2176, ISSN: 0025–1747.

Watkins, D. and Walker, S. (2021) Leadership Crisis Communication During the Pandemic of 2020. *Journal of Leadership, Accountability and Ethics* **18**, pp. 53–67.

Weick, K.E. (1988) Enacted Sensemaking in Crisis Situations [1]. *Journal of Management Studies* **25**, pp. 305–317.

Weick, K.E. (1993) The Collapse of Sensemaking in Organizations: The Mann Gulch Disaster. *Administrative Science Quarterly* **38**(4), pp. 628–652.

Younie, S. (2006) Implementing Government Policy on ICT in Education: Lessons Learnt. *Education and Information Technologies* **11**, pp. 385–400.

10 Leading a Large and Disparate School in Higher Education

Peter Wolstencroft and Track Dinning

Introduction

This chapter introduces the challenges associated with leading a large school in higher education. Because of the disparate nature of education, as well as the fact that the span of control, in other words, the number of people you lead, is very broad, more traditional leadership techniques are unlikely to be successful. Instead, leaders tend to look for more individual solutions to problems and focus on the broader situation in which the problem lies. Fairness is a key concept when using this type of leadership style, and it is always important to understand exactly what we mean when we talk about 'what is fair'.

By the end of the chapter, you should be able to explain what we mean by 'situational leadership' and able to apply this idea to a case study. You will also be able to explore the ways in which you can aim to ensure that your leadership style is fair for everyone and how you can communicate your ideas to those that you lead in the most effective and efficient way.

Setting the scene

Nine a.m., and there is a knock at the door, in walks the Social Butterfly, smiling, suggesting a coffee, and asking if you have heard who the next Head of the School of Education will be. Grimacing behind your fixed smile, you realise this might well be a lengthy conversation, and your bulging inbox will have to wait a little longer; you look at your watch and resolve to be back in the office in half an hour. Another email pings into your inbox; the Leader is suggesting a new initiative for the school and requesting resources from you. You grab your coat and accompany your smiling employee out of the door. Across the corridor you can see the Harsh Critic in animated conversation with the Introvert; you can hear your name being mentioned and you mentally prepare for a lengthy meeting later where you will remind the Harsh Critic that, despite their worries, they do a great job. As you reach the coffee shop a young, smartly dressed employee greets you with a cheery hello; the recent Graduate has clearly been in work for some time, unlike the hunched figure dashing through the building. Sighing you remember that the Procrastinator has still not provided you with a summary of their module evaluations.

LaSalle's (2022) typology of employees in the paragraph above might well be rather simplistic in nature, but the caricatures provided in it do give a useful illustration that, in any organisation, the people you lead are not all the same. Many books stress the importance of equity when dealing with employees, but it is equally important to understand that this does not mean that there is one

DOI: 10.4324/9781003321439-10

solution to all problems. As we can see above, there is a multitude of different sorts of employees and any team that you lead is likely to be *heterogenic* rather than *homogenous* in nature. As a leader of a diverse workplace, you need to show an ability to adapt your style of leadership to accommodate each of these types of employees, whilst maintaining fairness and equity. A common myth about leadership is that you need to ensure that you treat everyone the same in order to maintain fairness, but given the heterogenic nature of the average workplace, counterintuitively, treating people the same actually promotes a lack of equity as you will not be meeting all individual needs. Instead, just like a chameleon changing colour to adapt to its environment, equity is often best served by ensuring that approaches are adapted to the individual and each challenge faced. This is sometimes known as 'situational leadership' (Hersey and Blanchard, 1977) and relates to a flexible style of leadership that is popular in schools of education today.

The challenge of leading a large and diverse group of employees has been made even more difficult due to recent events. The Covid-19 pandemic has hastened the move towards a hybrid working model, which means that employees may not always be physically present in the building. From a productivity and staff well-being perspective, this can have significant benefits (Dale, 2020), but it does raise other challenges in ensuring that communication is maintained throughout the school and that there is consistency of culture when employees might only converse through virtual means. The situational leadership model often adopted, also presents a challenge when face-to face meetings are rare, as it is important that there are channels for people to use in order to communicate with anyone in a leadership position in order to ensure that any perceived unfairness is raised and dealt with at the earliest possible opportunity. The increased use of software such as MSTeams and Zoom has helped to facilitate an approach that has been described as 'Schrödinger's Leadership' (Wolstencroft *et al.*, 2021), where the leader can be present when needed, but remains hidden when not. Whilst this approach has gained supporters during the pandemic, it does require more energy from leaders to ensure staff are confident that there is support when called for, and that new staff are made aware of the ways they can be supported. As with so much of leadership, communication is paramount to ensure that everyone is kept fully informed.

In addition to the increase in remote working, there has also been a move towards larger departments and schools within universities. This is in part for sound business reasons: economies of scale afforded by greater numbers of employees can give both financial and organisational efficiency. However, there is also a pragmatic reason for this. The shortage of teachers in compulsory education is well documented (Gretton and Wolstencroft, 2021), but it is when recruiting for leadership positions that the lack of appointable people coming into the roles is most acute (Weale, 2020). This shortage is mirrored in universities and has been a key driver in the growth in size of departments and schools within higher education.

This chapter looks to assess the challenges posed by managing a large and diverse body of people in higher education. Key concepts explored are those of equity in leadership, diversity of employees, culture within the group and also communication. Throughout the chapter, a case study featuring Mariam, a senior leader in education, will be used to highlight the application of theory in practice.

Introducing situational leadership

At this point, it is important to talk a little more about situational leadership (Hersey and Blanchard, 1977). This theory suggests that there is no one 'right' way of leading. It differs from other theories that stress that a consistent approach works best and can be described as a 'pragmatic' approach to leadership. The priority in this approach is to work out what is best for the individual and the environment at any given time.

The situational leadership model was originally known as 'life cycle theory' and is split into four styles that can be used across four different situations. The basic concept is that the leader decides where the member of staff is at in the cycle and then adopts that style of leadership. Style 1 (S1) is where the leader needs to provide instructions to staff, taking a *directing approach* and telling staff how to complete a task. In this situation there is little input from the member of staff; the communication is all one way coming from the leader, and the leader is making the decisions. When using Style 2 (S2), the leader adopts a *coaching style*. This is useful when a member of staff needs guidance on what to do, but at the same time is fairly competent but wants to learn. The leader needs to allow time for a discussion with the member of staff, although ultimately the leader will still make the decision.

For a leader to adopt the third style (S3), the member of staff must be competent and have the skills and means to complete the task. The aim of the leader in this situation is to take on a *supporting role,* providing encouragement and building confidence. The leader might ask the member of staff how they envisage going about the task and asking if they need any help, but will leave the decision making to the member of staff.

Finally, the fourth style (S4). This style is only used when the member of staff is extremely knowledgeable, motivated and knows exactly how to perform the job. This is a *delegating style* where the leader can just leave the member of staff to get on with the job and to make all the decisions.

For example, some employees might know how to do the job and are competent, that a 'carrot' approach, often associated with S4, can provide motivation, while others need to be kept on task with a more directed 'stick' approach and S1 is more appropriate. Hersey and Blanchard also stress that the task to be completed needs to be taken into account when considering the leadership style. So, for example, a time-limited task might need more micro-management (where the performance of the person is monitored on a regular basis) than something where time is less of a factor.

A situational-based approach has many advantages and, given its focus on the task to be completed, is often seen as a very good way to 'get things done'. However, there are criticisms. The main issue raised is that it can cause a perceived lack of consistency of leadership. If different situations lead to different leadership approaches, then employees can feel unsettled as they are not sure what the reaction of a leader would be to any given event. Imagine if you were being checked up on when completing one task but left alone for another. Whilst there are good reasons for this, the worry is that it might lead to concerns about a lack of fairness. In this situation, the leader needs to ensure that lines of communication with staff are clear.

Questions for discussion

Can you think of a task when you want your manager at work to adopt each approach described above? Explain why.

Despite the problems of this approach, there are some significant advantages. Can you think of what they might be?

Situational leadership in practice

Getting communication right

Let's start with how communication is organised in a large school. This is often viewed as the most important part of the role of a leader because, without effective communication channels, it does not matter how good your decisions are, they won't get through to the people who matter; hence nothing will be actioned, and the status quo will be maintained. As an example, let's look at the use of a conduit to pass on important messages. In this situation, a very direct approach (maybe linked to S1) needs to be taken. The middle manager needs to be given the information and precisely what is expected of them so that it is disseminated across their team. In theory, this is a good idea: smaller groups can be gathered together and the workload spread. A typical approach to this would be that the leader would brief the middle managers, perhaps on a change that is required to working practice, and ask them to inform their teams. However, this approach only works when two things happen: first, that everyone actions the plan, and second, that the information is passed on in a way that the message is not distorted. These two points are absolutely crucial for the success of communication. Imagine finding out a week later that only half of your staff have been notified of a change. It would cause chaos and be likely to cause resentment. In short, it only needs one weak link for your communication plan to collapse.

Following the Covid-19 pandemic, communication has had an extra layer of complexity added to it with the greater prevalence of hybrid working (Dale, 2020): informal corridor conversations or chance encounters are less likely to occur and formal communication methods often encompass people spread over a wide geographic area. This does have some advantages as informal corridor conversations have been noted as causing anxiety with some staff when news spreads ahead of any official announcement (Crampton *et al.*, 1998). The added complications in hybrid working and the need to avoid unnecessary anxiety mean that a communication plan becomes a necessity in any large school.

Finally, as with students, staff have a preference as to how they like to receive information. The media available to a school to communicate with its staff has grown exponentially over the last few years. For many years leaders used face-to-face meetings and email, but now there is a growing choice such as MS Teams, Yammer or Slack, each with their own advantages and disadvantages, and means that leaders need to think about the medium used to communicate messages as well as the message itself.

A basic model of communication was suggested by Schramm (1954), who stressed that communication is a two-way process between a sender and a receiver. The key is to ensure that the message that the sender intends to give is understood by the receiver. This may sound obvious, but the intricacies of the English language mean that we tend to *encode* what we say. If we look at an example, we can see what we mean.

Imagine your lecturer saying to you: 'That's a very interesting approach you have taken'. What message would you take from this? For some people, they would be pleased that the creativity of their work is being recognised, and they would see the comments from the tutor as praise, but for others the meaning would be far more negative. The word 'interesting' is used in a variety of different contexts, sometimes as a 'softer' way of raising concerns. Hence, the same words can be decoded in two different ways. If we add in the cultural differences that occur in any international group of people, as well as what Schramm describes as 'noise' (which is anything that stops you hearing the meaning of the message), then you can see that communication is not as simple as a conversation between a sender and a receiver. This model also stresses the importance of any communication being two-way. Allows any decoding issues to be minimised and allows the flow of ideas from bottom to top, as well as vice-versa. Research also shows that this approach, allied with developing positive employee relations prior to any negative communication, can alter the way staff receive the message (Young, 2021)

As an illustration of the issues, please consider the following case study.

Mariam looked at the spreadsheet which listed everyone employed within her school: the final total was 150 people spread over four sites. She opened another tab: 30 of those people were fractional so they only worked specific days; others had teaching commitments, childcare issues and a few were either on annual leave or unwell. Next, she turned to the room booker, the maximum size of any room available today was 40.

Sighing, she looked again at the message that she had been asked to ensure that all members of staff were given immediately: there was going to be a restructure of the organisation and some people would be at risk of losing their jobs. Mariam knew that her staff would not be affected, but employment law meant that everyone must hear the message. It didn't seem right to simply send out an email with the details on it but.... how was she going to convey the message to such a disparate group of people?

Mariam's dilemma is a common one in any large organisation, and should be considered using four lenses:

1. Importance of message – given communication is something that happens constantly in our day-to-day lives, there needs to be some ranking of message in terms of how vital it is for it to be received and correctly decoded. A message regarding a temporary closure of a classroom could be sent as an email as the consequences of someone failing to read it are likely to be fairly minimal. However, in Mariam's case, a potential restructuring is something that is vital to be understood by everyone; so an email alone would not be an appropriate form of communication.
2. Immediacy of message – consider the difference between received a text message and an email. A text message has a high degree of immediacy in that the majority of people check their phones multiple times a day and are likely to respond when a message is received. With emails many people will answer them at a set time (often at either the start or end of the day) and hence, messages with a high degree of urgency are not likely to be sent by email.
3. Complexity of message – a risk with any form of communication is that the decoding will not be accurate and hence any messages where there is a high degree of complexity need special attention. A common method of communicating highly complex messages is to break it down into headlines and then add levels of detail behind the headlines so that people who want to delve deeper can do, but you can be sure that anyone who is not as thorough at least gets the key points.
4. Expectations of media – we are constantly bombarded with messages, so it is vital to ensure that the right media is used. Recent research suggests that many employees across

a range of professions either fail to open emails or ignore the contents if opened (De Gagne *et al.*, 2020); so using that as a method of communication might well result in the receiver not getting the message and communication being wasted.

These lenses help us understand Mariam's dilemma: her message is urgent, immediate, and complex, but the medium to be used is not straightforward as she can't rely on just one form. Due to the nature of the message, she can't merely email people, yet seeing them all face-to-face is not an option; so, alternatives need to be used. Remember that being a good communicator is a vital part of leadership.

Question for discussion

Now you have had time to read Mariam's dilemma, what would you do? Using the concept of situational leadership, outline a strategy to ensure that the correct message is received by as many people as possible. Ensure that any potential decoding problems are minimised.

The importance of culture

One factor that might help Mariam is our next topic for investigation: the culture of a department. It is undeniable that the culture within a school and a department has a strong relationship with how effectively the school is run. A department and school that values the development of its teachers, promotes collegiality and collaborative leadership is one that should demonstrate effectiveness (Gulsen and Celik, 2021). However, this is not always understood by all leaders: Warrick (2017) reports that many leaders lack the awareness of how significantly organisational culture can affect the workplace.

So, what exactly is culture? In simple terms, culture describes the environment in which we work, often characterised as 'the way we do things round here' (Bower, 2003). Most theory suggests that culture is set by the leadership of the organisation and is something that is seen as a 'construct'. This means that it is made up of lots of different pieces all of which contribute to an employee's perception of what the culture is. Whilst culture is something that is intangible in nature, there are clues that you can pick up when trying to identify what it is. Foremost amongst these is what people pay attention to and view as important. An organisation whose leaders stress the importance of the staff, will often have that culture embedded in policies, procedures and even the physical buildings (so for example a well-equipped staffroom or even a gym might be present), whilst one where leaders are focused on conformity and ensuring efficiency, is likely to be structured in a different way with narrower spans of control and a more regimented approach to work. It's important to stress that as culture is a construct, it can change; but for that to happen one of two things must occur. Either a recognition needs to take place that the people in the organisation want to change (this is the transformative change that Mezirow (1991) stressed was possible) or the people leading the organisation change.

As with many aspects of leadership, typologies are used to identify the many different forms of culture that might be present in an organisation. Often these are split into controlling, collaborative, cultivating and competence-based approaches. It is not our intention to look at every possible type of culture; instead, we will look at a few common forms found within education and see what challenges these would cause for Mariam

Cameron and Quinn (1999) suggested four different forms of culture, each of which can be found within education, and each will have a differing outcome to Mariam's dilemma. The first approach, which they called a 'Clan' approach, stresses teamwork and collegiality of approach and, as the name suggests, sees the school as a family as much as a workplace. The leader's role is that of either a benevolent matriarch or patriarch whose role is to offer guidance. In many ways this culture seems appealing, but when applied to Mariam's situation, there are risks involved. Whilst the news might well be accepted when coming from the leadership figure, any restructure could (potentially) be viewed as something which could mean a reframing of the clan, something which might well be viewed as traumatic. In addition, a delegated communication plan might well be seen as reducing the power of the authority figure.

The second culture, a 'Hierarchy' approach (Cameron and Quinn, 1999), focuses on procedures within an organisation. The advantage for Mariam in this approach, is that lines of communication are likely to be already clearly formed and hence passing the message to everyone is relatively straightforward. However, given the fact that success in this culture is measured in the smooth running of the organisation, anything that is likely to challenge this could be seen as destabilising.

A 'Market' culture, one which is results-oriented, has become increasingly common within education. Coffield and Williamson (2011) describe the way in which much of compulsory education has become an exam factory, and this, together with the increased datafication of education (Stevenson, 2017), has meant that the end result has become increasingly important to the culture of many places. Given employees are seen as cogs within a bigger machine in this culture, a restructuring is potentially something that could be viewed as a realignment of roles, something that could help Mariam when explaining the situation. However, there is a very real danger that employees might feel undervalued.

The final culture identified by Cameron and Quinn (1999) is 'Adhocracy', where an entrepreneurial approach is encouraged. This can have great benefits in terms of empowering people to pursue ideas that they believe are beneficial, but from Mariam's perspective there are numerous problems that it might raise. The disparate nature of this culture means that communication can be challenging with the engrained independence that the culture engenders. meaning that communication needs to be less hierarchical in nature and more driven by negotiation. This can be time-consuming.

The four cultures described above all have strengths and weaknesses, but there is one culture that can create multiple problems and one that needs to be avoided at all times: the toxic culture, which can often come from poor leadership. Let's return to Mariam; when we left her, she was working in a supportive, collaborative environment where she and her department were allowed to work as a team. They all had similar commitment levels to work, which is why it works, and there was always a sense of belonging in Mariam's team. Things, however, can change:

Six months on from her original dilemma and Mariam has begun to dread logging on to her emails. During the restructure, a new boss was appointed, and she quickly realised that they were very different from the outgoing one. From the start, Mariam and her team started seeing changes being imposed upon them, with a lot more structure and control coming down the hierarchy. In addition, work seemed to encroach far more into her life. Her old boss had a policy of never emailing at the weekend and insisting that when Mariam was on annual leave that cover should be provided so she could have a complete break, but her new boss had the expectation that everything should be actioned immediately, plans were changed at the last minute and Mariam had become used to phone calls in the evening asking her to sort something out for the next day. Mariam resented this approach and had caught herself snapping at some of her employees recently, not because of anything they had done, more borne out of frustration about the culture that had become embedded very quickly since the appointment of her new boss.

Culture from the top

Mariam's experience is a classic example of how culture starts at the top of the organisation and trickles down the structures. To many researchers, so much of what we do is down to learned behaviour, and this is done through observation, imitation, and modelling (Bandura, 1977). The theory suggests that if Mariam's boss starts behaving in a particular way, the likelihood is that everyone beneath them will do the same. Remember, our definition of culture came from Bower (2003), and if culture is 'the way we do things', then it is normal for people to look to leaders for clues about how to behave.

Culture is passed down, not just through the observation of what is important that employees undertake, but also through the recruitment of new members of staff. Leaders can stress characteristics that they view as important in job advertisements and then recruit 'in their own image' (Lumpkin, 2007). This will extend to any induction period that a new employee has. Using Vygotsky's Zone of Proximal Development as a model (Vygotsky, 1978), we can see that people are looking for a guide through any uncertainty, and it is upwards that they tend to look. This means that the culture reinforced by educational leaders tends to become established as the norm, as those around a leader seek to conform and ensure complementary communication (Berne, 1958). In practice, what this means is that if the leader adopts a (say) Clan cultural approach, then the strong likelihood is that this will permeate through each level as employees learn what is important and try to avoid crossed communications where people are looking to get different things out of the conversation, a situation that often leads to conflict.

At this point, it is important to reiterate the heterogenic nature of educational workforces. We have mentioned how situational leadership is often used to ensure that the needs of each individual are met. Whilst this sounds like a sensible approach and embraces the diversity inherent in education, the practical realities can be problematic. We return to Mariam for one last time.

Mariam looked at the request from the Recent Graduate and her brain began to whir. The request was to leave early on Friday to visit an elderly relative who had recently been hospitalised. The email outlined the extra work that they had undertaken to make sure that everything was finished in time for the weekend, and also the details of the cover they had arranged to ensure the one class they taught during this period was covered. The tone of the email was professional and there was no doubting at all in Mariam's mind that this was a request that she was happy to approve.

Half an hour later her heart sank as an email from the Procrastinator pinged into her inbox. The three-line request noted that they would not be in on Friday afternoon as they had a few things to attend to. The last line pointed out that, as she had approved Recent Graduate's request, they were sure that they would do the same to theirs.

Mariam checked her work folder; the Procrastinator still hadn't provided details of their module evaluations and checking their timetable she found that they were teaching all Friday afternoon. Sighing, she replied, turning down the request.

Five minutes later there was a knock on her door and in walked the angry Procrastinator.

This case study highlights the difficulties associated with being a leader. If we take the personalities out of the request, then the two emails are asking for exactly the same thing and hence should be treated as such. However, when the extra information is included then it is likely that most people would treat the two emails differently.

However, it is not just about the personalities that are included when deciding on a course of action; instead, the environment the leader works within needs to be taken into account. These could include the contract that employees sign; some are very detailed in terms of what acceptable time off is and what isn't; others are rather vaguer. The culture is also an important factor: Mariam is likely to be influenced by the approach taken by her boss and also by the degree of autonomy of decision-making she has.

Questions for discussion

How might this change in culture affect the staff and in particular their motivation to work? Would it affect their loyalty to the organisations? How would a change in culture relate to a situational leadership style?

Consider the changes a team will see if their work environment switches from one style of leadership to a more situational-based approach.

Fairness and equity through situational leadership

Fairness has been mentioned already in this chapter in terms of situational leadership but, as with so much of leadership theory, there is no simple consensus on what is actually meant by fairness. Earlier in the chapter, we have referred to the situational leadership style as best placed to align with the different type of employers within the school. However, at this point in your learning you may want to think about how you would promote equity in the workplace using this approach.

Before we move on any further, let's consider the terminology in this area. 'Fairness' can often be akin to two separate terms, equity and equality. It is important to understand the difference as we have so often heard them used intermittently yet they mean something quite different.

'Equality', which is often characterised by the word 'sameness', means that all staff will be treated the same, have the same resources, and same opportunities. This creates a great deal of consistency but does mean that individual needs and requirements can be ignored. The Equality and Human Rights Commission UK website has a range of useful recourses and guidance on the impact of The Equality Act (2010) in schools and universities. A key point is that not everyone has the same needs and wants; hence, providing the same thing to everyone does not always create a situation where every employee can thrive equally.

The second term used is 'equity', which tends to be referred to as 'fairness'. This approach recognises that all people are different and as such require different resources, different consideration in order to make things fair. It is this term that is of most important to educational leaders as it is important that, as leaders, there is an understanding of the terms and how practice within the school can be aligned to ensure 'fairness 'for all staff.

The importance of remembering that your workforce is heterogenic in nature is key and that every employee has their own specific needs and wants, but it is also vital to realise that there are specific groups that specifically can feel they are being treated unfairly. These might include minority ethnic groups, persons with disabilities, LBGTQ+ employees and those from a Roma background. The Fundamental Rights Report (2018) suggest that there is still a long way to go in ensuring fairness for all groups in the workplace, but by focusing on equity rather than equality, we can help all employees feel valued and that they have the resources needed to contribute to the workplace.

Many leaders in the sector adopt a transformational style to challenge the existing approaches to ensure ways are found to promote fairness for all staff. It is not enough to provide all staff with the same opportunities. The benefit of creating a fair workplace includes staff feeling safe, and very often will increase the employee's loyalty and investment into the workplace, resulting in less sickness and reduced turnover.

Returning to Mariam's original dilemma of having to relay an important message to all staff within 24 hours, when some were on fractional contracts, some had childcare commitment, were on annual leave or unwell. Sending one email to all staff, or holding a staff meeting with staff in work that day, as we have already deliberated, would not reach all staff in the time period needed, but it would meet the need for equality or 'sameness' as everyone as it would be seen that every member of staff has had the same opportunity to hear the news. Ensuring equity or 'fairness', however, would require a rather different approach as we can see when we look at those staff with childcare responsibilities.

It is widely thought that women with children are treated unfairly and can be held back from promotions (De Gagne *et al.*, 2020), making Mariam's dilemma very real for this group of staff. If Mariam decided to hold a staff meeting, late afternoon with just the staff in work on that day, she could quite easily have missed several staff who have a flexible approach to their work to allow them to collect their children from school. For equity to be achieved, Mariam would need to consider how she reaches those staff with childcare commitments and not in work in order to keep things fair. In addition to this, the new head of department's insistence on staff replying to emails and actioning things whilst on annual leave or outside of the working day clearly is not going to sit well with staff who have family commitment and enjoy their leisure time outside work. Very quickly inequality can creep into the workplace. Staff in a position to respond and action emails late can start to be favoured by the head of department.

To manage this, it is important to have in place a clear expectation of answering things such as emails+ and texts. This is now important as ever with hybrid working.

Question for discussion

Imagine that your school, currently the top recruiter in the UK for students, has recently seen a dip in applications and a drop in recruitment figures. The senior leaders within the organisation insist this needs to be reversed for the long-term survival of the organisation. What type of culture might be beneficial in this situation?

Conclusion

Given all of the factors discussed in this chapter, what advice can we give leaders when dealing with the problems associated with running a large and diverse school? There is certainly no single 'silver bullet' that will solve all problems. However, a number of points can be put in place which can help its smooth running.

The first point is the importance of having a coherent and effective communication plan. Making sure that everyone hears and then decodes your messages correctly is of vital importance when trying to ensure that your plans are put into action. Of course, the fact that your messages are heard by everyone does not necessarily mean that they will agree (or indeed action) with everything, but it means that the first hurdle is cleared and that you now have a chance of enacting your plans.

The second point is that you must remember that culture starts from the top. This means that what you stress as important and what you prioritise will be replicated in those you manage. The idea that you are a role model can be intimidating, but it needs to be remembered that your employees will not necessarily copy everything you do; instead, they will see the bigger picture and aim to treat others in a similar way to how you treat your employees, and they will make sure that what you are focusing on, is replicated throughout the organisation.

Thirdly, ensuring that you focus on equity rather than a more general equality approach can have beneficial effects on the school. By treating individuals as exactly that – sentient beings in their own right, rather than merely part of a collective – you are able to meet individual needs and ensure everyone feels valued.

Finally, we return to our starting point: leading a large school requires an acceptance that everyone will have their own needs, agendas, and characteristics. Some you will like, others may be less so, but they are all vital to the successful running of the school and hence, to ensure maximum performance, you as a leader need to look at the various components that make up a large and disparate School and draw them all together to work towards a common goal.

Summary points

- Any workforce is going to be heterogenic in nature.
- Lines of communication need to be clear and decoding minimal.
- The culture of the organisation generally comes from the senior leadership.
- 'Fairness' and 'equity' do not mean you treat people in exactly the same way.

Recommended reading

Blanchard, K. (2020) *Leading at a Higher Level: Blanchard on leadership and creating high performing organizations* (3rd Ed.). London: Prentice Hall.

References

Bandura, A. (1977) *Social Learning Theory*. Englewood Cliffs, NJ: Prentice Hall.
Berne, E. (1958) Transactional Analysis: A New and Effective Method of Group Therapy. *American Journal of Psychotherapy* **12**(4), pp. 735–743.
Bower, M. (2003) Company Philosophy: 'The Way We Do Things Round Here'. *The McKinsey Quarterly* **2**(1), pp. 100–117.

Cameron, K.S. and Quinn, R.E. (1999) *Diagnosing and Changing Organizational Culture: Based on the competing values framework.* London: Addison-Wesley Publishing.

Coffield, F. and Williamson, B. (2011) *From Exam Factories to Communities of Discovery: The democratic route (Bedford Way Papers, 38).* London: IOE.

Crampton, S., Hodge, J. and Mishra, J. (1998) The Informal Communication Network: Factors Influencing Grapevine Activity. *Public Personnel Management* **27**(1), pp. 569–584.

Dale, G. (2020) *Flexible Working: How to implement flexibility in the workplace to improve employee and business performance.* London: Kogan Page.

De Gagne, J., Yang, Y., Rushton, S., Koppel, P. and Hall, K. (2020) Email Use Reconsidered in Health Professions Education: Viewpoint *JMIR Medical Education* **6**(1).

Gretton, G. and Wolstencroft, P. (2021) *Thinking like a Teacher: Is the early career framework the answer to early career teachers' prayers?* BERA Blog. Available at: https://www.bera.ac.uk/blog/thinking-like-a-teacher-is-the-early-career-framework-the-answer-to-early-career-teachers-prayers (Accessed 25 May 2022).

Gulsen, F. and Celik, O. (2021) Secondary School Teachers' Effective School Perception: The Role of School Culture and Teacher Empowerment. *International Journal of Progressive Education* **17**(5), pp. 332–344.

Hersey, P. and Blanchard, K.H. (1977) *Management of Organizational Behavior 3rd Edition – Utilizing Human Resources.* Hoboken, NJ: Prentice Hall.

LaSalle Network (2022) *6 Types of Employees (and How to Manage Them).* Available at https://www.thelasallenetwork.com/lasalle-network-blog/6-types-of-employees-and-how-to-manage-them/ (Accessed 13 May 2022). +

Lumpkin, J.R. (2007) Recruiting and Retaining a Diverse Faculty. *Journal of Diversity Management* **2**(1), pp. 37–40.

Mezirow, J. (1991) *Transformative Dimensions of Adult Learning.* San Francisco, CA: Jossey-Bass.

Schramm, W. (1954) *The Process and Effects of Mass Communication.* Urbana, IL: University of Illinois Press.

Stevenson, H. (2017) The "Datafication" of Teaching: Can Teachers Speak Back to the Numbers? *Peabody Journal of Education* **92**(4), pp. 537–555.

The Equality Act (2010). Available at https://www.legislation.gov.uk/ukpga/2010/15/contents.

The Fundamental Rights Report (2018). Available at http://fra.europa.eu/en/publication/2018/fundamental-rights-report-2018.

Vygotsky, L. S. (1978) *Mind in Society: The development of higher psychological processes.* Cambridge, MA: Harvard University Press.

Warrick, D. D. (2017) What Leaders Need to Know About Organizational Culture? *Business Horizons* **60**(3), pp. 395–404.

Weale, S. (2020) Exodus of Exhausted Headteachers Predicted in England after Pandemic. The Guardian, 18 November, 2020. Available at https://www.theguardian.com/education/2020/nov/18/exodus-of-exhausted-headteachers-predicted-in-england-after-pandemic (Accessed 13 May 2022).

Wolstencroft, P., Kivits, R. and de Main, L. (2021) *Finding a Balance: Leadership in a time of chaos.* WonkHE. Available at: https://wonkhe.com/

Young, K. (2021) Building Organisational Resilience through Strategics Internal Communications and Organisation–Employee Relationships. *Journal of Applied Communications Research* **49**(5), pp. 589–608.

11 Leadership of International Schools

Mark T. Gibson and Lucy Bailey

Introduction

Although there is a range of International Schools, our definition is that they are typically fee-paying, offering a foreign language curriculum with the medium of instruction being a foreign language (frequently English). They are often staffed, particularly at senior level, by foreign nationals. For example, Copenhagen International School is a school in Denmark that delivers international programmes (the International Baccalaureate) in English to students from over 80 nationalities, whose parents have moved to Denmark for their work; The British School of Beijing enables children to study for international GCSEs and international 'A' levels (these are national qualifications in England and internationally, generally at age 16 and 18) in China. Globally, there has been a considerable growth in the number of schools referring to themselves as 'International Schools' in recent years, with a 40 per cent rise between 2012 and 2018, mainly in the Middle East and Asia. Projections are that the number of students who will attend such schools will reach seven million by 2023, the equivalent of a medium-sized country like England (Bunnell *et al.*, 2016). You may have student colleagues who attended an international school.

International schools are different to national schools, so it may not be a surprise that leading them has different challenges. This chapter explores these challenges, drawing upon our own recent research as well as the wider literature.

What is an international school?

The earliest international schools were founded by expatriate communities whose families wanted their children to experience a 'home school, away from home', whilst they were temporarily working in a different country. This would allow them to return to their home country and their children to the same national system of education. For example, the Alice Smith International School in Kuala Lumpur, Malaysia was founded in 1946 by a British mother, Alice Smith, originally operating from her own house.

The international school landscape has become more complex in recent years, and the definition of an international school is now contested (Bunnell *et al.*, 2016). Although international schools have predominately served the children of expatriate families, globally they now contain a higher proportion of host nation children; in a space of 30 years, international school places have gone from 80 per cent filled by expatriate children to 80 per cent host nation, local children (Brummitt and Keeling, 2013). These are averages, so some schools have no expatriate children, and others

DOI: 10.4324/9781003321439-11

no host nation children. These two groups, the internationally mobile global elite and the upwardly mobile host nationals, create international schooling that offers 'social and cultural reproduction for the globalising and cosmopolitan privileged' (Gardner-McTaggart, 2018: 149).

Hayden and Thompson (2013) created a typology of A, B, and C international schools, based around cohorts and curricula. Type A, 'traditional' international schools, frequently offer an English or US curriculum and serve expatriate communities and tend to be privately owned or run as parental co-operatives. Type B 'ideological' international schools differ in that they aim to bring a range of students together in order to foster world peace and develop international mindedness, typically with a curriculum based around the International Baccalaureate (IB). The final, Type C 'non-traditional' international school typically caters for host nation families, the economically advantaged who seek to give their children a social advantage. Of the three, they are the main growth area. These schools offer a curriculum and qualifications that assist students in their entrance to universities in Western countries; they exist for those who 'perceive a western education and fluency in English as a route to future success and prosperity in a globalised world' (Hayden and Thompson, 2013: 7). An additional distinction is that Type C schools tend to be privately owned businesses that are for-profit organisations. There are some difficulties with Hayden and Thompson's typology: for example, they do not refer to chains of schools operating under a single ownership, and we have critiqued this model and discussed the nature of ownership and governance elsewhere (Gibson and Bailey, 2021).

Individual/group task

Before reading further, see if you can list some of the areas that may be different about leading an international school compared to national schools.
What areas of leadership in international schools may be similar to national schools?

The range of ownership and governance models in international schools can make leading them challenging. There are two basic models of parent-run and privately-owned, but these can be distinguished further by not-for-profit and for-profit schools within groups. For-profit schooling operates on a commercial basis where the product they are selling is 'education'; not-for-profit schools are more like other social-based organisations such as charities, although some individuals may make personal financial gains in supposedly not-for-profit schooling (James and Sheppard, 2014). In more recent years, the growth of international schools has also included the expansion of 'chains' of schools, where an owner runs several schools, either within a single country, or across several countries. There has been a rise of corporate big players such as Nord Anglia, Cognita, and GEMS (Global Education Management Systems) that operate globally in many countries. Elite British and American schools have created franchises of their schools such as the Harrow International School in Bangkok (Bunnell, 2008).

Private international schools can operate with a single owner who controls the governing body and may be involved in running the school in many ways. This is similar in some ways to academy schools in England, and we have explored this elsewhere (Gibson and Bailey, 2021). However, they can also operate as a group of schools with a single governing board or even one where the HQ is in another part of the world. You could find yourself, for example, being the principal of an international school where the owner is in a different continent, is a local businessman or even the king of that country.

The structures of international schools can vary too and may be different to state-funded schools in the UK, although independent schools may also have a structural range. They may vary in size from a few dozen children in a converted villa to several thousand students spread over several sites. Frequently, international schools are 'through-schools', catering for children aged 3–18, and many have boarding facilities for older students. These through-schools are then often split into smaller schools or divisions by age, and leaders of these divisions may have the name 'Head of School', such as Head of Primary School and Head of Secondary School. There is normally one leader who has overall responsibility for the entire school; the name of this position varies, but we will refer to it as the 'principal'. Middle leadership positions occur for subject specialism and sometimes for cohorts of students.

Finally, there are some other key features of international schools that make them different from national schools. Blandford and Shaw (2001) identify areas such as high parental expectations, the range of governance models and autonomy given to principals and transience that differ from national schools. International schools may have transient principals and staff, with students, leaders and teachers moving on to another country after only a few years. Frequently, contracts for people working in international schools are fixed and short-term teacher contracts are typically for only two or three years before requiring renewal. One study cited an average principal's tenure is only 3.7 years (Benson, 2011). This transience may also refer to student populations, particularly for expatriate students whose parents may be posted to another country after a short period of time. International school principals are held accountable for their performance, reporting either to their owners or the governing body. Their Key Performance Indicators (KPIs) may be based around market-driven metrics such as student enrolment numbers (James and Sheppard, 2014) and a culture of business and profit margins (Machin, 2014). International school communities are typically diverse, and there may be local constraints on what can be discussed within the classroom, and any principal will need to be cognisant of the cultural appropriateness of their own behaviour and that of their staff. There are no organisations to support school workers such as trade unions.

In summary, there is a wide range of schools referring to themselves as international schools and we use the broad definition above. They are, by their definition, different from national schools and therefore leading them has differences too. In the remainder of this chapter, we look at some of the challenges of leading international schools and how they vary from national schools.

Challenges of leading international schools

Our research, based on interviews with international school leaders in Malaysia, has identified several ways that leading international schools differed from national schools including loneliness, transience, cultural differences, governance, business elements, and managing school composition (Bailey and Gibson, 2020, 2022; Gibson and Bailey, 2021, 2022). The leaders in our research study were all non-Malaysian; although not necessarily the case, it is typical for a non-national to lead an international school. We have given pseudonyms in order to protect their, and their schools, identity.

Loneliness

All school principals feel a sense of isolation; they have a type of professional loneliness in that they are the top of a pyramid, make decisions that can affect the whole school, and have the ultimate responsibility and accountability for the school. They must respect student and staff confidentiality, which may limit what they can discuss about their work. However, in international schools this can be amplified by the context. An international school is isolated; it is detached from the local host nation schooling system, following a different curriculum, and using a different language. The newly appointed international school principal may lack networks and find their social life is based around school, even living on the school campus, what Caffyn (2010: 328) refers to as the 'psychic prison mentality' of international schools.

In our work Sandra arrived with no family and found herself having no time to build an independent social life, her role was all consuming and she described working 14-hour days, including answering emails in school holidays. Even for the principals that had family, their children attended the school too, so the family focus became the school. The children were a daily presence at their parent's place of work, which could impact on the reputation of either.

There are professional organisation networks that exist for international school principals within countries and regions, and all of the principals in our research joined such groups. In addition, those in chains were frequently 'buddied' with a fellow principal from the country. They also all developed a professional confidante, a 'go to' person for confidential professional advice that they would 'sound out' before acting. It was particularly interesting that in the case where principals worked for a single owner, this confidante was a member of the owner's family who the principals trusted. This idea is not dissimilar to school principals in the UK having a 'critical friend', sometimes operating as a School Improvement Partner (SIP). Networking, then, seemed an important strategy to counter loneliness for such principals.

Individual/group task

What challenges might an international school principal have in these situations, and what do you think they could do to counter them?

> He/she does not speak the host nation's main language. The owning company is based in another part of the world.
> Their children attend their school.
> S/he leads a student body from over 80 nationalities.

Transience

A key challenge for international school principals is the transient nature of such organisations. There are three elements to transience: turnover of students, staff, and principals themselves. The different types of international schools have different levels of transient students; those with a higher proportion of local students tend to be more stable. Short-term staff contracts are the norm in international schools of all types (Lee *et al.*, 2012). This is due to a variety of reasons, but a significant one is that expatriate staff will require a working visa which will be fixed term, one of our principals particularly pointing out that her two-year contract was too short to impact on the culture of the school. Principals report adopting strategies for this transience: for example, employing staff with accompanying families who are thought more likely to stay longer than young, single teachers.

Transience in staff brought other issues too such as safeguarding. Not all countries have background check systems on potential employees available to employers such as the Disclosure and

Barring Service (DBS) in the UK. Principals reported on developing their own procedures to check the background of adults working with children. Networks with other principals were important here, with principals informally warning one another about teachers whose background may be of concern.

Transience was a key defining feature of international schools in the earlier literature (Blandford and Shaw, 2001), but it may be that in schools that have larger cohorts of host nation children, this may be less significant. Such schools in our research appeared to have less transient staff too, like the principal who, despite having a two-year contract, had been in place far longer than that. This school had over two-thirds host nation children and a high proportion of local staff too. It may well be that transience is not a defining characteristic of such schools in the future.

Cultural differences

The cultural differences between a national school experience and those of international schools are critical for international school leaders to appreciate; cultural intelligence is a key skill for international school leaders (Keung and Rockinson-Szapkiw, 2013). One of our research participants, Max, summarised this by saying that it was important when in a new post to gain an appreciation of the local culture, 'to get to know the people and the culture as quickly as possible. And understand that it's going to be different from other countries that you have been in… How you behave and what you say and how you say it'. For example, many of our research participants mentioned that 'losing face' was particularly important to consider in the Malaysian cultural context. If a colleague was openly criticised or contradicted, even mildly, in front of others they were said to 'lose face', they were professionally embarrassed. However, this was a strong feeling and should be recognised by expatriate leaders and avoided where possible.

Cultural differences will extend across relationships with colleagues, students, and parents. Another of our participants, Philip, referred to the range of cultural differences with parental expectations when he said:

> lots of different nationalities of parents, and we've all got a different view of whether they should have an input in schools or whether they shouldn't and there are some nationalities that you shouldn't question the leader and some who very much want to.

The management of these cultural differences also becomes complex in that parents have opted to send their child to an international school, often at great expense, and appreciate that there will be differences from host nation national schools; they may welcome those as, for example, better preparing their children for university education overseas. There may be cultural differences in pedagogy; in our sample all the leaders spent time explaining their teaching practices to parents. Additionally, even teaching materials can be problematic in a different cultural context. We are aware of an international school that was using a reading scheme from the UK in which one book had same-sex parents; this was seen as offensive in the country where the school was located.

Caffyn (2010) notes that these international school workplaces can become fractured with staff subcultures, enclaves and conflict and suggests, 'An understanding of the locational influences on the school, especially upon structures, individuals and groups, is critical for management to have' (p. 336). He quotes Bram Stoker's fictional Dracula to emphasise the point, 'We are in Transylvania, and Transylvania is not England'. One practice that we noticed creating potential inter-staff working relations difficulties was that of pay differentials, with local staff being paid less than their expatriate colleagues in Malaysia. One of our participants recognised this potential problem and employed exclusively expatriate staff, a practice that may contradict employment law in a country like the UK. Slough-Kuss (2014) points to the lack of cultural diversity among international school principals as a salient point in itself, the leadership of such schools being predominantly white expatriate.

Case Study 1: Comments from principals on host-nation people

The two quotes below are from two international school principals in our research talking about Malaysians to the authors. Malaysia has three distinct national ethnic groups, Chinese, Malays, and Indians.

The first quote is from John

our Chinese mums, who are largely unemployed, will gather at the school.... I'm sure you will understand the Chinese have been brought up in an education system that is very traditional, very demanding and very focused, and that's not the way we do things in teaching and learning anymore....after school activities, which for many of our parents are nothing more than child minding, allowing them to get themselves another latte before they come and get their kids, or get their maids to come and get their kids, or put them on a bus and cart them for 45 minutes across the other side of town. And I'm being cynical, but it's true.

The second quote is from Ryan

I've run into few people here that are proactive and not just reactive. Facility managers, contractors, people showing up on time, it's not laid back, it's not a laid-back Hawaii vibe, it's "I don't give a shit". You know, something's gotta get done. "Can you as a contractor get it done by this date? Yes, yes boss". But nothing, people don't show up, people just disappear. They're running out of people. Nothing happens on time.

Discussion

What do you think about these comments from the two principals in the light of the discussion about cultural differences above?

Governance and ownership

All schools have a form of governance, frequently a Governing Board, a set of people who run the school and are accountable for it. In international schools, the governance varies considerably from parental co-operatives to a single owner and his/her family. However, the lines between ownership and governance are frequently blurred in international schools. In national schools, there are structures, rules, and frequently laws surrounding the governance of schools; there are established parameters and procedures. Principals can move from one school to another within the same country and know broadly what to expect about their new school's governance. This is not the case with international schools. A principal could find themselves in a situation where there is no governing board at all, the principal talking directly to the single owner. There are a range of governance and ownership models in international schools and principals frequently need to negotiate their own role carefully. Some schools are for-profit, others are non-profit organisations. In our research, two principals from very different ownership models, one a for-profit, another a charity both emphasised the amount of trust the owner placed in them; they knew that such trust was essential to their continuing in post. Previous researchers have shown that the most common reason for a principal leaving an international school was the relationship with the school board (Benson, 2011).

There is wide variation over the autonomy principals have in international schools. Traditionally, international school principals have had considerable autonomy over such factors in the school as the curriculum and hiring and firing of staff; educational matters, whilst fiscal matters were frequently seen as areas for owners and governors (Hayden, 2006). The rise of for-profit schools and chains of international schools has changed that. Two experienced principals in our study described how they tried to establish boundaries from the outset of their posts, Sandra had a parental co-operative as owners and she ran the governing training herself, the not-so-hidden message here was that she was in charge. Keith on the other hand had a single, very 'hands on' owner (see case study 2 box) who he tried to limit, 'we had a few 'choice words' at the beginning but we managed to draw lines ...quite a bit of conflict at the beginning'. In these situations, principals need to also appreciate that the school is the private investment of the owner; it is their money that could be lost.

The traditional principal role of curriculum control was not always apparent in our work, and it may be changing as owners are more market aware. Keith's owner had bought into a franchise to deliver the Reggio Emila teaching approach (https://www.reggiochildren.it/en/reggio-emilia-approach/). Claire's owners had a market-led approach to their choice of curriculum; prior to appointing her, they had decided that the focus of the school would be on technology and the use of Singapore mathematics as their market research indicated that these would be popular with potential parents. With the increasing number of chains, along with developing niche market openings in a crowded marketplace, the traditional principal role in many international schools may be changing with less autonomy over curriculum decision-making. The reduction of autonomy for an international school principal within a chain may well be similar to that operating in some Multi-Academy Trusts (MATs) in England, where the chain owners control significant elements such as the curriculum, uniform and elements of staffing (Gibson, 2016).

Frequently in national schools a principal may have high levels of accountability, particularly measured using metrics such as student performance in high-stakes public examinations like GCSE. There are no performance 'league tables' for international schools and hard comparable data is rarely published, although the schools will indicate their highest achievers and, in particular, the numbers of students achieving university entrance especially when these are Western high-status universities. National school principals will undergo an annual performance review of some nature where targets are agreed and performance measured against. There appears to be little of this in international school settings, some of our sample for example saying they set their own targets and development plans. The main accountability measure across international schools appears to be the business bottom line; the number of fee-paying students on roll. Keith explained his appraisal:

> the ways things work at the moment it's purely numbers [student roll], because they were concerned with this ... but I would think that my only KPI [Key Performance Indicator] from this current round was based on numbers. So like once I reach 160 for the year, then I will get like a financial extra payment I think.

In summary, there are a range of ownership and governance models in international schools and frequently these operate in a very different way to national schools. International school principals will need to navigate their relationship with the governors and owner maybe more than in a national school.

Case Study 2: Working with a 'hands on' school owner

Keith was a principal who had a single private owner who also was a parent. She had her own office in the school, was in the school daily, walking in and out of lessons, attend all the staff meetings and reminded Keith publicly that he should be on the school gate to meet parents as it was lunchtime. In an unpublished research interview she stated that she was unhappy with the quality of management of one section of the school saying that she, not the designated teacher, was running that part of the school.

Trisha was from India and was internally promoted to the role of principal in the school. The owner suggested to her that she should no longer wear a sari to work but should dress in a more western manner.

The owner of Ryan's school employed several family members in administrative roles, which was not open to negotiation. Ryan was concerned about the quality of work of one family member who had a key role in finance.

Discussion point

How could a principal in each of these situations try and 'navigate' the relationship with the owner?

Business elements

In our research it was notable that the discourse surrounding business was strongly featured, with the principals frequently using terms such as 'competition', 'enrollment figures', 'marketing' and 'market-place'. Several participants appeared to be comfortable with what Machin (2014: 19) calls the 'simultaneous educational–commercial discourse'. Principals who worked for not-for-profit schools still used this language and in our study, one informed us that he felt schools had changed and 'nowadays you are a CEO...you are expected to deal with all of the things that anyone running a business organisation would need to do', another (in a for-profit school) had ensured those in charge of admissions and marketing reported directly to him as they are the 'driving force of the school'.

The competitive nature of the international school market, which some principals thought was over-saturated, resulted in international schools poaching students, sometimes teachers, from one another. There were business practices such as a building company that owned both the local housing stock and school, offering cut-price school fees as a 'loss leader' in order to sell its houses where it made greater profit. However, John, in our study, stressed the variability of the role of an international school principal:

> And having worked at four international schools, all of them have been quite different, where some want you to be at the grassroots level in the classrooms and others want you to be fulfilling more of the CEO type, more remote just simply by the pressure of paperwork and planning and strategy.

Such business elements can create ethical dilemmas for international school principals, such as removing good teachers from Malaysian schools, thereby reducing the pool of talent there. The for-profit notion particularly concerned our sample in a similar way to what Machin (2014) refers to as a contested role, professional educator or professional manager? In the home nations of our international school principals, which were predominantly Western countries like the UK or USA, schools are never for-profit. Our participants struggled with this dilemma; is it morally right to make a profit from schools? They discussed this idea at length, displaying what we referred to as 'affective dissonance'. They defended the for-profit notion by referring to the small margins the owning company makes or that the company is only in the education business. Words such as 'family', 'education business' and 'small' were used by different participants to defend for-profit schooling. Even one of our principals that worked in a not-for-profit school had strong opinions on for-profit status saying she would 'find it difficult in many, many cases to work in a [for-profit] environment... because resources are not spent for the students, but rather the bottom line is making money'. Martin, who led a for-profit school summarised what many felt:

> I'd be in danger of losing that moral purpose. I'd be in danger of just saying all I really care about is just having that three percent profit ... Whereas, if I can keep reminding myself why I'm doing this. I'm doing this because I want to make a difference to kids'.

Many principals in international schools, particularly those in for-profit organisations, embraced their education-commerce duality, although the extent to which they were involved in business elements varied. The notion of for-profit schooling can cause an ethical dilemma for international school principals that would not occur in a national school.

Individual/group task

Discussion

Why do you think the idea of working in a for-profit school seemed to concern the research participants? What areas of concern do you think they had?

Managing school composition

In most western countries there are legal constraints on the admissions of students into schools, in state-funded schooling it is frequently undertaken by an external regional body and the principal will not be involved. Even when the school is selective, the criteria will be transparent and the school principal will not be involved. The literature on international schools emphasises the importance to leaders of maintaining school numbers (Gardner-McTaggart, 2018), however our work suggests principals may well focus on not simply how many are admitted, but also *who*.

Principals in our study referred to managing the cultural composition of the teaching staff and student body. One principal identified maintaining a different cultural balance in the school as his biggest challenge; he did not want students with a shared language other than English to flock together. Another school restricted the number of students from China for a similar reason and emphasised the 'international' make-up of the students. A third had a policy that no nationality could go above 25 per cent of the students in order to maintain its internationalism. Andrea had clear parameters, not going above 40 per cent of host nation students and requiring teachers to be British trained, although they were not required to be British passport holders. She defended this in order to be able to market the institution as a true 'British School'.

The racial composition of the student body was part of the identity and marketing of some international schools in Malaysia, one school having an explicit cap of 35 per cent of places being reserved for students who carried passports from the (Anglophone) 'founding nations' of the school. Another principal, Alistair, used the school's colonial past as a marketing strategy, saying, 'We do actively manage the demographics. That is quite a key part of the mission of the school; we look to actively market to those families through the connections with our trustee organizations'. The staffing too reflected an identity in some schools, Claire felt that before she arrived at her school it marketed using white staff, and according to her this was common in the sector. She explained that 'international schools want white faces' for marketing reasons, adding 'it's just overwhelming with selling whiteness'. She described the conflict she had with the owners when she challenged such marketing materials. In such ways, it seems that some international schools appear to construct themselves as postcolonial sites, and we have discussed this elsewhere (Gibson and Bailey, 2022).

Meeting the needs of students with special educational needs is not always seen as the responsibility of international schools. Most of the schools limited the number of special educational needs children, Trisha for example was clear and open that her school did not accept children with special educational needs and refused to admit one boy for wearing an earring and another for having his hair in a ponytail. Other principal's limited numbers of students with special needs to ensure they did not become 'The Special Needs School' and this sat uncomfortably with the background they were from, Ryan saying, 'That's the hard part. As a public educator, it's a different role. It's business. That's probably the biggest personal challenge. Not to just fling your arms open and take them all in'.

The idea that the role of the principal is to actively manage the school community in terms of ethnicity, nationally, first language and special educational needs are very different to the expectations of national school leadership in Western countries, where most of these principals came from; indeed, such practice is likely to be unlawful in those countries.

Conclusion

This chapter has explored some of the key differences between international schools and schools serving a national context. These differences have implications for leadership, and international school leadership appears to be different in at least six ways, including loneliness, transience, cultural differences, governance, business elements, and managing school composition.

It is also of interest to draw attention to some aspects of school leadership that are salient in national contexts did not appear in our interviews at all. None of the principals referred to managing student behaviour in taking up their time for example. Nor did any of them mention challenges of stimulating parental involvement; the opposite was occurring with many of them referring to ways they actively reduced parental roles to provide demarcation lines. In summary, whilst there are a number of challenges that appear to be specific to international school leadership, there is equally a number that occurs more in national contexts.

You may be interested in leadership styles and models and their effects on schools. This is a complicated area and may well become more complex with a cultural mix of an international school. There is not enough space to discuss such ideas in this chapter but a good starting point for reading around such leadership concepts is the Bush and Glover (2014) article in the recommended reading below, you may wish to read it and consider how such models apply to international schools.

If you are interested, and read further around the research literature on international schools, you will see it has changed over the years from accounts that tended to describe such provision to studies that are more critically analytical. People who lead such schools are likely to face professional ethical questions such as are international schools promoting 'international mindfulness', 'globalisation', or Westernisation? And are they producing new elites, such as globally mobile elites or new elitism, privilege, and division within host nations?

There are also of course, shared experiences between the leadership of international and national schools. International school leadership may be similar to national schools in staffing structures, curriculum, a collegiate environment and leading people. Fundamentally school leadership is about leading people to achieve their best, and one of our participants, Philip, described his driving principle as basing his decisions on 'what's right for the children'. Whatever the type of school being led, this principle is surely the driver of all successful leadership?

Individual/group task

Discussion

How might a potential international school leader prepare for their role? [Bailey and Gibson (2020) may help with this]

Student Presentation
You may have student colleagues who studied at an international school, and they may be willing to give a presentation of their experiences of them.

Summary points

- International schools are ones that are typically fee-paying, offer a foreign language curriculum with the medium of instruction being a foreign language (frequently English). They are often staffed, particularly at senior level, by foreign nationals.
- There has been a significant rise in international schools globally in recent years, particularly in the Middle East and Asia.
- There are different types of international schools but recent changes involve a greater number of host nation children studying at them.
- International school leadership may be similar to national schools in staffing structures, curriculum, a collegiate environment and leading people.
- The leadership of international schools may differ from national schools in the following ways: loneliness, transience, cultural differences, governance, business elements, and managing school composition.

Recommended reading

Bailey, L. (2021). *International Schooling: Privilege and power in globalized societies*. London: Bloomsbury.

Bush, T. and Glover, D. (2014) School Leadership Models: What Do We Know? *School Leadership and Management* **34**(5), pp. 553–571.

Hayden, M. (2011). Transnational Spaces of Education: The Growth of the International School Sector. *Globalisation, Societies and Education* **9**(2), pp. 211–224.

Kim, H. (2019). *How Global Capital Is Remaking International Education: The emergence of transnational education corporations*. Singapore: Springer.

References

Bailey, L. and Gibson, M. T. (2020) International School Principals: Routes to Headship and Key Challenges of Their Role. *Educational Management Administration & Leadership* **48**(6), pp. 1007–1025.

Bailey, L. and Gibson, M. T. (2022) International School Principals in Malaysia: Local and Global Factors Impacting on Leadership. In T. Bush (Ed.), *School Leadership in Malaysia*. Abingdon: Routledge.

Benson, J. (2011) An Investigation of Chief Administrator Turnover in International Schools. *Journal of Research in International Education* **10**(1), pp. 87–103.

Blandford, S. and Shaw, M. (2001) The Nature of International School Leadership. In S. Blandford and M. Shaw (Eds.), *Managing International Schools*. Abingdon: Routledge.

Brummitt, N. and Keeling, A. (2013) Charting the Growth of International Schools. In R. Pearce (Ed.), *International Education and Schools: Moving Beyond the First 40 Years*. London: Bloomsbury.

Bunnell, T. (2008) The Exporting and Franchising of Elite English Private Schools: the Emerging "second Wave". *Asia Pacific Journal of Education* **28**(4), pp. 383–393.

Bunnell, T., Fertig, M. and James, C. (2016) What Is International About International Schools? An Institutional Legitimacy Perspective. *Oxford Review of Education* **42**(4), pp. 408–423.

Caffyn, R. (2010) We Are in Transylvania, and Transylvania Is Not England': Location as a Significant Factor in International School Micropolitics. *Educational Management Administration & Leadership* **38**(3), pp. 321–340.

Gardner-McTaggart, A. (2018) International Schools: Leadership Reviewed. *Journal of Research in International Education* **17**(2), pp. 148–163.

Gibson, M. T. (2016) Sponsored Academy School Principals in England: Autonomous Leaders or Sponsor Conduits? *International Studies in Educational Administration* **44**(2), pp. 39–54.

Gibson, M. T. and Bailey, L. (2021). Navigating the Blurred Lines Between Principalship and Governance in International Schools: Leadership and the Locus of Ownership Control. *International Journal of Leadership in Education*, pp. 1–18.

Gibson, M. T. and Bailey, L. (2022). Constructing International Schools as Postcolonial Sites. *Globalisation, Societies and Education*, pp. 1–12. https://doi.org/10.1080/14767724.2022.2045909

Hayden, M. (2006) *Introduction to International Education: International schools and their communities.* London: Sage.

Hayden, M. and Thompson, J. (2013) International Schools: Antecedents, Current Issues and Metaphors for the Future. In R. Pearce (Ed.), *International Education and Schools: Moving beyond the first 40 years.* London: Bloomsbury.

James, C. and Sheppard, P. (2014) The Governing of International Schools: The Implications of Ownership and Profit Motive. *School Leadership & Management* **34**(1), pp. 2–20.

Keung, E. and Rockinson-Szapkiw, A. (2013) The Relationship Between Transformational Leadership and Cultural Intelligence: A Study of International School Leaders. *Journal of Educational Administration* **51**(6), pp. 836–854.

Lee, M., Hallinger, P. and Walker, A. (2012) Leadership Challenges in International Schools in the Asia Pacific Region: Evidence from Programme Implementation of the International Baccalaureate. *International Journal of Leadership in Education* **15**(3), pp. 289–310.

Machin, D. (2014) Professional Educator or Professional Manager? the Contested Role of the for-Profit International School Principal. *Journal of Research in International Education* **13**(1), pp. 19–29.

Slough-Kuss, Y. (2014) Cultural Diversity Among Heads of International Schools: Potential Implications for International Education. *Journal of Research in International Education* **13**(3), pp. 218–234.

12 Leadership for Flourishing Schools: From Research to Practice

Andy Wolfe and Lynn E. Swaner

Introduction

In 1811, a church leader in London, Joshua Watson, gathered together a group of like-minded individuals with a vision for their churches to create free educational institutions to serve the children of their parishes. At that point in time, there was no access to education for families who could not pay for it. Thus, the Church of England globally pioneered the provision of schooling for families of every socioeconomic background by opening schools which grew quickly in size and popularity and spread across England through the Church of England's parish system. It was a culture-changing moment of social justice which would change the nation's approach to education and go on to influence educational provision on a global scale.

Over two hundred years later, the Church of England oversees just under 5000 schools in 41 dioceses, and as such is the largest provider of schools in the country. In total, the Church of England educates over one million students, representing approximately 20 per cent of the English education system. In 2016, the Church of England published its vision for education, entitled *Deeply Christian, Serving the Common Good*, which outlines the core purpose of education around four themes:

- **Educating for Wisdom, Knowledge, and Skills** – Fostering discipline, confidence, and delight in seeking wisdom and knowledge (including a healthy and life-giving tension between knowledge-rich and biblical wisdom curriculum approaches) and fully developing talents in all areas of life.
- **Educating for Hope and Aspiration** – Seeking healing, repair and renewal, coping wisely with things and people going wrong, opening horizons and guiding people into ways of fulfilling them.
- **Educating for Community and Living Well Together** – Ensuring a core focus on relationships, participation in communities and the qualities of character that enable people to flourish together.
- **Educating for Dignity and Respect** – Ensuring the basic principle of respect for the value and preciousness of each person, treating each person as a unique individual of inherent worth.

This is a vision that is for the whole education system, not simply Church of England schools. It has underpinned the national Statutory Inspection of Anglican and Methodist Schools (SIAMS) inspection framework and has been used by thousands of schools and multi-academy trusts (MATs) to explore

DOI: 10.4324/9781003321439-12

the relationship between a school's vision; its day-to-day lived experience, and ethos-enhancing out-comes. At the core of this framework is a central question: "How effective is the school's distinctive Christian vision, established and promoted by leadership at all levels, in enabling pupils to flourish?" This chapter examines research on flourishing in schools to frame this question, and concludes with reflections on leadership dispositions and practices for flourishing in schools.

The broader educational context

Quite understandably, a significant amount of attention has been given to the description, analysis, and measurement of the achievement of children in schools. In many countries, this has resulted however in a reductionist view of education and overall schooling experience. More recently, some have called for an expanded view of educational success, including one based in the concept of 'flourishing' – rooted in Aristotelian virtue ethics, character education, positive psychology, and well-being: 'Schools today exist in an era of heightened accountability for educational outcomes, measured almost exclusively via standardised testing... 'flourishing' offers a more expansive view of the purposes and processes of education' (Swaner et al., 2019).

When considering flourishing schools as whole institutions, it is important to highlight the impor-tance of the flourishing of adults alongside, and interacting with, children. Schools are not simply collections of discrete programmes and classrooms run by individuals who operate independently of each other. Rather, schools involve webs of relationships and reciprocal actions between leaders, teachers, staff, students, families, and others who engage with and in the school community. This recalls the words written by the Rev. Dr Martin Luther King, Jr, in his letter from a Birmingham Jail (1963): 'We are caught in an inescapable network of mutuality, tied in a single garment of destiny'. This ecology of flourishing is a vision of interdependence of all parts of the school system, for without flourishing adults, there will be few flourishing children.

And yet across much of education, flourishing is often far from the norm. In fact, it seems that many factors serve to inhibit flourishing in schools. These include external factors like economic pressures, students' struggles outside of school, and societal rifts related to inequality and injus-tice. Structural factors common in educational systems also work against flourishing, such as an underlying competition model (with students and schools competing on the basis of academic achievement, and schools and individual teachers competing for resources). Schools are also impacted by reductionist views of the purposes of education, reflected in shallow definitions and measures of success for which our societies have settled. For example, gateway exams restrict access to higher education, while at the same time most school curricula are exclusively designed as preparation for university attendance; this not only creates an educational funnel that restricts opportunity for many students within a given system but also restricts the educational system's definition of 'success' in both school and life. Thus, while schools' mission statements may be loftily expansive, the daily experience of leaders, teachers, and students alike reflects a much narrower story around education.

By engaging with a broader vision for educational flourishing, educational leaders will find fresh vision and energy to re-imagine their schools – and themselves – as what they desire them to be. This begins with the understanding that the health of everyone in the educational ecosystem matters to the health of everyone else. Put simply, students, educators, and school communities flourish together, or not at all.

Questions for discussion

1. How does the current educational context and system limit schools' abilities to address holistic learning and growth for students?
2. In what ways do external pressures for accountability, often enacted through standardised testing regimes, constrict the work of leaders and teachers in schools?
3. What outcomes might an educational system that is designed for human flourishing prioritise?

Domains of flourishing: Insights from research

The research-based vision for 'Flourishing Together' (Swaner and Wolfe, 2021) shared in this chapter has emerged from a long-term quantitative analysis of the components of flourishing undertaken across over 120,000 leaders, teachers, students, alumni, and school families since 2017, in North America as well as in international schools around the world. This Flourishing Schools research initiative resulted in the development of the Flourishing Schools Culture Model (FSCM), shown in the model below (Swaner et al., 2019) (Figure 12.1).

This model, validated in 2020 by Cardus (an independent think tank and research organization in Canada), outlines five interacting domains of flourishing: *Purpose; Relationships; Learning; Resources;* and *Well-being.* These five domains do not work alone in shallow silos but together in deep interdependence, at the level of the student, the educator, and the school itself, as shown in the centre of the model. The FSCM thus encourages school leaders to reflect deeply on these elements of school life, with a particular call to consider the flourishing of adults and children together,

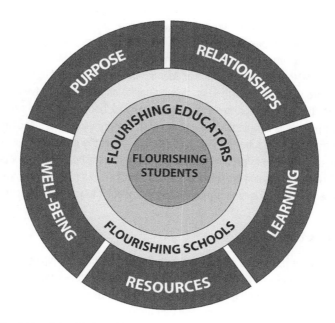

Figure 12.1 The Flourishing School Culture Model

which leads to the flourishing of the school as a whole. The next section of this chapter examines these five domains in greater depth.

The purpose domain

A clear understanding of a school's shared purpose – *why* leaders, teachers, and students are together at school – sets schools on the path to flourishing. A common purpose helps all constituents unified around clear goals and to work toward a 'greater good' to which they aspire together. For example, the Flourishing Schools research found that flourishing outcomes were positively linked with everyone within the school – from trustees to administrators to teachers to staff members – having a shared sense of *responsibility*. Responsibility implies much more than agreement or even buy-in, but rather involves leaders and teachers interpreting purpose in and through their daily lives and work. Rather than being dictated, shared responsibility must be cultivated through collective dialogue and reflection. The Flourishing Schools research also found that a school's purpose must extend beyond the school walls – involving more than a calling held just by those who work in the school – to a genuine *partnership* with school families. The Flourishing Schools research showed that when families feel they are a part of the school's mission, and that their involvement with the school is truly valued, there is a positive link with greater flourishing outcomes.

For students, the Flourishing Schools research identified *holistic learning* as a key construct linked to student flourishing, which entails teaching 'the heart and soul, as well as the mind'. In other words, holistic learning involves more than just cognitive and academic growth. Most educators recognise that students are complex individuals who think, feel, act, and relate to others, and an education that is holistic in nature attends to all of these facets of the human person. This includes the arts and sports, of course, but also depending on the mission of the school, might include character development, morality and ethics, or spiritual formation.

While an education that prioritises flourishing would also prioritise these dimensions of humanity through holistic learning experiences, most educational systems across the world are driven by discretely measured academic outcomes. Additionally, for most schools regardless of sector, programmes and personnel that are deemed 'non-academic' are usually the first to be reduced or cut when financial pressures are exerted. Nevertheless, an incomplete education can have little hope of making a significant and positive contribution to the wholeness of mind, body, emotions, and relationships that contribute to flourishing. This is reflected, at least in part, in increasing stress and anxiety among students and in high degrees of teacher burnout and attrition. While the growing emphasis on social and emotional learning and trauma-informed instruction in recent years is heartening, deeper conversations are needed to ask how schools and classrooms can be structured as places for holistic learning, up to and including how educational success is measured for students, teachers, and schools.

The relationships domain

Flourishing is dependent upon who people are with – together in community. As relational beings, the degree to which people value, honour, and care for each other – students, teachers, leaders, and families alike – impacts mutual flourishing. School communities that are characterised by a sense of belonging are places where everyone can flourish together. This includes all members of the school community, as they relate with and to one another.

Along these lines, the Flourishing Schools research points to the importance of proactively building positive relationships with the community immediately connected to the school, first by *engaging families* of students. The research found this involves teachers getting to know parents, guardians, or other significant adults in students' lives through frequent and effective communication. The research also found evidence that flourishing is linked with *community engagement*, specifically when leaders engaged with the surrounding community by regularly tapping into community resources, including networking and resource-sharing with other schools. Other research has identified positive outcomes linked to school engagement with parents, community agencies, and organisations, in terms of school improvement and student achievement (Murphy, 2016; Reynolds *et al.*, 2014; Shannon and Bylsma, 2007).

Similarly, diversity in the student body is linked positively to flourishing outcomes. This confirms that diversity is not just a good idea in principle, but that flourishing together in schools is related to the degree to which 'together' is inclusive. The research also clearly showed, however, that diversity remains a challenge for many schools. For this reason, schools need to be intentional in recruitment and admissions processes, as well as ensure that the school environment is welcoming and inclusive of students from varying backgrounds when they matriculate and throughout their school experience.

When it comes to the relationship among leaders within a school, the Flourishing Schools research identified the importance of collective leadership, first through *leadership interdependence,* where all leaders, including the board of trustees, come from diverse backgrounds, are transparent about their weaknesses, and rely on others to offset those weaknesses. Second, collective leadership also relies on building relational trust between leaders. Specifically, the research found that *supportive leadership* – evidenced by all staff members agreeing that leaders are trusted and 'have their backs' and that they empower staff to make decisions – was positively linked with flourishing outcomes.

The next type of educator relationships is that between teachers. The Flourishing Schools research found that *collaboration* between teachers was correlated with positive outcomes for flourishing, when defined as teachers' belief that learning from, and with, other teachers inspire and propels them to grow and become better in their craft. Other research has shown that teacher collaboration on how to teach what students need to learn – in activities like unpacking standards, mapping curriculum, designing lessons, constructing assessments that measure mastery of lessons – is correlated with academic improvement (Chenoweth, 2007, 2015). By collaborating with colleagues, educators can, as Peter Senge articulates, 'continually expand their capacity to create the results they truly desire, where new and expansive patterns of thinking are nurtured, where collective aspiration is set free, and where people are continually learning how to learn together' (Senge, 1990: 12).

When it comes to relationships between teachers and students, the Flourishing Schools research linked flourishing with *mentoring students*, defined pointing out talent in each student, being aware of students' struggles at school or home, and truly coming to know students on a personal level. While relationships are crucial for the flourishing of all students, they are absolutely critical for the most vulnerable students. Along these lines, the Flourishing Schools research found that a *caring environment*, in which students feel safe and are protected, is positively linked with flourishing outcomes. This is especially true in the case of adverse childhood experiences – such as trauma, loss, abuse, or neglect – which can result in insecure attachments for students, often manifesting in schools as behaviour issues or failure to progress. Louise Bombèr's (2007) work on trauma-informed education underscores the need to understand each student with these experiences on a personal level and, on the basis of that relational knowledge, adjust how we teach and care for each one. A caring environment must also prevent and protect students from bullying, which is a common source of trauma *in* schools. Bullying is typically not an isolated incident between two people, but rather 'a dynamic social relationship problem' that requires a broader, school-level approach in addition to an interventional approach with individual students (Kyriakides *et al.*, 2013: 453). On this point, the Relational Schools Foundation found that where healthy relational systems and processes are intentionally put into place at a school, bullying levels are lower and student well-being is higher (Loe, 2016).

The learning domain

Undoubtedly, learning is what students are supposed to do at school, and the quality of that learning is supremely important. At the same time, student learning is intricately linked to the learning of educators and the school itself as an organisation. When all learn together in a 'community of practice', as a group of people who 'share a concern or passion for something they do and learn how to do it better as they interact regularly', all grow together (Wenger and Wenger-Trayner, 2015: 1). Indeed, the Flourishing Schools research points to the importance of developing a collective *learning culture* that is future-focused and marked by continual improvement.

A key part of this is an *outcomes focus* on the part of leaders, which entails a consistent prioritising of learning activities that make a difference for students; while this may seem intuitive, classrooms are busy places, with a host of needs and pressures competing for the attention of leaders, teachers, and students alike. Related to this, leaders and teachers need to use *data-informed instruction* to improve student learning on a continual basis. Again, this may be easier said than done: in schools where data is sought primarily for accountability purposes, a shift is needed in terms of broadening the outcomes examined and in using the resulting data to inform everyday practice. Data sources should be qualitative as well as quantitative and may be generated by varied practices such as conducting formative and varied assessments of student learning, evaluating teacher practices, and involving students in designing their own assessments as co-learners on the educational journey. And leaders' use of *systems thinking,* or the ability to see situations from a holistic perspective, is linked positively with school flourishing. This entails considering the potential impact on students, educators, and the overall school when planning for change, thereby helping leaders to better address the source of complex problems and improve the likelihood they can lead their teams in mapping out sufficient strategies and solutions.

Along these lines, one of the strongest linkages in the Flourishing Schools research was between flourishing outcomes and *feedback on teaching* that enables real-time adjustments in practice. Although for leaders this may bring to mind the practice of formal observations as part of teacher supervision and evaluation, this is not necessarily what is meant; rather, research suggests that peer observation – with teachers providing constructive feedback offered in real-time – is more powerful for teacher learning (Reeves, 2008, 2010). The input of teaching and learning coaches, as well as peer mentors, can likewise be effective means of providing feedback on instruction.

Peter Senge and colleagues assert that where there is no student engagement, there is no learning (Senge *et al.*, 2012). The Flourishing Schools research likewise found that *engaged learning* for students is linked to flourishing. In considering what engaged learning looks like, it is helpful to mention that other researchers and practitioners employ different adjectives to modify the word 'learning' (such as 'deeper', 'authentic', 'transformational', etc.). While there may be differences in the specific pedagogies encompassed or endorsed by each, they all involve two similar goals: first, to differentiate between the 'learner as passive knowledge receiver' approach and more active, collaborative, learner-centred, and student-directed approaches; and second, to broaden the scope of learning from the exclusively academic or cognitive to include social-emotional, spiritual, physical, artistic, and other outcomes.

Additionally, the Flourishing Schools research found that a strengths-based or *individualised learning* approach – involving metacognition, or students' learning how they learn best – is positively linked with flourishing. This requires encouraging reflection, or helping students to think about their learning and growth and engage in self-discovery. Other research shows that when students are encouraged to reflect on their learning through journaling, discussion, learning portfolios, and other methods, 'knowledge retention is higher, and students are able to make stronger connections across curricular areas' (D'Erizans and Bibbo, 2015: 80). Finally, the ways in which schools work toward inclusion for students with disabilities is correlated with flourishing. Specifically, the Flourishing Schools research found a positive link between flourishing outcomes and a school's responsiveness to the needs of students with disabilities – defined as teaching staff working together to support students appropriately, aided by processes and resources for identifying and responding to students' needs.

The resources domain

Schools are shaped by access to physical, technological, and human resources, which in turn shapes people's experiences at school – students, educators, and families alike. Not surprisingly, the Flourishing Schools research identified the importance of *resource planning* where financial planning was a strength of trustees for school flourishing. The research also confirmed that having *qualified staff* at a school, defined as those who are credentialed and have sufficient professional experience, is linked with flourishing outcomes.

In addition to these constructs, the Flourishing Schools research also found that leaders' beliefs about resources can play an inhibiting role when it comes to school flourishing. Specifically, the research identified as significant the construct of *resource constraints* – a belief held by leadership that the school could be more effective if not for fiscal restraints, and that the school lacks the resources to make changes. While lack of resources is a problem for schools everywhere, this belief focuses the attention of leaders on what their schools do not have. This might be considered as a school-level equivalent of Carol Dweck's (2016) 'fixed' versus 'growth' mindset, whereby leaders who are focused on what is lacking in their schools may not have the mindset to consider creative solutions with the resources their schools do have. A growth mindset toward resources may lead to openness to repurposing space in unconventional ways; sunsetting programs that have enjoyed historic success to make way for innovative offerings; and reassigning staff based on strengths and opportunities for growth versus seniority or rank.

While mindset toward resources matters, the research also shows that having *sufficient resources* – including classroom materials, technology, and school buildings in good condition – are all positively linked to flourishing. This is an unsurprisingly but still significant finding, as the reality around much of the world is that gaping disparities in resources exist between schools in different communities and settings. These worldwide gaps can be caused by educational funding systems and schemes that produce inequity, by lack of economic opportunity and mobility within a community, by violence or cycles of poverty fuelled by institutionalised racism and gender bias, and by the crises of genocide, war, and displacement. Where these issues and resulting disparities exist in communities, they often manifest in schools through dropout rates, mental health issues, bullying and violence, and student and family disengagement. Ultimately, this is a question of how societies steward the potential of children and young people who are their most valuable resource.

Leaders create the possibility for remedying action when they ask whose potential is maximised through access to resources like excellent school choices, enrichment opportunities, safe housing, quality medical care, and technology. They can then ask whose potential is inhibited by lack of access to the same – to the detriment not just of individual children and young people but also of families, neighbourhoods, communities, and entire countries. Leaders also need to ask what schools, educators, and students can do – together – to work toward removing disadvantage in institutions, communities, and societies. Educators would be remiss if they did not involve students centrally in all of these efforts, perhaps through service-learning, student-led outreach, and partnerships with community groups and houses of worship. As school constituents engage in these efforts together, students can learn how to advocate for themselves and others, address disparity of resources wherever they find it in their lives and communities, and develop perseverance in the face of what may seem to be insurmountable challenges at the core of society. Undoubtedly, these are all skills the next generation will need in abundance if they are to lead the way toward flourishing together.

The well-being domain

The Children's Society in the UK defines well-being in its annual *The Good Childhood Report* as '"how we are doing" as individuals, communities and as a nation, and how sustainable this is for the future' (Children's Society, 2020a: 3). The physical and emotional health of students, characterised by healthy habits and developing resilience, is critical to whether – and how – students flourish. The same holds true of teachers and leaders. Those in helping professions like education can only help others out of a place of abundance; otherwise, educator burnout and poorly educated students will result. For this reason, flourishing schools prioritise the well-being of all members of their community.

The question of well-being in schools has become a particularly challenging one in recent years. Most leaders would readily identify a decline in student well-being and its impact on learning, the classroom environment, and the school overall. This would appear to be supported by statistics; for example, The Children's Society also found that in 2020, 18 per cent of children in the UK were deemed to have low well-being, which was the highest percentage in the last five annual household surveys and reflects declines in children's happiness with life overall, as well as with their appearance, schools, and friends' (Children's Society, 2020a). A supplemental report on the impacts of the COVID-19 pandemic in the same year showed increases in feelings of isolation and adverse effects on cognitive well-being for children (Children's Society, 2020b). Further, the UK children's mental health charity Place2B notes that one in eight children have diagnosable mental health problems, many of which continue into adulthood (Place2Be, 2020).

For students, the Flourishing Schools research identified *resilience* as an important construct linked specifically to well-being. Resilience can be described as 'the existence of assets and protective factors in the social context, the ability to adapt to combat adversity, or the developmental outcomes that result from coping positively with adversity' (Briggs et al., 2011: 171). A high level of resilience is associated not only with better academic performance in school but also with higher levels of critical thinking and a range of non-cognitive outcomes, including greater opportunities in life (Bali and Sharma, 2018; Blackburn, 2018). Thankfully, resilience has been receiving increased attention in schools in recent years; across educational sectors, schools are incorporating social and emotional learning goals as well as training faculty and staff in ways to nurture resilience through research-informed practices (Tomlinson, 2013).

The importance of well-being in schools is not limited to students, however. Data suggests that close to half of teachers report the highest levels of professional stress – at the same rate as nurses and higher than physicians – and that four-fifths of teachers report feeling both physically and emotionally exhausted every day. Nancy Lever and colleagues identify a *symbiotic relationship* between the well-being of educators and students in school, as 'teacher burnout is predictive of student academic outcomes, including being correlated with lower levels of student effective learning and lower motivation… [Moreover] teacher burnout appears to affect the stress levels of the students they teach' (Lever *et al.*, 2019: 6).

Not surprisingly, the Flourishing Schools research found that *stress* for both teachers and leaders – defined as experiencing constant feelings of being overwhelmed, accompanied by a lack of time to prepare or to focus on health – is negatively correlated with flourishing in schools. In reducing leaders' stress, strategies can include sharing responsibilities through collective leadership, careful examination of workloads, increasing leaders' agency and decision-making power, and making mental health a priority (DeWitt, 2020). Failure to address stress in systematic ways not only represents a missed opportunity to nurture educators' well-being but also reinforces enduring stigma around mental health and unhelpfully relegates stress-related challenges to questions of performance and supervision. When it comes to addressing stress, opening up communication will be key: schools may need to utilise community resources, such as the assistance of qualified mental health professionals, to initiate and sustain conversations around educator stress.

The Flourishing Schools research also identified *healthy living* as positively linked with flourishing outcomes. This construct includes adequate rest, nutrition, and physical activity. Importantly, a programme 'here and there' does not always add up to an overall school environment that promotes well-being – rather, an integrated and intentional approach is needed. This might start with a well-being 'audit', in which a cross-constituent team convenes to discuss issues of concern in the school environment and daily schedule, as well as target and prioritise areas for improvement. Such a team should include students who, in addition to providing valuable insight, can also gain practical problem-solving experience and meet various learning objectives related to health, science, psychology, and other subjects. The guiding question for such efforts should move us from viewing well-being in schools as something to address 'if only we can find the time' to something that is a primary emphasis because it creates the preconditions for learning, growth, and overall flourishing together.

Questions for discussion

1. How might a holistic model of flourishing in schools, like the one identified in the Flourishing Schools research, be used by school leaders in their practice?
2. When looking at the five domains of flourishing (*Purpose, Relationships, Learning, Resources, and Well-being*), which ones are most challenging for school leaders in today's educational context?
3. How could school leaders build consensus around a holistic model of flourishing among all school constituents, including teachers, trustees, parents and guardians, and students themselves?

Leadership dispositions for flourishing

Cultivating an ecology of educational flourishing will lead educators to reassess priorities, change rhythms, and re-imagine practices so they better align with a vision for flourishing together. This is because any focus on the development of flourishing students and adults in flourishing schools needs to focus on the very practical outworking of this leadership thinking. To help in this transformational process from research to leadership practice, three essential dispositions – or qualities of character – can be identified for leaders. These are being *'called', 'connected',* and *'committed'* to flourishing. These dispositions emerged from the core leadership document published by the Church of England in 2020 (Ford and Wolfe, 2020). This document unpacks in detail the kind of model of leadership that is important to flourishing schools.

The first disposition for flourishing is a sense that leaders are *called* to lead flourishing schools. The word 'called' is used in the sense of the word 'vocation' – that there is a goal worthy of one's life's work, one that is deeply meaningful and for which one is well-suited, and one that will produce fullness in one's own life as it is pursued. This is true for children and young people, for leaders and teachers, and for schools and communities. This echoes Angela Duckworth's (2016: 149) parable in her book *Grit*:

Three bricklayers are asked: 'What are you doing?'

The first says, 'I am laying bricks.'
The second says, 'I am building a church.'
And the third says, 'I am building the house of God.'
The first bricklayer has a job.
The second has a career.
The third has a calling.

This sense of vocation is not limited to individualised pursuits, but one that can be explored and developed together. It can help define a community's 'why' – the motivation and underpinning structures of thought and language which ultimately define practice and pursuit of outcomes. This dispositional view enables leaders to re-envision the holistic nature and process of education and to move beyond efforts to reform, improve, or otherwise change schools based on a narrow set of criteria. It permits leaders to re-imagine schools as places that are designed, organised, led, managed, evaluated, and known for flourishing together.

Secondly, leaders are *connected* to lead flourishing in schools. In her virtual address to Oak National Academy during the global coronavirus pandemic, the Rt Revd. Rose Hudson-Wilkin (2020), Bishop of Dover, defined this disposition:

> There is a Zulu word called *ubuntu*. It means 'I am, because you are.' In other words, we are a people together. We are interdependent. We do not exist by ourselves. No one really flourishes unless we flourish together. Black and white, young and old, rich and poor, with and without disability. We are all God's children.

This vision is not solely for students, nor educators, nor schools, but the three interacting together. The three need each other, in times of plenty and in times of want. They are 'all parts of the same body' as the apostle Paul observed in his letter to the church at Corinth (1 Corinthians 12:25-26); they are the different sections of the orchestra playing as one; they are conversing guests eating together the same table; they are fellow labourers in the same garden. They can only exist in the same place – in a school – because of one another. And each one's flourishing is dependent on their flourishing together, which requires fundamental shifts in grammar in schools – from 'I' to 'we', and from 'me' to 'us.'

Thirdly, leaders must be *committed* to flourishing together in their educational contexts. Educators know intuitively that flourishing takes time. Moreover, the journey to flourishing is often circuitous instead of direct – meaning that students and adults may look very much as though they are 'failing' at something, but if given the opportunity to grow through setbacks, they can acquire important skills like patience and build essential capacities like resilience. It is crucial then to see flourishing not just as a state of being but also as a long-term process – one to which leaders must be fully committed. Having a long horizon for flourishing is perhaps the biggest challenge to the way educational systems are currently designed, as most prioritise immediate, observable results, as well as every identifiable efficiency to obtain those results. Effecting change as leaders will require a commitment to an ecological understanding of the time it takes for children and young people to learn and develop, as well as the uniqueness and unevenness of the process for every individual.

Questions for discussion

1. As a leader, describe whether and how you feel 'called' to your role and to education in general.
2. How can school leaders participate, develop, or otherwise engage with networks of other leaders, so that they can be connected with other leaders for their own flourishing?
3. Given the challenges facing schools today, how can leaders develop the long-term vision, resiliency, and self-care to sustain their commitment to education?

Conclusion

Ultimately, re-imagining schools as sites for flourishing together will require leaders to push beyond various illusions of the industrial and information revolutions, many of which have obscured very important realities about what it means to be human – and in turn, what it means to educate human beings. Where those illusions have shaped practice in schools, leaders need to commit to questioning, dismantling, and re-imagining those practices, so that students, educators, and school communities can truly flourish. In their place, leaders must develop a range of new leadership practices grounded in the dispositions of being called, connected, and committed. These include leading learning, removing disadvantage, sustaining vision, building resilience, accepting vulnerability, and learning love.

Finally, leaders must also encourage and hold each other accountable to a more expansive vision of educational flourishing. This is why the Church of England's inspection schedule prioritises flourishing in its overarching question: again, 'How effective is the school's distinctive Christian vision, established and promoted by leadership at all levels, in enabling pupils and adults to flourish?' When reformulated and particularised for the unique vision of each school, this question can help guide leaders in their re-imagination of educational practice in the domains of flourishing – from a school's purpose, held and enacted together; to mutual relationships that engender belonging; to collective learning; to wise and generous stewardship of resources; to holistic and interdependent well-being. This question can also generate the inspiration and courage leaders, and their teams will need for transformative change as they reflect on their shared calling, connectedness, and commitment to flourishing together.

Summary points

- In place of a reductionist view of education and overall schooling experience – with success principally defined by academic achievement and solely measured by standardised testing and university placement – the concept of 'flourishing' offers an expanded view of educational success and a foundation for more holistic education.
- Because the flourishing of leaders and teachers in schools is interdependent with the flourishing of students, there will be few flourishing students without flourishing educators; this means that schools must prioritise the learning, growth, and well-being of staff alongside children and young people.
- The research-backed and validated Flourishing School Culture Model outlines five domains of flourishing for educators, students, and schools: *Purpose; Relationships; Learning; Resources;* and *Well-being.*
- Three essential dispositions – or qualities of character – can be identified for leaders of flourishing schools; these are being 'called', 'connected', and 'committed' to flourishing.
- Leaders must seek to develop a range of new leadership practices grounded in a view toward educational flourishing and the dispositions of being called, connected, and committed; these include leading learning, removing disadvantage, sustaining vision, building resilience, accepting vulnerability, and learning love.

Recommended reading

Ford, D.F. and Wolfe, A. (2020) *Called, Connected, Committed: 24 leadership practices for educational leaders.* London: The Church of England Education Office.
Swaner, L.E. and Wolfe, A. (2021) *Flourishing Together: A christian vision for students, educators, and schools.* Grand Rapids, MI: Eerdmans.

References

Bali, D. and Sharma, A. (2018) Art of Fostering Resilience in Adolescents. *Indian Journal of Health and Well-Being* **9**(1), pp. 73–75.

Blackburn, B.R. (2018) Five Ways to Strengthen Student Resilience. *The Education Digest* **83**(5), pp. 47–50.

Bombèr, L.M. (2007) *Inside I'm Hurting: Practical strategies for supporting children with attachment difficulties in schools*. London: Worth.

Briggs, K., Akos, M., Czyszczon, P. and Eldrige, G. (2011) Assessing and Promoting Spiritual Wellness as a Protective Factor in Secondary Schools. *Counseling and Values* **55**(2), pp. 171–184.

Chenoweth, K. (2007) *It's Being Done': Academic success in unexpected schools*. Cambridge, MA: Harvard Educational Publishing Group.

Chenoweth, K. (2015) How Do We Get There from Here? *Educational Leadership* **75**(2), pp. 16–20.

Children's Society (2020a) *The Good Childhood Report*. London: The Children's Society.

Children's Society (2020b) *Life on Hold: Children's well-being and covid-19*. London: The Children's Society.

D'Erizans, R. and Bibbo, T. (2015) Time to Reflect: E-Portfolios and the Development of Growth Mindsets. *Independent School* **74**(2), pp. 78–85.

DeWitt, P. (2020) We Should Be Concerned About the Mental Health of Principals. *Education Week*, August 25, 2020. Available at: https://www.edweek.org/leadership/opinion-we-should-be-concerned-about-the-mental-health-of-principals/2020/08. (Accessed 7 October 2022).

Duckworth, A. (2016) *Grit: The power of passion and perseverance*. New York, NY: Scribner.

Dweck, C.S. (2016) *Mindset: The new psychology of success*. New York, NY: Ballantine Books.

Ford, D.F. and Wolfe, A. (2020) *Called, Connected, Committed: 24 leadership practices for educational leaders*. London: The Church of England Education Office.

King, M.L. Jr (1963) *Letter from a Birmingham Jail*. Available at: https://kinginstitute.stanford.edu/king-papers/documents/letter-birmingham-jail. (Accessed 7 October 2022).

Kyriakides, L., Creemers, B., Papastylianou, D. and Papadatou-Pastou, M. (2013) Improving the School Learning Environment to Reduce Bullying: An Experimental Study. *Scandinavian Journal of Educational Research* **58**(4), pp. 453–478.

Lever, N., Mathis, E. and Mayworm, A. (2019) School Mental Health Is Not Just for Students: Why Teacher and School Staff Wellness Matter. *Report on Emotional and Behavioral Disorders in Youth* **17**(1), pp. 6–12.

Loe, R. (2016) *The Relational Teacher* (2nd Ed.). Cambridge: The Relational Schools Foundation.

Murphy, J. (2016) *Leading School Improvement: A framework for action*. West Palm Beach, FL: Learning Sciences International.

Place2Be (2020). Improving Children's Mental Health in Schools. Available at: https://www.place2be.org.uk. (Accessed 7 October 2022).

Reeves, D.B. (2008) *Reframing Teacher Leadership to Improve Your School*. Alexandria, VA: ASCD.

Reeves, D.B. (2010) *Transforming Professional Development into Student Results*. Alexandria, VA: ASCD.

Reynolds, D., Sammons, P., Fraine, B., Van Damme, J., Townsend, T., Teddlie, C. and Stringfield, S. (2014) Educational Effectiveness Research (EER): A State-of-the-Art Review. *School Effectiveness and School Improvement* **25**(2), pp. 197–230.

Senge, P.M. (1990) *The Fifth Discipline: The art and practice of the learning organization*. New York, NY: Doubleday/Currency.

Senge, P., Cambron-McCabe, N., Lucas, T., Smith, B., Dutton, J. and Kleiner, A. (2012) *Schools That Learn: A fifth discipline fieldbook for educators, parents, and everyone who cares about education*. New York, NY: Crown Business.

Shannon, G.S. and Bylsma, P. (2007) *Nine Characteristics of High-Performing Schools*. Olympia, WA: Office of Superintendent of Public Instruction.

Swaner, L.E., Marshall, C.A. and Tesar, S.A. (2019) *Flourishing Schools: Research on christian school culture and community*. Colorado Springs, CO: Association of Christian Schools International.

Swaner, L.E. and Wolfe, A. (2021) *Flourishing Together: A christian vision for students, educators, and schools*. Grand Rapids, MI: Eerdmans.

Tomlinson, C.A. (2013) One to Grow On: Growing Capable Kids. *Educational Leadership* **71**(1), pp. 86–87.

Wenger, E. and Wenger-Trayner, B. (2015) Communities of Practice: A brief introduction. Available at: https://scholarsbank.uoregon.edu/xmlui/bitstream/handle/1794/11736/A%20brief%20introduction%20to%20CoP.pdf?sequence=1&isAllowed=y.. (Accessed 7 October 2022).

13 A Practical Exploration of Non-teaching Leadership Roles within the Further Education and Skills Sector (FES)

Brendan Coulson, John Everson, and Sheridan Brown

Introduction

The further education and skills (FES) sector provides education to 1.6 million adult and young adult learners in England (Association of Colleges, 2022) and offers a wide variety of academic and vocational courses to students aged fourteen and above. These courses are delivered in a range of large and small educational settings, such as further education colleges, private training providers, sixth-form colleges, apprenticeship providers, universities, prisons, and adult education.

To provide a competitive and high-quality learning experience for students, FES providers need to employ the right people in a range of positions, including in non-teaching leadership roles.

This chapter provides a practical exploration of non-teaching leadership roles within the FES sector. It considers roles within four areas of work:

- Leadership in supporting learners and learning;
- leadership in encouraging and supporting employer engagement;
- leadership of activities that support staff; and
- leadership of corporate systems.

The importance of employability to FES

In the UK, a significant measure of the success of an educational setting is the progression of its students. Within post-16 education, the focus is on progression to further study and/or employment. For post-18 education, greater emphasis is placed on graduate employment (Office for Students, 2021).

For more than a century, government policy has focused on skills-based approaches to improve employment outcomes. For example, Samuelson's 1884 report was commissioned to inquire into technical skill instruction in several countries to inform UK skills policy. And in 2022, the government published the Skills and Post-16 Education Act to enshrine, in law, reforms to transform education and training. This aimed to support more people to enter the job market, and to address the UK skills shortage. In the context of an ever-evolving labour market, it is essential to identify what skills are needed to succeed in a particular sector. The same is true of the FES sector, and the non-teaching leadership roles within it.

In recent years, theorists have tried to explain the complexity of thinking around employability through models that go beyond skills development to encompass personal qualities, attitudes, and behaviours. These models can support graduates to understand the wider requirements of

DOI: 10.4324/9781003321439-13

a role, reflect on their existing abilities and identify areas for development. Graduates can use an employability model to visualise themselves in a role, focus their career aspirations and guide their personal development.

Theoretical employability models

To frame a discussion of what skills are needed to enter and progress within non-teaching leadership roles in the FES sector, three theoretical employability models will be considered. Please refer to the reference list at the end of this chapter to find full details of each model's publication, and these also include graphical representation of each model.

The Career Edge Model was suggested by Dacre Pool and Sewell (2007) to describe the concept of employability. The model is used internationally as a framework for enabling graduates to reach their employment potential. There are five equally important aspects that combine to enhance employment prospects, these include:

- **Career** Development Learning – acquiring knowledge, concepts, skills, and attitudes which will equip individuals to manage their careers.
- **E**xperience (Work and Life) – work experience and other life experiences that support progression into a career.
- **D**egree Subject Knowledge, Skills, and Understanding – developing subject knowledge and a passion for learning.
- **G**eneric Skills – supporting the development of enterprise skills, such as communication, team working, problem-solving, and digital literacy.
- **E**motional Intelligence – develop abilities in emotional awareness, relationships, well-being, and so forth.

The model illustrates the need to address all aspects, without which potential employability is reduced. The model suggests that an individual should be given the opportunity to experience all the components, which they then reflect upon and evaluate. The main aim is to support the development of self-efficacy, self-esteem, and self-confidence, in order to enhance their employability.

The Graduate Capital Model is Tomlinson's (2017) more recent articulation of employability, against which educational settings can map their curriculum and learning outcomes. Each component inter-relates and is of equal importance in preparing graduates to achieve longevity within their career. The components are defined as follows:

- **Human Capital** – developing knowledge and skills to be confident in the labour market.
- **Social Capital** – establishing networks and social relations to improve knowledge and to gain access to employers.
- **Cultural Capital** – being able to present oneself in a creditable manner, and appreciating the different culture of sectors and organisations.
- **Psychological Capital** – being able to move into and adapt within a fluid job market, and to manage the challenges and pressures of working.
- **Identity Capital** – interpreting experiences, values, and achievements to support the development of a professional profile and strategies to achieve career goals.

*The **Psycho-Social Model*** developed by Fugate *et al.* (2004) represents employability as three interlinking dimensions:

- **Personal Adaptability** – the ability to adapt to changing situations within employment.
- **Career Identity** – understanding how people define themselves in a particular work context.
- **Social and Human Capital** – understanding the benefits to individuals and organisations of making investments in social and human capital in the workplace.

This model encapsulates the common dimensions that influence a graduate's ability to actively adapt within their chosen career.

Each of these models recognises the importance of skills development to employability. But they also emphasise the importance of developing one's personal qualities, attitudes, and behaviours through both life-long and life-wide learning (Jackson, 2008).

To be a competent life-long and life-wide learner, one needs to foster an enduring aptitude for recognising opportunities for holistic development that may exist in any aspect of life (life-wide). Supporting one's personal, academic, and career development, requires reflection, and making conscious decisions about what to study, the activities to involve oneself in, and in what capacity. It also requires some consideration of potential future opportunities and occupations that may be desirable. Finally, it requires a permanent commitment to learning, either informally or through formal methods, as well as developing skills and personal qualities through a variety of experiences.

Reflecting the emergence of more expansive models of employability, government policy is beginning to look beyond skills development alone. For example, apprenticeships and higher technical qualifications are aligned to the knowledge, skills, and behaviours (KSBs) of sector-focused occupational standards (Institute for Apprenticeships and Technical Education, 2022). In view of this, the terms *knowledge, skills,* and *behaviours* will be used because of their alignment with the language of theoretical discussions around employability and because of their increasing currency in the employment market.

Knowledge can be defined as the information and technical detail that one must have to successfully meet the requirements of a role. *Skills* enable the application of one's knowledge; this is the 'doing' aspect of the role. Finally, *behaviours* are concerned with the mindset, attitude and approaches required for one to be competent within a specific occupation. While knowledge is often relevant to a specific role, skills and, even more so, behaviours are transferable; for example, being adaptable, proactive, and a team player would all be useful across many disciplines.

Non-teaching roles in further education and skills

Questions for discussion

Which theoretical employability model resonates with you? How would you use concepts from these models within your own educational journey to support your development of knowledge, skills, and behaviours?

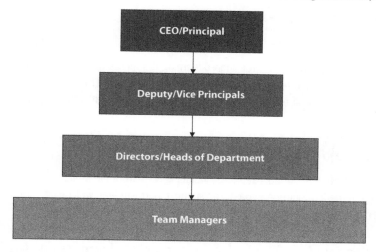

Figure 13.1 College Hierarchy

The remainder of the chapter will use knowledge, skills, and behaviours as a lens through which to explore a range of non-teaching leadership roles in the FES sector. The reader will be encouraged to consider how their own KSBs might prepare them, and need to develop, to secure such a role in the future.

Generally, an FES college follows a hierarchical management structure (Figure 13.1) typical of large businesses and organisations. The Chief Executive Officer or College Principal is at the top of the structure. Beneath them are distinct levels of management, including senior leadership and middle management. Together they are responsible for a range of operational areas and teams. This is an example of a tall organisational structure, where each level of management has a clear line of responsibility and control; allowing decision-making to flow from the top, down.

Non-teaching roles within a college can loosely be divided into four areas of work:

- supporting learners and learning;
- encouraging and supporting employer engagement;
- activities that support staff; and
- corporate systems.

By demonstrating the KSBs for a particular area of a college's work, graduates can progress through to leadership within that field. Different leadership positions will share some commonality in terms of KSBs. However, some will vary according to the focus and responsibilities of an area of work; this is discussed below.

Explanation of leadership roles and professional profiles

To create the four professional profiles used in this chapter, we asked a group of current leaders in FES to tell us about their careers, and the knowledge, skills and behaviours that have proved significant to their success. We have synthesised their responses into fictionalised profiles, which capture their experiences in FES.

Leadership in supporting learners and learning

Learning resources

Leaders of this area are responsible for shared learning resources across an FES institution, including: library; learning technologies; virtual learning environment; careers and employability hubs; and sustainability resources, and ensuring the exams office is compliant with the policies of the Joint Council for Qualifications.

Student support and safeguarding

This area oversees student support services, including: classroom learning support; learner attendance and engagement monitoring; pastoral support and student well-being; safeguarding; and equality, diversity and inclusion.

Carrie: Professional profile of a leader supporting learners and learning

My name is Carrie and I work as a Safeguarding Team Leader in a private training provider that offers training opportunities to young people who find mainstream college a challenge. Before I came to this role, I co-ordinated a team of additional learning support staff at a large college of FES. Safeguarding is a critical part of college life; it is essential that we do all we can to keep our young people safe and to comply with Ofsted expectations.

One of my main responsibilities is to ensure I stay up to date with any safeguarding legislation and agendas. I use this knowledge and understanding to help me develop ongoing training materials and CPD events for staff, to ensure they are fully conversant with safeguarding protocols in the organisation. I also write a monthly newsletter, which helps staff to react to any new developments. All staff should know who our 'Designated Safeguarding Leads' are, and it is my job to appoint, train, and monitor these leads. I also chair the organisation's Safeguarding Board, which reviews cases and shares practice.

In addition to ensuring that all staff are up-to-date with the latest safeguarding training, I also co-ordinate safeguarding information and messages aimed at students, including at induction, and through ongoing promotion of advice and guidance campaigns around our organisation.

Over the years, I have had to develop my skills in terms of being able to research and analyse the latest safeguarding policies and data, and to write reports which feed into safeguarding boards, self-assessment plans and strategic planning. Being a good communicator (both verbally and in writing) is a central part of my role.

The role of Safeguarding Team Leader can be quite harrowing – but I have a dogged sense of doing what is right. I have had to develop my ability to be unemotional, when needed, and to understand the limitations of my role. It is important that I am non-judgemental and compassionate, and aware of any potential biases that might be present in my thinking.

My advice for someone interested in this area of work would be: don't be afraid to start in a supportive role; don't turn down any opportunities to expand your experience; and don't be afraid to work out of your comfort zone. Make sure you are approachable and build up good contacts to help to develop your knowledge and skills.

Leadership in encouraging and supporting employer engagement

Apprenticeship and business engagement

Those with responsibility for leading this area manage all business engagement and income generation activities with small and medium-sized enterprises, large employers, local councils, local enterprise partnerships, chambers of commerce, and international partners.

An important aspect of this area of work is the oversight of work-based learning, for example apprenticeships, Skills Bootcamps, alignment with local skills improvement plans, and local funding offered to employers to upskill their workforce.

Amrit: Professional profile of a leader in encouraging and supporting employer engagement

I am Amrit and I lead on business and commercial engagement activities in a large college of FES. I manage a team of business engagement advisors. Prior to this role, I worked in hospitality and customer services.

Our department is required to develop strong links with employers. Our team is set targets to increase the number of apprentices and government-secured contracts, for example, European Social Fund, Skills Bootcamps, and employer-funded commercial activities.

This area of work requires solid communication skills and sales acumen, in order to create strong links with employers. Most of our day-to-day activities require us to network with businesses; this might include everything from attending employer networking events through to cold-calling activities. The initial objective is to secure an appointment with an employer.

Once contact has been made, we research their individual business in preparation for a conversation about how the college can support them to meet their training needs. The main objective of our team is to ensure that we are providing the training that a business requires; this is through the creation of a training plan. Once approved, this plan leads to us designing a recruitment strategy to attract a potential apprentice to the vacancy. We provide a full service, from initial recruitment to tailored off-the-job training.

If the business wants to develop their existing staff, we tailor training plans which include apprenticeship or non-apprenticeship routes. We meet regularly with the employer to address any issues relating to the training, and to offer further opportunities where necessary.

Everyone on our team must keep up to date on the apprenticeship funding rules, and any government initiatives that we can promote with employers. This relies on a good knowledge and understanding of business engagement, along with knowing how courses are designed and delivered. This is to ensure we are clear on the limitations of a course and training package.

Overall, this is an extremely rewarding role, but very challenging. You have to be resilient to withstand when employers do not want to engage with you, but proactive enough to respond quickly when they do. I have developed great networking, communication, and research skills. I am confident to discuss complex funding streams in simple terms to avoid confusing our clients. And I have developed strong analytical skills to work out timeframes, costs of delivery, and to calculate an employer's return on investment.

My advice for someone interested in this area of work is to be curious and passionate about providing training solutions to businesses. Seek exposure to as many situations as possible to become a confident speaker, networker, and salesperson. And look for opportunities where you can develop your communication and numeracy skills, as well as your ability to research and analyse into areas that you don't know much about.

Leadership of activities that support staff

IT support

This department oversees all information technology (IT), including the IT infrastructure, computer networks, servers, systems security, software management, IT maintenance, General Data Protection Regulation, system compliance, systems administration, and technical support.

Administrative support services

Administrative Support Services handle the smooth running of their institution by managing clerical teams and operations that secure efficiency and comply with institutional policies. These include: co-ordinating and minuting meetings, managing office supplies, course administration, front-of-house engagement with learners and visitors, student admissions, withdrawals, and transfers, maintaining student records, data analysis and reporting, and governance support.

Quality and staff development

Leaders of this area are responsible for all aspects of cross-college quality and improvement. Examples of work in this field include: monitoring the quality of teaching and learning through learning walks, lesson observations and work scrutiny; evaluating student surveys and course retention and achievement rates; and co-ordinating cross-college continuing professional development.

They ensure that courses adhere to standards laid out in assessment regulations and manage processes by which courses and the overall institution self-assess and plan improvement. Furthermore, the quality and staff development team will manage Ofsted visits and awarding body compliance.

Joe: Professional profile of a leader of activities that support staff

My name is Joe, and I am employed in a city further education college as Head of Quality. I started my professional life lecturing in functional skills English and mathematics, before moving into a middle leadership position, where I was responsible for leading the curriculum and line-managing others. My interests in coaching and quality assurance led to me moving into the Quality Team. As Head of Quality, I am part of the senior leadership team, with overall responsibility for quality assurance and improvement within my institution.

My main responsibility is for cross-college teaching and learning. I devise a strategy for quality in teaching and learning, which aligns with the college's vision and values. Then I lead the Quality Team in operationalising the strategy, by developing quality systems and processes, planning and delivering training to departments across the college, and fostering a culture of accountability. Consequently, I need to keep abreast of policy changes and innovations in teaching and learning, as well as being fully aware of the strengths and weaknesses of current practice in the college.

I am also responsible for the management of all inspections and reviews by external bodies, including acting as the college's nominee for Office for Standards in Education (Ofsted) inspections and leading on our accreditation as a provider of the Department for Education's matrix standard for assuring the delivery of high-quality information, advice, and guidance. This is 'high-stakes' work because it impacts on how the college is perceived externally. And its success relies on accurate self-evaluation and ambitious improvement planning.

One of the most rewarding aspects of my role is working to develop my colleagues. Professional development, including staff induction and initial teacher education, fits within my remit. We mentor and coach all colleagues to improve their teaching and learning; tailoring programmes to meet the needs of individual staff, making effective use of the GROW coaching model, and encouraging reflective practice.

To succeed in this kind of role, I think it helps if you have experience across a range of different institutions. This equips you with a broad knowledge of curriculum, pedagogy, and assessment. You also need to develop a clear understanding of quality assurance and improvement mechanisms.

In terms of the skills required of the role, you need to be able to articulate a clear and ambitious vision for quality improvement. You need to think and plan strategically. You need to have excellent relationship management skills so that you build strong, trusting, professional relationships and 'take others with you'. You need to have an eye for detail, as you systematically review performance and developments. And you need to support, challenge, and hold others to account.

I have found that it is vital to strike a balance between being assertive and being approachable. You're expected to ensure compliance and drive forward improvement, but this is easier if you've always got time to listen to, learn from and work with your colleagues. I am passionate about teaching and learning and supporting teachers to do the best job they can for our learners. It also helps if you're curious (maybe even nosey) about finding out what people in your own institution and beyond are doing. In this way, you can spot what's working and exciting new ideas, and then promote them to others.

My advice for someone interested in this area of work is to take every opportunity to see teaching and learning happening, reflect on what you see and identify what works and what could work even better. And do as much professional development of your own as possible!

Leadership of corporate systems

Human resources

Human resources (HR) is responsible for recruitment and workforce management, including writing HR policy, staff contracts, employment disputes and complaints, essential training of staff, staff performance processes, employee benefit schemes and pensions, compliance with employment law, governance, and legal advice.

Finance

Financial leadership maintains the overall financial position of the institution, including financial forecasting, monitoring and reporting, cross-college budgets, payroll, suppliers, internal and external audits, lettings, purchasing, and financial returns to governing and funding bodies such as the Education Skills Funding Agency.

Marketing

Leaders in this area are responsible for examining the FES market through competitor analysis and labour market intelligence. This is shared with course teams to inform course creation, development, and currency. The marketing team promotes an institution and its courses through the website, social media campaigns, hardcopy materials (for example, the prospectus) and general marketing. They engage with prospective learners in local schools and community-based organisations and organise events such as open days. They encourage existing and alumni students to progress to other courses.

Facilities and estates

This department manages the institution's premises and related services. These include general maintenance, cleaning, catering, car parking, security, and health and safety, through compliance with the Health and Safety Executive.

Simona: Professional profile of a leader in corporate services

I am Simona and I work within Corporate Services. This area consists of many functions, but I lead on marketing and communication.

The team I lead is the Student Recruitment Team. Members of my team are required to understand the local and national market, to ensure that our courses provide students with progression pathways through to employment or to a higher level of study. We analyse labour market intelligence in order to identify trends in employer needs, student demographics, current interests, and competitor offerings. This helps to keep us agile and responsive to employer and student needs.

We actively promote our courses to target groups, depending on student age, eligibility for funding, employment status and interest group. We tailor marketing activities to target audiences, including school leavers; adult learners; those wanting to retrain; and employer-led courses.

We plan and co-ordinate in-college open days and outreach events in local schools and community centres. These involve talks and 'stands' where prospective students can make enquiries. For employer-related courses, such as apprenticeships, we arrange events that encourage employers to visit the college to discuss what opportunities we have on offer. We also target marketing through sponsoring local chambers of commerce, and business awards events.

Working within the college, we also promote progression routes to our current students. This can be through in-class talks, our website and poster campaigns around the college. As our college offers both further education and higher education courses, our marketing actively seeks to encourage students to 'step-up' to higher education within the college, once they have completed their further education route.

Our marketing campaigns involve lots of social media advertising, as well as making hardcopy materials available, such as leaflets and prospectuses. We design advertising on a bigger scale, such as billboards and promotions on buses, showcasing the student experience. We also create videos, demonstrating how the college supports students to succeed. And we use these videos through our website, on social media campaigns and during talks, to demonstrate how the college can impact students, employers, and the wider community.

One major responsibility of our team is maintaining our course listings through our pro-spectus and website. We manage all aspects of the website, such as following up on any enquiries by directing them to the relevant departments. We work with all teams across the college to promote the work we are doing through student success stories, performances and anything that will draw attention to the college and encourage more traffic to our website.

My advice for someone interested in this area of work is to be creative. Learn how to market yourself. Be willing to put yourself forward for things where you will get to speak to people and businesses. Make sure you develop good IT skills and learn how to use marketing tools such as Photoshop and Illustrator. Improve your written communication skills and learn how to write for different audiences. Find out about FES and the courses that are on offer in local learning providers.

Leadership roles and knowledge, skills, and behaviours (KSBs)

The most common knowledge identified within the professional profiles is having and maintaining in-depth sector-related knowledge in your chosen area of work. This can be achieved through actively staying up-to-date with current policies, initiatives and agendas, engaging with research and, where necessary, making use of networking opportunities.

Furthermore, there are many skills which are common to most areas of work in FES. These include having high levels of written and verbal communication, and the ability to adapt communication to different audiences. Alongside this, prospective leaders in FES should ensure they have excellent digital skills and be able to make confident use of role-specific software. Data analysis skills are also common to many areas of work within the sector, as is the ability to use this data to inform decision-making. Being able to translate complex figures and statistics into understandable formats is a further skill valued in some areas of FES.

What is noteworthy is the importance that each professional profile places on developing your behaviours and associated attitudes and personal qualities, such as self-determination, adaptability, and career identity. Common behaviours identified by our leaders in FES include being open to new experiences, being curious and having the willingness to try out new things outside your comfort zone. This includes taking every opportunity to work or network with different people, and to learn from them. Being willing to start in a supporting role and 'working-your-way-up' in a particular field is also identified as a positive behaviour.

The prominence attributed to professional behaviours is not to suggest that the development of knowledge and skills is of less importance; on-the-contrary, these are essential. However, it recognises that knowledge and skills will, in time, become dated. Therefore, to be successful in any career, you need to be aware of this, and able to adapt knowledge and skills to meet the demands of an ever-changing labour market. Openness to change and adaptability are key behaviours that can enable this progression. This resonates with the theoretical employability models above, which all go beyond the notion of only developing knowledge and skills and give equal parity to the development of behaviours.

Questions for discussion

Having read the case studies, can you identify knowledge, skills and behaviours that are common, or unique, to different non-teaching leadership roles in the FES sector? To what extent are these KSBs inherent or learnt? And how well do they align to your existing KSBs? What could you do to develop your KSBs to align with areas of leadership to which you are attracted?

Planning your future in further education and skills leadership

For graduates considering a non-teaching leadership role in FES, the GROW coaching model is a useful mechanism for translating an employability theory into practical action. First introduced by Sir John Whitmore in 1992, GROW supports decision-making, problem-solving and goal-setting, by utilising self-reflection that leads to small manageable steps towards achieving a personal or career aspiration.

The acronym GROW outlines the key stages in a successful coaching conversation, including **G**oal-setting, understanding your current **R**eality, identifying the **O**ptions, and determining what **W**ill need to happen and by when.

GROW supports personal development, usually through dialogue with, and active listening by a coach. However, the model can also be used to scaffold personal reflection. Its use enables you to improve aspects of your KSBs, first through the identification of what you want to achieve or improve upon. This is then followed by an assessment of your current ability and the potential for progress towards achieving the goal. Next, any barriers to meeting the goal are identified, and related options for overcoming them are considered. Finally, a plan of action is constructed, using Specific, Measurable, Attainable, Relevant, and Time-based (SMART) targets that help focus your efforts and increase your chances of achieving the set goal.

Questions for discussion

Start a personal reflection to determine the next steps that will support you in pursuing a career in a non-teaching leadership role in the FES sector. You could answer the following questions, which are framed around the GROW model (Whitmore, 2009), remembering to retain a clear focus on your KSBs.

Goal-setting	What do you want to achieve?
	How will you know that you have achieved your goal?
Reality	What is your position now?
	Have you taken steps towards your goal?
Options/obstacles	What are your possible next steps?
	What are the advantages and disadvantages of these options?
	What obstacles exist, and how might you overcome them?
Will/way forward	What will you do and when?
	When will you review your progress?
	How will you stay motivated?

Conclusion

This chapter demonstrates the breadth of the FES sector and of the non-teaching leadership roles within it. It underlines the opportunities the sector presents for establishing and developing a varied and stimulating career that encompasses multiple areas of work.

Graduates are encouraged to use employability models to support them to think holistically about the knowledge, skills, and behaviours they have gained through their life-long and life-wide learning, and how these prepare them for an entry-level role within the FES sector. The professional profiles are intended to prompt further thought about how careers in the sector can develop and enable progression into non-teaching leadership roles.

The GROW coaching model is recommended as a tool for personal reflection. Translating this thinking into the setting of goals and identification of clear milestones can move graduates towards achieving their career aspirations.

Summary points

- There is a wide range of non-teaching roles within the FES sector.
- There are opportunities to experience multiple areas of work and for progression into a leadership role.
- Contemporary employability models go beyond *knowledge* and *skills* to give equal parity to the development of *behaviours*.
- Non-teaching leaders in the FES sector recognise that knowledge and skills will become dated. Openness to change and the ability to adapt knowledge and skills are behaviours that enable progression.
- Using the GROW model enables the setting of goals that can give graduates the confidence to move towards achieving their career aspirations.

Recommended reading

Cole, D. and Coulson, B. (2022) Through and Beyond COVID-19, Promoting Whole Person, Lifelong and Life Wide Learning. *Journal of Innovation in Polytechnic Education* **4**(1), pp.45–50.

Jackson, N.J. (2008) A Life-Wide Curriculum: Enriching a traditional WIL scheme through new approaches to experience-based learning. Proceedings of the WACE Symposium. Sydney.

Whitmore, J. (2009) *Coaching for Performance* (4th Ed.). London: Nicholas Brealey Publishing.

References

Association of Colleges (2022) [Online]. Available from: https://www.aoc.co.uk/about/college-key-facts (Accessed 24 October 2022).

Dacre Pool, L. and Sewell, P. (2007) The Key to Employability: Developing a Practical Model for Graduate Employability. *Education and Training* **49**(4), pp. 277–289.

Fugate, M., Kinicki, A.J. and Ashforth, B. (2004) Employability: A Psycho-Social Construct, Its Dimensions, and Applications. *Journal of Vocational Behaviour* **65**, pp. 14–38.

Institute for Apprenticeships and Technical Education (2022) [Online]. Available from: https://www.instituteforapprenticeships.org/occupational-standards/what-is-an-occupational-standard/ (Accessed 5 October 2022).

Jackson, N.J. (2008) A Life-Wide Curriculum: Enriching a traditional WIL scheme through new approaches to experience-based learning. Proceedings of the WACE Symposium. Sydney.

Office for Students (2021) Graduate Employment and Skills Guide. Online. Available from: https://www.officeforstudents.org.uk/employment-and-skills (Accessed 5 October 2022).

Tomlinson, M. (2017) Forms of Graduate Capital and Their Relationship to Graduate Employability. *Education and Training* **59**(4), pp. 338–352.

14 Charitable Education Organisations in England: The Case of Teacher Educators

Bethany Kelly and Deborah Outhwaite

Introduction: Government involvement in teacher education

The education of new teachers in England is in the midst of a massive upheaval known as 'The ITTE Market Review'. The impact of turbulent governmental changes has been felt across the entirety of the teacher education landscape, with over 30 higher education institutions (HEI) at present having been removed from the provision of PGCE programmes nationally (DfE, 2022a). From the mid-1990s there was a focus on re-establishing traditional approaches in the classroom, with an emphasis on the importance of knowledge and all students benefiting from a return to a more traditional curriculum. Ball (2021) describes the changes that have taken place in the last fifty years as 'epistemic', and he goes on to say that these changes 'represent a fundamental shift in organising principles, from welfare education, based on the principles of public service, to neo-liberal education, based on the principles of market exchange and competition' (Ball, 2021: 1). Debate has raged over the work of teachers and, as a result, the work of those who train teachers.

The publicity around NIoT, summer 2022

Teacher training has often been described in terms of equipping practitioners with a knowledge of the theory that is needed to ensure effective practice in the delivery of lessons (Moore, 2000). How this happens has been hotly debated. In the 1990s, the discussion focused on 'competencies' (Moore, 2000: 263). It was at this time, 1992, when the Council for the Accreditation of Teacher Education was replaced by the Teacher Training Agency (TTA), marking a shift, not only in the name of the profession, but in the nature of the work. Prospective teachers were no longer being educated about the profession: they were being 'trained'; in other words, told what to do and how to do it. Whitty *et al.* (2007) referred to this stage in the development of teacher training as the de-professionalisation of the teaching profession.

Questions for discussion

Which of these phrases best describe teachers and teaching: 'the charismatic subject', 'the competent craftsperson', or 'the reflective practitioner'? (Moore, 2000: 8).

What would you feel was the most important aspect of teaching to learn before becoming a teacher?

DOI: 10.4324/9781003321439-14

When the Conservative Coalition Government was formed in 2010, Michael Gove was appointed as the Secretary of State for Education. The focus on a traditionalist approach to teaching and learning was supported by a number of key voices in education promoting a knowledge-rich curriculum. The way to deliver this curriculum was through 'Direct Instruction'. If the emphasis for teachers was being directed to particular approaches in the classroom, it is not surprising that this also had an impact on teacher education. This chapter examines how the landscape of teacher education has changed over the last twelve years, particularly by considering the political impact through the involvement of charitable organisations in teacher education. The changes have been mirrored by the privatisation of particular aspects of education provision. Ellis *et al.* (2020: 2) argued that 'different relations of power and interdependence represent a new political economy of teacher development in England'.

What's in a name? Educator or trainer?

The shift in name from the education of teachers to the training of teachers has continued to be a concern for many in the profession. Since 2019 teacher preparation has been required to follow the ITT (Initial Teacher Training) Core Content Framework provided by the DfE. There is a clear focus on its being evidence-based with research being used to support teacher *training* rather than teacher *education*. The change has caused some academics to suggest that the process of preparing teachers is 'too prescriptive' and lacking academic rigour (Booth, 2022). Lofthouse (2018: 3) suggests that 'the language of training rather than education is potentially reductive. How we talk about teacher education can be lost in the different perspectives involved in the debate today. There is a danger of having overly simplistic definitions of teaching as "craft"' (Czerniawski *et al.*, 2019: 185). This highlights the expectations of the education process taking place. Are teacher educators educating prospective teachers about the research and strategies of teaching, or are they trainers showing them how to teach? Reflected here is a fixed perspective of research to be delivered rather than as a process to engage with that is fluid and evolving. Czerniawski *et al.* (2019) suggest that how those involved in the preparation of new teachers identified themselves was also a reflection of context. They posited that those who are university-based identify themselves as educators, whereas those based in schools saw themselves as teachers and their work as training. These opposing perspectives contributed to the perception of teacher trainers as 'removed from the "ivory tower"' (Czerniawski *et al.*, 2019: 175). Research by Czerniawski *et al.* (*ibid*) found that there was an association of university-based teacher educators as those with 'knowledge *of* teaching' rather than the school-based trainers having 'knowledge *about* teaching'. This distinction reinforces the point that there is a confusion over the identity of all teacher educators, but particularly that of the university-based teacher educator. The perception of some, including colleagues faced with the same task of preparing teachers, is that university-based teacher educators are removed and academic, lacking direct experience, despite often decades of their own teaching experience in schools.

Questions for discussion

What's in a name? Does it make a difference whether to train rather than educate teachers?
   List some of these differences. How might they impact the next generation of teachers?
Does it matter where teachers are trained: in schools, in universities, or a combination of both?
What are the differences in focus of each approach?
What other considerations may prospective trainees have in choosing where to study?

What is the role of charitable organisations?

The interwoven nature of the political agenda set out by different governments and the direction and purpose of teaching has been evident, particularly since the second world war and in particular in relation to questions of welfare and equity for all children. This agenda has become further complicated in the last twenty years through the advent, of a number of charitable organisations involved in education. The promotion of social mobility by Conservative governments since 2010, has been presented as the driving force for redesigning the education of teachers in England: evidence of the way in which the political agenda has been interwoven with financial priorities for state-funded education. The Schools' White Paper, *The Importance of Teaching* (DfE 2010), regarded as the start of this drive for social mobility, presented education as liberation from societal constraints.

Since 2010, a range of organisations have been actively encouraged by the DfE through a variety of policy enactments to become involved in the training of teachers. Consequently, the development and training of teachers has been outsourced to a number of privately-owned organisations that work to ensure the political agenda is met. These include, for example:

- Teach First (TF, Founded 2002).
- Ambition Leadership (AL, Founded 2006).
- Teacher Development Trust (TDT, Founded 2012).

What role has these charitable organisations played?

Organisations such as Teach First provided an alternative entry point for Teacher Education, and this organisation was awarded £3.9 million from the Teaching and Leadership Innovation Fund in 2015. Whilst they were able to deliver teacher training, they still had to use Higher Education Institutions for validation. Ambition School Leadership, on the other hand, was founded in 2006, later becoming the Ambition Institute. Originally awarded a government contract, they were later involved in a dispute with the DfE over loss of income from the loss of the contract. Ambition Institute made a claim for three-quarters of a million for wasted costs, resulting in a financial settlement with the DfE (Dickens, 2022).

In 2012, the Teacher Development Trust (TDT) was founded by 'a former director of the government's National Centre of Excellence in the Teaching of Mathematics, Dr Mark McCourt' (Ellis *et al.*, 2020: 29). The work of the TDT was particularly focused on the professional development of teachers, and in 2017 they were awarded £1.3 million to develop 'excellence hubs', occurring months after the DfE (2011) White Paper, *Training our Next Generation of Outstanding Teachers,* setting out intended reforms for ITT. Both the TDT and the White Paper aimed to shift the focus from higher education institutions to school-based training through teaching schools hubs.

Teacher education in England has also been changing rapidly since the COVID-19 pandemic. When teaching and learning were forced online, the Government was prompted to fund organisations that could provide easily accessible resources for schools, one result being the establishment of Oak Academy, which in September 2022 was awarded a contract for £43million to be paid over the next three years, which the All-Party Parliamentary Group (APPG) for the Teaching Profession has stated amounts to the mass politicisation, not only of initial teacher training and education (ITTE), but also to lesson planning and, in effect, curriculum control (Waterman, 2022).

Questions for discussion

What problems can emerge when politics, economics and education are combined?
Do you think independence from government is important when training teachers for the
    delivery of a state system of schooling? Why and why not?

How does this all fit together: The Golden Threads?

The DfE see teacher training as part of a bigger picture, referred to as the Golden Threads (ref). These threads are illustrated in the diagram below, starting with recruitment into ITT, [not Initial Teacher Education (ITE)], leading to the Early Career Framework (ECF), and then on to Continuing Professional Development (CPD) provided by the curriculum hubs in behaviour management: computing, maths, phonics, and science. Finally, are the National Professional Qualifications (NPQs) suite of Leadership programmes (Figure 14.1).

In September 2022, ITT was reviewed through a two-stage DfE accreditation process that resulted in the number of teacher training providers being reduced from 240 to 179 (DfE, 2022a). Only 83 per cent of universities were able to continue providing teacher training, and in the published list of approved providers, there is evidence of a shift to government-supported institutions, including the National Institute of Teaching (NIoT). Some notable HEIs were left out, such as the University of Cumbria, which educates many beginner teachers from the North-West and Northern Ireland (Spendlove, 2021).

What is the role of NIoT?

First announced in 2019 in order to create 'World Class Teacher Education' (DfE, 2019), NIoT faced a fierce fight back from many organisations, including the APPG for the Teaching Profession, a professional umbrella group, the Universities Council for the Education of Teachers (UCET) representing university teacher educators, and the National Association of School-Based Teacher Training (NASBTT). The sector understood that giving degree-awarding powers to non-HEIs would change the future direction of teacher education, potentially creating a different type of market, one that was seen as extending the remit of 'charitable' organisations (listed above) further than before. Such organisations are directly accountable to the DfE. In other words, a non-HEI remit is created by these policy changes. For universities it looked as though they were being cut out of the ITTE routes altogether (UCET, 2022) unless the new body chose to engage with them. What was on offer for the first time was an alternative to the HEI route. However, the NIoT cannot provide the numbers of new teachers required. This led to uncertainty in the sector. The result was a 'knock-on effect' to teacher recruitment,

Figure 14.1 'A Lifetime of Opportunity' from the Spencer Teaching School Hub
Source: Ovenden-Hope (2022: 257).

alongside traditional challenges associated with recruiting teachers, traditionally: workload and rigidity of employment (no annual leave, or ability to make appointments during the day, for example).

What does this mean for teacher education and university education departments?

In 2002, Chris Woodhead, then the Ofsted Chief Inspector of Schools, published the document *Class War: the state of British Education*. It made claims that the majority of academics were left-wing and used the term 'the Blob' to describe teacher trainers and educational researchers. This term was then picked up by Secretary of State Gove (Craske, 2021) and used again just over ten years later. As part of the newly appointed Coalition government in 2010, policies were introduced to challenge perceived urgent issues of teacher education. The belief was that progressive agendas were being peddled by teacher trainers along with the abandonment of any rigour:

> The themes of diversification, freedom and choice in the school system are also consistently present in speeches by Michael Gove in opposition and in government and later in government by Nick Gibb (Minister of State for Schools 2010-2012).
>
> Childs and Menter (2013: 104)

Under the auspices of 'improving' teacher education, changes included widening access to teacher training. Routes into teaching were added: for example, for graduates who otherwise would have considered a career in industry and business, or Troops to Teaching for service personnel leaving the armed forces. Charitable organisations such as Teach First were expanded to replace existing Graduate Training Programmes (GTP). Gove argued that these organisations, in contrast with higher education Institutions, were generating a culture that went beyond existing provisions and were therefore offering something better.

The need for Government-led CPD marked the end of creating a 'Masterly-led' profession with the HEIs and the National College for School Leadership (NCSL) that had existed under the New Labour Governments until 2010 (Outhwaite, 2016). First, the National College for School Leadership was changed to the National College for Teaching and Learning in 2013, then it was incorporated directly into the DfE in 2018, and finally disbanded altogether in 2019. As Gunter (2012) has argued, the original NCSL was far from perfect, but it ploughed large amounts of university-led investment into teaching, encouraging senior staff to take masters, and doctorates. Instead of higher education institutions providing further qualifications to continue teacher education, charitable organisations such as TDT were ear-marked early on under the Coalition Government as the replacement providers of NPQs, so that HEIs did not need to be involved: universities have, in effect, been written out of the DfE's Golden Threads, as these CPD qualifications remain with the marketised providers.

Eight hundred or so Teaching Schools, or Teaching School Alliances (TSAs) responsible for the liaison between schools and universities were scrapped in the summer of 2021, and Teaching School Hubs (TSHs) were created, charged with delivering and signposting the Golden Threads from September 2021, in the middle of the COVID-19 pandemic. As part of this wide re-structuring of teacher education, from recruitment through training, to CPD, to leadership development, the DfE decided to scrap the Newly Qualified Teacher (NQT) status and replace it with that of the two-year Early Career Teacher (ECT) programme. Appropriate Bodies (AB), the organisations that have a role in checking that Early Career Teachers are receiving a programme of support and training based on the ECF (DfE, 2022b) became part of these Golden Threads, but again capacity was an issue. TSHs were new, and many of these hubs had no experience of delivering the appropriate body role. Local Authorities, for the present at least, remain providers alongside these hubs, in the important role of inducting new teachers into the profession, and 'signing-off' their early career teacher (ECT) status, but have to use the ECF materials, delivered by these charitable organisations.

Questions for discussion

Who would you say were the AB to support teachers new to the profession?
What kind of support would be most useful for teachers in the first few years of their work?
Look up the organisations that provide the ECF and the NPQs. What do you notice?

This marginalisation of higher education institutes in teacher training in favour of these charitable organisations who benefited from high levels of funding to deliver professional qualifications on a large scale. Brown (2015) defines the paradox of neoliberalism as:

.... structuring markets it claims to liberate from structure, intensely governing subjects it claims to free from government, strengthening and retaining states it claims to abjure. In the economic realm, neoliberalism aims simultaneously at deregulation and control. (*ibid*: 49)

No universities or local education authorities were awarded funding in these ways. This shift away from the academic underpinning provided by universities seemed to be in marked contrast to other disciplines. Whilst education moved away from academic collaboration, law, medicine, engineering, and other disciplines moved towards academic partnerships. Whereas many medical courses have been lengthened and formalised in universities, for example, in nursing, teacher education courses have often been shortened.

Questions for discussion

Would you feel happy going to a doctor or a lawyer who had not gone to university for their training?
Why do people not see teachers as specialists in the same way?

What does this mean for schools?

TSHs have been presented as organisations designed to lead the way in teacher training and development in the latest set of government reforms. This has placed schools-based training in opposition to university-based training, despite there being examples of both approaches being combined. For schools themselves, they are ever more involved in trainee/student placements and require staff to oversee them and liaise with local universities or the providers who will use the new National Institute of Teaching (NIoT). Some may think that nothing has really changed, but in fact the philosophy that underpins the way in which the system worked, has been fundamentally altered, not by NIoT and other non-university providers in the system.

What now for the PGCE?

Politicians appear to have little interest in the Postgraduate Certificate of Education. The focus from Ofsted and the DfE is on Qualified Teacher Status (QTS), and the creation of an iQTS for international teachers (DfE, 2021). This has been made even more evident through the ITT re-accreditation process. In the first round, two-thirds of providers failed to meet the criteria set out by the DfE. Whilst more went through in the second round, the numbers of teacher training providers were still reduced with a number of universities excluded from future delivery, as out-lined above.

The focus on teachers as curriculum experts would appear to be reinforcing the profession, but the reality of new processes such as the implementation of the ECF has not resulted in the retention of teachers that had been anticipated. With new measures coming into effect in 2024, the reduced number of teacher training providers now has to present their intended resources for scrutiny. The centralisation of teaching, already seen in some multi-academic trusts (MATs), could go further still where teachers are simply instructed on what to deliver, and when, with no professional autonomy encouraged at all. Leadership in schools achieved through appointment from within central organisations could lead to an educational inbreeding of poor practice without academic criticality.

Many PGCE programmes are now delivered at masters (Level 7) standard, which requires critical-ity, debate, evaluation, and synthesis. Instead of being able to engage with the educational debates surrounding strategy, pedagogy and theory, teacher training is changing into a form of professional development almost entirely focused on subject knowledge. The loss of the PGCE could have a significant impact on teaching in future years.

What does this mean for the future of teaching?

Government-preferred models of teaching focus on the importance of delivering a knowledge cur-riculum that provides pupils with a foundation of factual knowledge. Testing processes that meas-ure this knowledge show an increase in results, but the focus remains firmly on how rather than why. As with the NIoT, there appears to be an increased focus on the importance of underpinning research, but it has been limited and controversial. The Department for Education has invested £350 million in the 'What Works? Centre for Education', funding the Education Endowment Fund (EEF) (EEF, 2022) and a particular 'model' of pedagogy, heavily influenced by the understanding of metacognition. However, it has left no space in the system for discussion about students find-ing schooling challenging because of austerity and poverty, and puts forward a mantra of not accepting excuses in order to drive up standards. Teachers and leaders argue that the politicisa-tion of education, and lack of realism about students' lived experience, is what is driving staff out of teaching. Certainly, the English education system has a recruitment crisis (Ovenden-Hope and Passy, 2021).

Questions for discussion

Why would governments consider outsourcing activities such as teacher training to charitable organisations? What are the merits/demerits of such a strategy?

Should charitable organisations in the education sector be independent of the government or work closely with them? Why, why not?

What can you think of that has changed, in wider society, in the last ten years or more? Did we always have Food Banks? Do other sorts of Banks now exist that you know of? Why have these come about?

Does it have to be this way? What could England learn from other countries?

Discussion relating to what role teacher-educators play is not unique to England. In America, Olsen and Buchanan refer back to Goodlad's study (1990) where teacher educators felt that they had a 'low status' with their work being considered as 'low prestige and non-scholarly' (1990: 10). This certainly seems to align with developments in England. Olsen and Buchanan (2017) themselves argue that the teacher educator role itself is not seen as a distinct career path, and their conclusion is to recommend that the professional identity of teacher educators needs further research focus and reflection. When writing about 'native and non-native EFL Teacher Educators', Mannes argues that their professional identity is 'confused' (2020: 385). The demands of the role require teacher educators to have a dual focus of teaching and researching. Perhaps it is this confusion that creates a perceived distance between universities and teaching.

Gunn et al. (2016) examine the way in which the work of teacher educators has changed in New Zealand. The authors suggest that, rather than a dual focus, there have been three 'trajectories' for teacher educators: firstly, as an expert practitioner contributing their career experience, but not necessarily having an expectation of carrying out research; secondly, a 'traditional academic' who may not be a qualified teacher; or one who has both the teaching qualification and has also been engaged in research (Gunn et al, 2016: 306). New Zealand's Ministry of Education was looking at ways to increase the 'status and effectiveness of the teaching profession' (Gunn et al. 2016: 307) with the result of teacher education having an increased postgraduate focus. This shift to university-based teacher education, in line with approaches found in other countries such as Norway and Finland, has an impact on the professional identity of teacher educators. Again, this seems to emphasise a possible sense of professional identity shift that can happen within teacher education, with a sense that the teacher educator faces the biggest challenges when moving from to academia. In England, this move from the classroom to the university has resulted in many teacher educators being chastised (particularly on social media) for clinging to their own experience as teachers. For example, those in teacher education cannot become Members of the Chartered College of Teaching, as this is only open to those in schools.

In Norway, Høydalsvik (2019) explains that the expectation is that most teacher educators will be qualified to doctoral level. The link made with qualifications may reflect the need for the individual to invest themselves in this new role, recognising that it requires its own professional development. This is the direction of travel that the previous New Labour Government in the UK was going in by aiming for an all-masters profession, but this is now long gone: staff in schools are encouraged to go only as far as the Golden Threads permit, and further funding is no longer available to teachers to become better qualified. Charitable organisations in the education sector in England are effectively delivering prescribed, for-profit, solutions encouraged by government policy, whilst university teacher education is in rapid decline.

Those involved in teacher training still see their role as encouraging teachers to engage with research and debate regarding the integration of theory to practice. Whether the charitable organisations are equipped to provide training at the level required is yet to be seen. Many will be happy to concentrate on seeing teaching as a craft with a number of skills to be acquired, whilst others will want to engage with the education debate that this involves and to be critically reflective practitioners. Either way there are likely to be yet further changes to teacher training in England in the years leading up to the major structural changes that are taking place from 2024 and beyond.

Questions for discussion

Where does this leave the sector, and how does it reorganise?
Do teacher educators need to be teachers, or academics, both or neither?

Summary points

- The landscape of teacher training and education has been changing since the Second World War, but there have been significant philosophical changes in the last 10–20 years.
- In the light of these changes, those involved with teacher training have had to think about the impact of these ideas, specifically:

  o The difference it makes to talk of teacher training rather than teacher education.
  o The extent to which the political agenda sets the direction of teaching and ultimately the autonomy of teachers.
  o The impact of the DfE's Golden Threads for teachers' CPD at every stage of their careers.
  o The questions that need to be asked of the charitable education organisations that win the bids to deliver this CPD.
  o The role that higher education institutions will play in the future, if the academic expectations continue to shift away from them.
  o How the structure of education and schools will evolve away from external, independent HEI accreditation to schools and the work of government-funded organisations.

Recommended reading

Ball, S (2017) *The Education Debate (Policy and Politics in the Twenty-First Century)*. London: Policy Press.
Claxton, G. (2021) *The Future of Teaching*. Abingdon: Routledge.
Ellis, V., Mansell, W. and Steadman, S. (2020) A New Political Economy of Teacher Development: England's Teaching and Leadership Innovation Fund. *Journal of Education Policy* **36**(5), pp. 605–623.
Moore, A. (2000) *Teaching and Learning: Pedagogy, curriculum and culture*. Abingdon: Routledge.

References

Ball, S.J. (2021) *The Education Debate: Policy and politics in the twenty-first century*. Bristol: Policy Press.

Booth, S. (2022) 'Cambridge refuses to reapply for teacher training over 'prescriptive' reforms' *Schoolsweek*, 25 February, 2022, https://schoolsweek.co.uk/cambridge-refuses-to-reapply-for-teacher-training-over-prescriptive-reforms/ (Accessed 3 March 2022).

Brown, W. (2015) *Undoing the Demos: Neoliberalism's stealth revolution*. Cambridge, MA: MIT Press.

Childs, A. and Menter, I. (2013) Teacher Education in 21st Century England. A Case Study in Neoliberal Public Policy. *Revista Española de Educación Comparada* **22**, pp. 93–116.

Craske, J. (2021) Logics, Rhetoric and 'the blob': Populist Logic in the Conservative Reforms to English Schooling. *British Educational Research Journal* **47**(2), pp. 279–298.

Czerniawski, G., Kidd, W. and Murray, J. (2019) We Are All Teacher Educators Now: Understanding school-based teacher educators in times of change in England. In J. Murray, A. Swennen and C. Kosnik (Eds.), *International Research, Policy and Practice in Teacher Education*. Zurich: Springer.

DfE (2010) *Importance of Teaching*. London: DfE. Online. Available at https://www.gov.uk/government/publications/the-importance-of-teaching-the-schools-white-paper-2010 (Accessed 1 September 2022).

DfE (2011) *Training Our Next Generation of Outstanding Teachers*. London: DfE.

DfE (2019) *Initial Teacher Training (ITT): Core content framework*. London: DfE. Online. Available at https://assets.publishing.service.gov.uk/government/uploads/system/uploads/attachment_data/file/974307/ITT_core_content_framework_.pdf (Accessed 1 September 2022).

DfE (2021) *Introducing International Qualified Teacher Status*. London; DfE. Online. Available at https://www.gov.uk/government/publications/international-qualified-teacher-status-iqts/introducing-the-international-qualified-teacher-status-iqts-pilot (Accessed 20 October 2022)

DfE (2022a) List of Providers Accredited to Deliver ITT from September 2024. Online. Available at https://www.gov.uk/government/publications/accredited-initial-teacher-training-itt-providers/list-of-providers-accredited-to-deliver-itt-from-september-2024 (Accessed 1 October 2022).

DfE (2022b) *Appropriate Bodies Guidance*. London: DfE. Online. Available at https://assets.publishing.service.gov.uk/government/uploads/system/uploads/attachment_data/file/991723/Appropriate_bodies_guidance_induction_and_the_early_career_framework.pdf (Accessed 1 September 2022).

Dickens, J. (2022) DfE Settles with Ambition over £121m Institute of Teaching Contract Dispute. Online. Available at https://schoolsweek.co.uk/dfe-settles-with-ambition-over-121m-iot-contract-dispute/ (Accessed 1 September 2022)

EEF (2022) DfE confirms funding to enable the EEF to continue its work evaluating and spreading best practice for at least another decade. Centre for Education (EEF). Online. Available at https://educationendowmentfoundation.org.uk/news/dfe-confirms-funding-to-enable-the-eef-to-continue-its-work-evaluating-and-spreading-best-practice-for-at-least-another-decade (Accessed 27 October 2022).

Ellis, V., Mansell, W. and Steadman, S. (2020) A New Political Economy of Teacher Development: England's Teaching and Leadership Innovation Fund. *Journal of Education Policy* **36**(20), pp. 1–19.

Goodlad, J. (1990) *Places Where Teachers Are Taught*. San Francisco, CA: Jossey-Bass.

Gunn, A.C., Hill, M.F., Berg, D. and Haigh, M. (2016) The Changing Work of Teacher Educators in Aotearoa New Zealand: A view through activity theory. *Asia-Pacific Journal of Teacher Education* **44**(4), pp. 306–319.

Gunter, H.M. (2012) *Leadership and the Reform of Education*. Bristol: The Policy Press.

Høydalsvik, T.E.L. (2019) The Hidden Professionals? An Interview Study of Higher Education-Based Teacher Educators professional Identity. *Nordisk tidsskrift for utdanning og praksis* **13**(2), pp. 93–113.

Lofthouse, R.M. (2018) Re-Imagining Mentoring as a Dynamic Hub in the Transformation of Initial Teacher Education: The Role of Mentors and Teacher Educators. *International Journal of Mentoring and Coaching in Education* **7**(3), pp. 248–260.

Mannes, A. (2020) The Confused Professional Identity of Native and Non-Native EFL Teacher Educators: Are They Teachers or Researchers? *Athens Journal of Education* **7**(4), pp. 385–396.

Moore, A. (2000) *Teaching and Learning: Pedagogy, curriculum and culture*. Abingdon: Routledge.

NIoT (2022) School-Led Development Trust Appointed to Lead New Flagship Teacher and Leader Development and Research Institute. Online. Available at https://blog.niot.org.uk/2022/05/launch/ (Accessed 11 September 2022).

Olsen, B. and Buchanan, R. (2017) Everyone Wants You to Do Everything: Investigating the Professional Identity Development of Teacher Educators. *Teacher Educator Quarterly* **44**(1), pp. 9–34.

Outhwaite, D. (2016) British Educational Research Association (BERA) Blog on Masters in Education. Online. Available at https://www.bera.ac.uk/blog/developing-a-cohesive-strategy-for-leading-learning-inside-education (Accessed 29 October 2022).

Ovenden-Hope, T. (2022) *The Early Career Framework: Origins, outcomes, and opportunities*. Woodbridge: John Catt Publishers.

Ovenden-Hope, T. and Passy, R. (Eds) (2021) *Exploring Teacher Recruitment and Retention: Contextual challenges and international perspectives*. Abingdon: Routledge.

Spendlove, D. (2021) 'Golden thread of distraction: It doesn't have to be this way!' Online. Available at https://davidspendlove.wordpress.com/ (Accessed 29 October 2022).

UCET (2022) *Promoting Quality in Teacher Education*. London: UCET. Online. Available at https://www.ucet.ac.uk/policy (Accessed 1 September 2022).

Waterman, C. (2022) *Schools Bill (HL Bill 1) and Explanatory Notes: A plain guide*. London: Iris Press.

Whitty, G., Furlong, J., Barton, L., Miles, S. and Whitiing, C. (2007) Researching Initial Teacher Education in England in the 1990s. In J. Feeman-Moir and A. Scott (Eds.), *Shaping the Future: Critical essays on teacher education*. London: Brill.

Index

Aas, M. 46
Academies 2, 15, 81–82, 90
Activism 30–31, 72, 74–75, 79
Ada, S. 54
Administration 1–3, 15, 83, 146
Advocacy 71–72, 74–76, 79
Aguilar, E. 42
Akpolat, E. K. 47
Allison, E. 42
Amineh, R.J. 91
Arbour, M. 76
Association of Colleges 140
Attainment/pupil attainment 4, 96
Authentic leadership 10, 76, 133
Autonomy 3–4, 15, 62, 65, 81, 83, 86, 110, 116, 120, 159, 161
Aydın, İ. 50
Ayyıldız, P. 54
Azorín, C. 61

Bailey, L. 115–116, 123–124
Balcı, A. 47, 52
Bali, D. 135
Ball, S. 15, 16
Ball, S.J. 153
Balogun, J. 92
Bandura, A. 37, 109
Barth, R. 47
Başaran, İ.E. 50
Baxter, J. 91–94, 96
Baxter, J.A. 99
Bayrakdar, S. 63
BBC News 25
Beabout, B. 98
Behaviour management 66
Beltman, S. 65
Bengtson, E. 47
Bennett, B. 59
Bennett, N. 18
Bennis, W. 48
Benson, J. 116, 120
Berne, E. 109
Bertalanffy, L.V. 48

Black Lives Matter 28–29
Black, K. 92
Blackburn, B.R. 135
Blandford, S. 116, 118
Boin, A. 92
Bolam, R. 16
Bolman, L. 50
Bombèr, L.M. 132
Booth, S 154
Boronski, T. 25
Bottery, M. 12
Boudes, T. 94, 97
Bourdieu, P. 84
Bourgeois L.J. III 91
Bower, M. 107, 109
Brock, A. 77
Brown, W. 158
Brummitt, N. 114
Bruner, J.S. 92
Bryson, J. 52
Building-up approach 66
Bundy, J. 67
Bunnell, T. 114–115
Bursalıoğlu, Z. 48, 51
Bush, T. 3, 4, 10–11, 14, 18, 47

Caffyn, R. 117–118
Çalıkoğlu, A. 51
Cameron, K. S. 108
Campbell-Stephens, R. 24
Carlyle, T. 1
Casey, A. J. 90–92
Catalytic leadership 73
Chapman, C. 82
Charitable organisations 154–158, 160–161
Chenoweth, K. 131
Chia, R. 90–91
Children's Society 134
Childs, A. 157
Church of England 6, 86, 127, 136
Church of England Foundation for Educational Leadership 86
Clarke, J. 3

Clarke, S. 17
Classical management 49, 51–52
Classroom management 59–60, 62
Closed systems 18, 20, 48
Clough, P. 94
Coaching/peer coaching 7, 39, 41–43,
    64–65, 72–74, 104, 146–147, 150–151
Coffield, F. 108
Coldron, J. 82–83, 85
Collaborative leadership 12–14, 20, 62, 107
Collective leadership 12, 14, 19, 131, 135
Colley, K.M. 46
Communication 6, 35, 38, 42, 47, 50, 64, 94,
    103–109, 112, 131, 135, 141, 145–146,
    148–149
Communities 12, 19, 23–24, 28–30, 34,
    40, 42, 46, 68, 75–77, 79, 92, 114–116,
    127–128, 130, 134, 136, 138
Communities of practice 75–77, 79, 92
Competencies 54, 153
Comte, A. 52
Connolly, M. 2, 5
Continuous quality improvement 71, 76, 79
Coordination 49–51
Core purpose 5–6, 127
COVID-19 6, 39–40, 59, 62, 64–68, 81–82,
    84, 89–90, 92, 96–97, 99, 103, 105, 134,
    155, 157
Cox, K. 12
CPD 1, 62, 65, 67, 69, 144, 156–157, 161
Crampton, S. 105
Craske, J. 157
Crawford, M. 34, 41
Crisis leadership 67, 89
Critical race theory 29
Critical reflection 77–79
Cultural differences 105, 116, 118–119,
    124–125
Culture 4, 6, 9–10, 14–15, 18–19, 23, 25,
    34, 38, 42, 46–48, 50, 53–55, 59, 63,
    71–72, 75–76, 78–79, 89, 92–93, 96,
    103, 107–112, 116–118, 127, 129, 132,
    138, 141, 147, 157
Curriculum x, 3–4, 26–28, 53, 62, 66, 84, 95,
    99, 114–115, 117, 120, 124–125, 127,
    131, 141, 146–147, 153–156, 159
Czerniawski, G. 154

D'Erizans, R. 133
Dacre Pool, L. 141
Dale, G. 103, 105
Daly, J. 77
Day, C. 33, 35–36, 42
De Gagne, J. 107, 111
De Grauwe, A. 48
Deal, T. 46, 50

Decision-making 3, 11, 13–14, 25, 49, 54,
    61, 104, 110, 120, 135, 143, 150
Demirtaş, Z. 47
DeWitt, P. 135
DfE 7, 25, 27, 82, 90, 154–159
Dickens, J. 155
Digital learning 89–90, 95–96, 99
Dimmock, C. 11
Disability 24–25, 27, 30, 137
Disability rights 24
Discourse x, 10, 12–13, 18–19, 21, 28, 121
Distributed leadership 6, 11, 13, 20, 43, 53,
    61, 68, 71–75, 79
Diversity x, 6, 16, 23–24, 30, 103, 109, 119,
    131, 144
Doğan, E. 52
Doğan, S. 53
Domains of flourishing 129, 136, 138
Doohan, L. 54
Douglass, A. 75
Drucker, P.F. 48
Drury, S. 53
Duckworth, A. 136
Dunford, J. 12
Durna, U. 49
Duverger, M. 48
Dweck, C.S. 133
DWP 26

Earley, P. 35
Early career framework 5, 156
Early career teachers 158
Early childhood education 7, 71, 79
Educating 59, 127, 154
Educational leadership x, 1–3, 5–7, 10, 60, 67
Educational management 2–3, 52
EEF 159
Effective leadership 48, 61
Effective school management 46–47, 49–50,
    54–55
Eickelmann, B. 89
Eisenbach, R. 53
Elliot, J. 94
Ellis, V. 154–155
Emotional intelligence 36–37, 141
Employability 140–142, 144, 150–151
Equality x, 6, 23–31, 110–112, 144
Equality of access 6
Eraslan, L. 53
Erdem, A.R. 54
Eren, Z. 49–50, 54

Fairman, J. 61
Farmer, T. A. 38
Featherstone, K. 86
Flourishing schools 6, 128–136, 138

Followership 1, 10
Ford, D.F. 136
Framework/s 2, 4–6, 15, 19, 28, 30, 34,
    52–53, 90, 92–94, 127–128, 141, 154,
    156
Fry, L.W. 54
Fryer, P. 28
Fugate, M. 142
Fullan, M. 3
Fuller, K. 85

Garbe, A. 63
Gardner-McTaggart, A. 115, 123
Gender 24, 26–27, 30, 82–83, 85–86, 134
Gibbon, M. 12
Gibson, M. T. 40–41, 115–116, 120,
    123–124
Glanz, J. 14
Glatter, R. 15
Global communities 23
Golden threads 156–158, 161
Goldman, E. F. 90–91
Goleman, D. 37
Goodlad, J. 160
Goodson, I. 12
Gov.UK 27
Governance/governing 6, 115–116, 119–121,
    124–125, 146, 148
Greany, T. 40
Greenhow, C. 59
Greenleaf, R.K. 53
Gretton, G. 103
Gronn, P. 9
GROW 147, 150–151
Gül, İ. 50, 52
Gulick, Luther. 49, 51
Gulsen, F. 107
Gümüş, E. 52
Gunn, A. C. 160
Gunter, H. M. 13, 157

Hall, D. 12–13
Hallinger, P. 53
Hanson, E.M. 49
Hargreaves, A. 47
Harris, A. 13, 60–61, 64, 68
Hartley, D. 13
Hatch, M.J. 51
Hatcher, R. 13
Hayden, M. 115, 120
Head/Headship/Headteacher 6, 11–14,
    19–21, 61, 74, 81–87, 94, 97
Heikka, J. 73
Henderson, L. 76
Hersey, P. 103–104
Hickman, G.R. 73, 75
Higham, R. 11–12, 15

Higher Education x, 6, 102–103, 128, 149,
    153, 155, 157–158, 161
Hinde, E.R. 47
HM Government 24, 25, 29
Holism 12
Hollins, E.R. 47
Hopkins, D. 11
Hordern, J. x
Hoy, W.K. 47
Høydalsvik, T.E.L. 160

ICT 89
Ideological international schools 115
Ilgar, L. 48
Inclusion 23–24, 30–31, 133, 144
Inequalities 6, 23–24, 74
Influence 1–5, 11, 13, 18, 23, 35, 48, 50,
    61–62, 72–73, 77–79, 82, 85, 98–100,
    127, 142
Inner London Education Authority 26
Institute for Apprenticeships and Technical
    Education 142
Instructional 64–65, 69
Instructional leadership 53
International schools 6, 14–125, 129
Invisible leadership 71–73, 75, 79

Jackson, M. 12
Jackson, N, J. 142
James, C 115–116
Jones, A. 60, 64, 68
Jordan-Daus, K. 65

Kafalı, U. 46
Karadağ, N. 46–47
Karip, E. 51
Keskinkılıç, K. 47–49
Keung, E. 118
Kılınç, A.Ç. 53
King, Jr, M.L. 128
Koç, U. 50
Koçel, T. 48, 51
Köse, S. 46
Kuru Çetin, S. 50
Kyriakides, L. 132

LaSalle Network 102
Leadership dispositions 128, 136
Leadership for remote learning 60
Leadership in encouraging employability 7,
    140, 145
Leadership in supporting learning 7, 140, 144
Leadership of corporate systems 7, 140, 148
Leadership preparation 6, 38
Leadership roles x, 7, 42, 62, 140–141, 143,
    149–151
Leadership styles 7, 33, 35, 43, 59, 124

League tables 15, 120
Learning communities 12, 19
Lee, J. 63
Lee, M. 117
Legislation 23–26, 28–31, 144
Leithwood, K. 4, 11, 13, 35–37, 53, 60
Lever, N. 135
Life-cycle theory 104
Loe, R. 132
Lofthouse, R. 39
Lofthouse, R.M. 154
Loneliness 116–117, 124–125
Lorenc, A. 63
Lugg, C. A. 38
Lumby, J. 12
Lumpkin, J. R. 109
Lunenburg, F.C. 49–50

Macdonald, I. 19
Machin, D. 116, 121–122
Maitlis, S. 92
Making up approach 66
Mangla, N. 47
Mannes, A. 160
Maroy, C. 84
Masculinist discourse 14
Masten, A. S. 35
May, C. 94
McCarley, T. A. 47
McLeod, S. 40, 61, 68
Medical model 25
Memduhoğlu, H.B. 51
Mentoring/peer mentoring 39–43, 72–73, 131
MeToo movement 26–27
Mezirow, J. 92, 107
Milgram, S. 60
Millett-Gallant, A. 25
Modelling 33, 42, 72–73, 109
Mongon, D. 10
Moore, A. 153
Mullins, L.J. 46
Multi Academy Trusts/MATs 6, 82, 84, 86, 93–94, 120, 127, 159
Murphy, J. 52, 73, 131

National contexts 5, 124
National curriculum 3
National Professional Qualifications x, 5–7, 75, 86, 156
Neeleman, A. 3
Neo-classical management 51
Neo-liberal/neoliberalism 15, 153, 158
Netolicky, D. 61
New management 51
New public management 3–4, 15
Newman, S. A. 47
Nicholson, J. 77

NIoT 153, 156, 159
Non-teaching leadership roles x, 7, 40–143, 145, 150–151
Non-traditional international schools 115
Not-for-profit 7, 115, 122, 133

O'Mallay, K. 27
O'Sullivan, J. 13, 74, 78
OECD 1, 2, 3, 5
Office for Students 140
Ofsted 27–28, 65
Olsen, B. 160
Olusoga, D. 28–29
Open systems 20, 48
Oplatka, I. 52
Organisation schemas 92–93, 96
Organisational culture 46–47, 50, 54, 71–73, 75–76, 79, 107
Organisational goals 35
Organisational structures 1–2
Organising 49–51, 59, 64, 153
Outhwaite, D. 68, 157
Ovenden-Hope, T. 86, 156, 159
Özdemir, M. 46–47, 49
Özer, N. 53
Özevren, M. 52

Pandemic x, 6, 39, 41, 59–62, 64–65, 67–69, 81, 89–90, 95, 98, 103, 105, 134, 137, 155, 157
Patterson, J. L. 34, 36–38, 41, 43
Patterson, W. 94
Paullay, I. 50
Pedagogical leadership 7, 71–79
Penty, W. 61
Personality trait theory/trait theory 33–35
Pfeffer, J. 49
Piaget, J. 92
Place2Be 135
Planning 6, 12, 49–51, 59, 65, 76, 90–91, 94, 96, 98, 122, 132–133, 144, 147, 150, 155
Plowden, B. 83
Plowden Report 83
Policy 3–4, 7, 11, 14–15, 18, 21, 26, 30, 52, 62, 72, 75, 81–87, 89, 98–100, 108, 125, 140, 142, 147–148, 155–156, 161
Policymakers 2–3, 16, 81
Post-graduate Certificate of Education (PGCE) x, 84, 153, 159
Potter, I. 17, 19
Power 10–12, 16, 18, 23, 30, 35, 40, 60, 71, 73, 75, 83, 85–86, 92, 98, 100, 108, 135, 154
Primary headship 6, 83, 85–86
Principal/school principal 33, 41–43, 46–48, 115–118, 120–123, 143

Professional leadership roles 7
Professional profiles 141, 144–146, 148, 150
Professionalism 11–12

Qualified teacher status (QTS) 159–160

Race 24, 28–30
Race equality 24, 28
Race Relations Act 28–29
Reddy, L. A. 65
Reeves, D.B. 132
Renold, E. 27
Resilience 7, 33–44, 62, 67, 75, 134–135,
    137–138
Resilient schools 42–43
Responsibility 2, 14, 23, 25, 28, 49, 52–53,
    61, 63, 72, 116, 123, 130, 143, 145, 147,
    149
Reynolds, D. 131
Rhodes, C. 33–34, 39
Rieser, R. 26
Ritchie, M. 19
Robbins, P.S. 46
Robertson, J. 16
Roethlisberger, F.J. 46
Role models 61, 112
Ross, F. 51
Rubin, H. 14

Sardar, H. 39
Scheerie, E.L. 49
Schein, E. H. 46, 72
Schemas 92–93, 96–97
School administrator 47
School autonomy 3
School composition 116, 123–125
School improvement 3, 6, 9, 11, 13, 82, 85,
    17, 131
School leaders 1, 3–4, 6, 12–14, 16–17,
    19–21, 33, 36–40, 42–43, 59–60, 62–68,
    90, 92–94, 98–99, 116, 118, 129, 136–137
School management theories 50
School system 14, 18–19, 81–82, 87, 128, 157
Schramm, W. 105
Schrödinger's Leadership 103
Self-efficacy 36–41, 43, 141
Self-improving system 13, 19–20
Senge, P. 132
Senge, P.M. 11, 18, 20, 131
Sepuru, M.G. 47
Sergiovanni, T. 46
Servant leadership 53
Sex equality 26–27
Shafritz, J.M. 49
Shannon, G.S. 131
Sharp, C. 66, 68
Shibuya, K. 48

Silva, A. 1
Simkins, T. 16
Simon, C.A. x
Simon, H. 49
Simon, S. 40–42
Sims, S. 65
Situational leadership 102–105, 107, 109–110
Slough-Kuss, Y. 119
Smailes, N. 66
Social distancing 63–64
Social justice/socially just 19, 127
Social model 25
Society 3, 23, 25–26, 31, 42, 46–47, 72, 75,
    79, 83–86, 89, 134, 160
Solo-leadership 9, 12, 16, 20
Spears, C.L. 53
Special educational needs 25, 123
Spendlove, D. 156
Spillane, J.P. 13, 53
Spiritual leadership 54
Stakeholder/s 4, 12, 46, 49, 81, 92
Staufenberg, J. 85
Stephen, C. 71
Stevenson, D. 89
Stevenson, H. 108
Steward, J. 38–39
Stogdill, R.M. 1
Stolp, S. 46–47
Strategic thinking 91–92, 94, 97
Strategy 13, 60, 90–94, 97–100, 107, 117,
    122–123, 144, 147, 159–160
Strategy as learning 90–94, 97–100
Super-head 13
Sustainability 2, 41, 47, 144
Swaner, L.E. 128–129
System leadership 6, 11–14, 16, 18–19
Systems 2–3, 6–7, 9, 14, 16, 18–19, 21, 25,
    30–31, 39, 48, 51, 60, 63–64, 82, 89, 91,
    115, 117, 128, 132, 134, 137, 140, 143,
    146–148
Systributed leadership 6, 19, 21

Tait, M. 35
Teacher education x, 147, 153–154, 156–158,
    160–161
Teacher leadership 6, 53, 60–62, 64, 67
Teaching School Alliances 157
Teaching School Hubs 155, 157
Technology 27, 52–53, 59–60, 62–63, 65,
    67–69, 90, 120, 133–134, 144
Thürmer, J.L. 92
Tierney, W.G. 54
Times Educational Supplement 27
Timperley, H.S. 47
Tomlinson, C.A. 135
Tomlinson, M. 141
Traditional international schools 115, 119

Transactional leadership 5, 10
Transience 116, 118, 124–125
Tschannen-Moran, M. 52

UCET 156
UK Parliament 30
United Nations 23, 27
Universal Declaration of Human Rights 23, 30

Values x, 4–5, 33, 36–38, 43, 46, 54, 60–61,
    67, 81, 107, 141, 147
Vision 5–6, 31, 34, 49, 52–53, 72–74, 76,
    84, 97, 127–129, 136–138, 147
Visionary leadership 53
Vitality 7, 33, 41–44
Vygotsky, L. S. 109

Wanburg, C. 46
Ward, S. x
Warrick, D. D. 107
Waterman, C. 155

Watkins, D. 97
Weale, S. 103
Webster, L. 25
Weick, K.E. 91–92
Wellbeing 6, 25, 65, 84, 97
Wenger, E. 132
Western, S. 10, 16
White, D. 50
Whitty, G. 153
Witcher, S. 25
Wolstencroft, P. 103
Woodrow, C. 74
Woods, P. 18, 81
Wright, D. 86

Yates, D. 29
Young, K. 106
Youngs, H. 18
Younie, S. 89

Zalenzik, A. 10